Reconsidering Tocqueville's
Democracy in America

DE LA

DÉMOCRATIE

EN AMÉRIQUE,

PAR

ALEXIS DE TOCQUEVILLE,

AVOCAT A LA COUR ROYALE DE PARIS,

L'un des auteurs du livre intitulé :

DU SYSTÈME PÉNITENTIAIRE AUX ÉTATS-UNIS.

Orné d'une carte d'Amérique.

—

TOME PREMIER.

PARIS,

LIBRAIRIE DE CHARLES GOSSELIN,

RUE SAINT-GERMAIN-DES-PRÉS, 9.

M DCCC XXXV.

Reconsidering Tocqueville's
Democracy in America

EDITED BY

Abraham S. Eisenstadt

RUTGERS UNIVERSITY PRESS
New Brunswick and London

The following two essays are reprinted with the permission of their respective publishers: Arthur Schlesinger's, which was originally presented at the Brooklyn College-City University of New York Tocqueville Conference and has appeared in a variant form in *The Michigan Quarterly Review* (Summer 1986); and Robert Nisbet's, which has appeared, also in a variant form, in *The World and I* (November 1986).

Library of Congress Cataloging-in-Publication Data

Reconsidering Tocqueville's Democracy in America.

Includes index.
1. Tocqueville, Alexis de, 1805–1859. De la démocratie en Amérique. 2. United States—Politics and government. 3. United States—Social conditions—To 1865. 4. Democracy. I. Eisenstadt, Abraham Seldin, 1920–   .
JK216.T7193R42 1988   321.8′042′0973   87-23489
ISBN 0-8135-1298-0
ISBN 0-8135-1299-9 (pbk.)

British Cataloging-in-Publication information available

Frontispiece: Title page of *De la Démocratie en Amérique*, 1835. Courtesy of the Yale Tocqueville Manuscripts Collection, Beinecke Rare Book and Manuscript Library, Yale University.

Contents

v

Acknowledgments

THE CONTRIBUTORS to this volume, except for Robert Nisbet, were participants in a two-day conference in October 1985, commemorating the sesquicentennial of the first part of Alexis de Tocqueville's *Democracy in America*. The conference was held under the auspices of the Brooklyn College Humanities Institute and the City University of New York Academy for the Humanities and Sciences. The making of the conference and of this book owes much to the advice of James T. Schleifer of the college of New Rochelle. I am grateful too for the suggestions of Harold Proshansky, President of the Graduate Center of C.U.N.Y., Glenn C. Altschuler of Cornell University, and Robert Viscusi, Director of the Brooklyn College Humanities Institute.

I am particularly indebted to those members of the Rutgers University Press who cordially assisted me in all stages of preparing the book for publication: Kenneth Arnold, the director; Marlie Wasserman, the editor-in-chief; Marilyn Cambell, the managing editor; and Cynthia P. Halpern, who did the copyediting. A paleolithic planner/editor who has unreasonably delayed entering the word-processing age, I thankfully acknowledge the help of two marvelous typists (now restyled, so I understand, as "data entrants"): Ruth Karp and Arleen Sepulveda. And because in the making of books there is surely no end of intermediating by one's family-as-association (Tocqueville would never have phrased it that way, but he certainly would have tried to explain it), I am very pleased to record my considerable debt, for all impromptu counsel rendered, to my daughters, son, and son-in-law, and most especially to my wife.

Obviously, my largest debt is to the scholars who richly contributed to this joint ventures in ideas and to the great intellect who inspired the venture: Alexis de Tocqueville.

Abraham S. Eisenstadt
New York City
June 1987

Contributors

BERNARD E. BROWN is Professor of Political Science at Lehman College and the Graduate Center of the City University of New York. His publications include *American Conservatives: The Political Thought of Francis Lieber and John W. Burgess* (1951); *New Directions in Comparative Politics* (1963); *Protest in Paris, Anatomy of a Revolt* (1974); *Intellectuals and Other Traitors* (1980); *Socialism of a Different Kind: Reshaping the Left in France* (1982); and (editor) *Great American Political Thinkers*, 2 vols. (1983).

SEYMOUR DRESCHER is University Professor of History of the University of Pittsburgh and Visiting Distinguished Professor at the Graduate Center of the City University of New York. His many books include *Tocqueville and England* (1964); *Tocqueville and Beaumont on Social Reform* (1968); *Dilemmas of Democracy: Tocqueville and Modernization* (1968); *Econocide* (1977); and *Capitalism and Antislavery* (1987). Of his several articles on Tocqueville, particularly notable is "Tocqueville's Two *Démocraties*," *Journal of the History of Ideas* (1964).

ABRAHAM S. EISENSTADT is Professor of History at Brooklyn College and the Graduate Center of the City University of New York. His publications include *Charles McLean Andrews: A Study in American Historical Writing* (1956); *American History: Recent Interpretations*, 2 vols. (1963; 1970); *The Craft of American History*, 2 vols. (1966); and (co-editor) *Before Watergate: Problems of Corruption in American Society* (1978).

GITA MAY is Professor of French and Chair of the Department of French and Romance Philology at Columbia University. Her books include *Diderot et Baudelaire, critiques d'art* (1957); *De Jean-Jacques Rousseau à Madame Roland, Essai sur la sensibilité préromantique et révolutionnaire* (1964); *Madame Roland and the Age of Revolution* (1970: Van Amringe Distinguished Book Award); and *Stendhal and the Age of Napoleon* (1977).

ROBERT NISBET is Albert Schweitzer Professor of the Humanities, Emeritus, of Columbia University. Among his numerous publications are *The Quest for Community* (1953); *The Sociological Tradition* (1966); *Tradition and Revolt* (1968); *Social Change and History* (1969); *The Degradation of the Academic Dogma* (1971); *The Social Philosophers* (1973; rev. 1983); *The Sociology of Emile Durkheim* (1974); *Twilight of Authority* (1975); and *History of the Idea of Progress* (1980). His noteworthy article, "Many Tocquevilles," appeared in *The American Scholar* 46 (Winter 1976–77): 59–75.

MELVIN RICHTER is Professor of Political Science at Hunter College and at the Graduate Center of the City University of New York. His publications include *The Politics of Conscience: T. H. Green and His Age* (1964) and *The Political Theory of Montesquieu* (1977). His article, "The Uses of Theory: Tocqueville's Adaptation of Montesquieu," appeared in *Essays in Theory and History: An Approach to the Social Sciences*, ed. Melvin Richter (1970).

DANIEL T. RODGERS is Professor of History at Princeton University. His works include *The Work Ethic in Industrial America, 1850–1920* (1978: Frederick Jackson Turner award) and *Contested Truths: Keywords in American Politics since Independence* (1987).

JAMES T. SCHLEIFER is Professor of History at the College of New Rochelle. His publications include *The Making of Tocqueville's Democracy in America* (1980: Merle Curti Award; Spanish translation, 1985); and a new French edition of the 1835 *De la Démocratie en Amérique* (Pléiade series, 1988). His most important articles on Tocqueville are "Tocqueville and Some American Views of Liberty" and "Jefferson and Tocqueville" (both in press), "*De la Démocratie en Amérique aux Etats-Unis*," in *Tocqueville* (Collection bouquins: Paris, 1986); "Tocqueville and Centralization," *Yale University Library Gazette* 58:1–2 (October 1983):29–39; and "Tocqueville and Religion: Some New Perspectives," *The Tocqueville Review* 4:2 (Fall 1982): 303–321.

ARTHUR SCHLESINGER, JR., is Albert Schweitzer Professor of the Humanities at the Graduate School and University Center of the City University of New York. His extensive writings, which have won him many distinguished awards, include: *The Age of Jackson* (1945: Pulitzer prize for history); *The Age of Roosevelt* (3 vols., 1957–60: Francis Parkman and Bancroft prizes); *The Imperial Presidency* (1973); *Robert Kennedy and His Times* (1978: National Book Award); and *Cycles of American History* (1986). In 1967 he received the National Institute of Arts and Letters Gold Medal for History, and in 1983 the Fregene Prize (of Italy) for Literature.

SEAN WILENTZ is Professor of History at Princeton University. He is the author of *Chants Democratic: New York City and the Rise of the American Working Class, 1788–1850* (1984), which received the Albert J. Beveridge award and the Frederick Jackson Turner award.

Reconsidering Tocqueville's
Democracy in America

Introduction

ABRAHAM S. EISENSTADT

OR THE past decade, America has been conducting an elaborate exercise of celebration whose grand theme is the bicentenary of the nation's birth. Occasional anniversaries have come up, such as that of erecting the Statue of Liberty, which have added further luster to the ceremonies of patriotic remembrance. Great deeds and documents of America's revolutionary age have drawn special acclaim, as of course have her foremost leaders. But men from other shores have invited our attention as well, and none more significantly perhaps than one man and his distinguished book: Alexis de Tocqueville and *Democracy in America*. The vogue of Tocqueville, already vital in earlier decades, has if anything become more vital during the bicentenary years. The present collection of essays, which undertakes to reconsider Tocqueville's *Democracy*, is in some measure part of the republic's salutation to its founding. But there are two principal reasons for the vogue of Tocqueville that lie well beyond the rites of celebration. First: the substance and premises of the *Democracy* invested it with enduring significance for the age that was ushered in by the transatlantic democratic revolution of the late eighteenth century. Second: it is a document that is particularly relevant to the issues facing America and western Europe in our own age.

In reconsidering the *Democracy*, we would do well to distinguish its importance from its vogue. Its importance inheres in the substance and quality of its inquiry into the basic problems of political society. Its vogue expresses its immediate concern with current issues in the politics of a particular period. Ever since its appearance, the *Democracy* has had an enduring importance in the Western world, if not a continuous vogue. Designed to educate European statesmen, and particularly French, it was a book about democracy, and particularly American.

With its double theme and purpose, the two parts of *Democracy*, which appeared in 1835 and 1840, were in effect really two distinct books bound by one title. For the same reason, its appeal to Europeans has differed from its appeal to Americans. In liberal Europe, the vogue of the *Democracy* remained vital throughout the decades of democratization; it declined from around 1880 to 1930; and has resumed its earlier vitality in the age of totalitarianism and the cold war.[1] In America, the *Democracy*, if hardly a very popular book, always found its place among scholars, politicians, publicists, and students in graduate and undergraduate academic institutions.[2]

In what way did the substance of the *Democracy* invest it with significance for the century that began with the attack on the ancien régime in the late eighteenth century throughout the Western world? *Democracy in America* is at bottom a discourse on the modern Western state: the state whose identity was redefined and transformed by the American and French revolutions. Tocqueville rightly perceived these revolutions, which challenged the rationale and continuity of aristocratic society, as manifesting the central tendency of modern politics. America served him merely as a point of departure, a model by which to understand what was happening in France, as well as where the French future lay. His grand subject was an analysis—in all its aspects—of democracy's driving force: the idea of social equality.[3] That the democratic revolution was irresistible he took as the central fact of his time. To question its advent was, he thought, self-deceiving and wasting valuable time.[4] The only valid enterprise for political leaders was to be everywhere concerned with the transmuting effects of democracy.[5] Because he saw all too clearly the vastly expanded domain of sovereignty that democracy could claim, his preoccupying interest was to ensure the survival of liberty.[6]

This gave his book its most enduring theme: the grave threat that democratic despotism posed to democratic liberty.[7] It was precisely because he discovered this antithesis in democracy that he ventured to call himself "a liberal of a new kind."[8] He wished to define the problems of the modern polity in new terms. Fully conscious of the issues that had troubled European politics in earlier times, he essayed a contemporary answer for contemporary problems: quite literally, a new science of politics for an age quite new. Because he saw equality as a dynamic and transforming force, his subject was in effect that of modernization. That is what, in considerable measure, has made the *Democracy* a continuously relevant book.

No less than its subject, the *Democracy*'s premises have given the book a perennial appeal. Tocqueville's thought took shape in the turbulent ideological terrain of Orleanist France, which formed a wavering bridge between a society that was ending and one whose contours were uncertainly taking shape. Who could say for sure just what the bridge linked: was it agrarianism and industrialism, patriotism and nationalism, localism and centralization, aristocracy and democracy, orthodox faith and heterodox, mercantilism and capitalism, collectivity and individualism, establishmentarianism and liberalism, or whatever other grand duads the social philosophers could propose? That they were prolix in their proposals was evident enough from the many plans that everywhere abounded for building the new Western world. Tocqueville was only one among the many prophets of Paris (but Paris was not their only habitat, in fact) who were busy in their ideational manufactories forging schemes for the new age.[9] One has to cite but some of their names to remember how imaginative and radical the social inventors were: Saint-Simon, Fourier, Sismondi, Blanc, Bentham, Owen, and of course Marx and Engels, the most memorable joint partners of that intellectually inventive age. Each fashioned a new society, and no less a new past with which to rationalize and validate the society he wished to introduce. For the new social currency they hoped to put into circulation, playing tricks with the past was only the other side of the coin of playing futures with the present.

Inhabiting the same milieu, spurred by the same social up-
heavals, Tocqueville was at bottom rather different, and it was
this difference that gave a more lasting resonance to his *Democracy*. He had no grand scheme for setting up the new commonwealth. He did not so much plan the future as fear for it.
He gave rather much to the supervening role of Providence and
rather little to inexorable laws of social change. In trying to
understand the tendency of his times, he kept his vision wide
and his reasons flexible. He did not fit them to a procrustean
chronology. The aristocratic age was waning, the democratic
age was waxing: because he did not set a date on either, what
he said about them had a continuing contemporaneity. He
hardly attempted to prove his basic premise: that the regime of
democracy, long in the making, was irresistible. He took this as
a given, on the basis of a highly sensitive intuition rather than
of extensively amassed evidence.[10] The prodigious facts embedded in their writings on social reform bound and dated
many of his contemporaries; the relative absense of such facts
from the *Democracy* liberated and revitalized Tocqueville. Far
from trying to prove the coming democratic age, he ascribed it
to Providence and he had merely to invoke it. He devoted his
life's work not to "discussing the evidence, much less finessing
it, but, on the contrary, exploring its consequences."[11] Working from intuition, Tocqueville took a leap in the dark into the
democratic future. That the future evolved as it did both sustained his intuition and validated his leap.[12]

Tocqueville built the grand structure of *Democracy in America* out of three elemental ideas—democracy, revolution, and
liberty.[13] He explored these elements in all their permutations
and combinations, ceaselessly contemplating, ruminating,
speculating. Writing a variety of scripts for the evolving future,
he never insisted on the inevitability of any one of them. He
kept his options open, intently resisting dogmatism.[14] This
mind-set gives the *Democracy* its special nature. It is in many
respects an intellectual log book in which Tocqueville takes the

reader on a shared, almost personal adventure of inquiry about the new democracy. One can almost hear him discussing the book's key themes with his principal contemporaries: men such as Royer-Collard, Chateaubriand, Guizot, even Thiers.[15] But while everywhere alive to the actualities of his day, Tocqueville wished to push beyond them. However much it is based on his close knowledge of July monarchy, the *Democracy* transcends the immediate scene of Orleanist France. Tocqueville willfully tried to liberate himself from his time and place. That was why, in measure, he refrained from acknowledging his debt to ideas he had surely picked up from his contemporaries. And that was why, suiting his intellect and temperament, the *Democracy* was not so much a book of answers as a book of questions. It was not that he began to think before he had learned anything, but that every fact he learned opened up a panorama of questions and hypotheses. Jean-Claude Lamberti puts one aspect of this very well: "He was a great inquirer, rather than a great reader."[16] In sum, the broad scale of his inquiry, his startling intuition, his refusal to dogmatize, his unremitting questions, his persistent hypothesizing: these formed the premises of the *Democracy*, giving it a sustained importance for the generations that followed Tocqueville.

If the *Democracy* had a continuing meaning for the modern Western polity, that meaning was greatly enhanced by the totalitarian revolutions of the 1920s and 1930s. The Nazi regime reminded Europe how dangerous German authoritarianism could be. Buttressed by widespread popular support and well-nigh universal plebiscitary sanction, Hitler could claim he was the agent of a democratic sovereignty.[17] He executed, to a degree that would have startled even the amazingly prescient Tocqueville, both a savage suppression of liberty by "democratic despotism" within his own state and an even more savage assault by "democratic despotism" on Germany's neighboring states. In May 1945 peace came to Europe only in a limited sense. The Western powers, including the United States, very soon understood that Stalin's Soviet Union, an only slightly variant form of despotism, was no less threatening and belligerent than Nazi Germany had been. If Tocqueville had hardly predicted the specific features of twentieth-century totalitarianism, he had surely considered that the body politic of democracy could bring forth a behemoth.[18] He had read Rousseau carefully; from his own family's experience in the Revolution, he understood all too well what power Rousseau's disciples could claim and what acts they could commit in the name of democracy.[19] Under the ancien régime, he said, centralized administration exercised very great power; revolution further enhanced the power the state could exercise; and democracy established by revolution could leave the individual virtually no breathing space for liberty. The concluding chapters of the *Democracy* focus precisely on the despotism that democracy could introduce.[20] The *Democracy* was far from being a book of predictions about totalitarianism. But the monstrous power and deeds of totalitarianism gave the *Democracy* a remarkably new significance. The reason was simple enough. Its principal theme, indeed Tocqueville's almost obsessive fear, was that central power marching under the sanction of democracy could all but extinguish liberty.

Tocqueville was hardly less important for the age following the downfall of the fascist powers and their allies. Totalitarianism dissolved many of the distinctive elements of the nineteenth-century polity. A revolution of the type that Tocqueville had understood and dreaded, it radically restructured power and society. Its sweeping premises were equality, centralization, nationalism, autarchy, warfare, and despotism. Where totalitarianism went down to defeat, a new polity had to be created, whose leaders faced the task of proposing a new science of politics for their new age. Liberal democracy necessarily figured in their proposals. Tocqueville, who had long contemplated what kind of democracy the new democracy could be, almost inevitably served as their guide and mentor. He had, after all, by anticipating the new democracy, reckoned with a liberalism of a new kind.

In the totalitarian states, where liberty carried no visa, where indeed its very idea was revolutionary, the *Democracy* gained no entry. But where its message was allowed, it took on new life, and particularly in three Western polities: France, the Federal Republic of Germany, and the United States. As the *Democracy* assumed an enhanced importance, it was natural enough for France to wish to celebrate the teachings of one of her most illustrious figures. But the reason for Tocqueville's appeal was more compelling than that. The crises he had seen in the France of his own day were, in slightly altered form, continuing to beset her. It is hard to put an exact number on the great trials France has experienced during the past two centuries in her passage through four monarchies, five republics, two empires, and a series of revolutions, civil wars, and world wars that historians could not certainly count. It was France's profound instability in the century before him that spurred Tocqueville's ideas; the instability continued during the century after his death. Unable to work out her organic laws, vacillating between the conflicting claims of the center and of the localities, France never successfully solved the problem that had so much troubled Tocqueville: how to set up the delicate balance between the mores of liberty and the governance of democracy.[21]

Fashioned by the Western democracies as a counterstate to Soviet-run East Germany, the German Federal Republic wished to impose restraints upon those internal forces that regularly inclined Germans toward authoritarianism. The American polity offered valuable guidance on how to fracture power and control the center. But no one had been more aware than Tocqueville of the immense strength that a continental state could exercise, and no one more alert to the problem that, in fact, seemed to trouble the Germans far more than the French: how to infuse the mores of liberty into attitudes and habits of the heart that gravitated toward authority. Tocqueville's gospel to the French was particularly important for the Germans. Liberty is not a legacy, it is an acquisition; it is not a growth of nature, but an art; it is not a genius, but a mastery. Libertarians are not born, they are made. After the Second World War, the Federal Republic of Germany went to school in the textbooks of liberty, and of these few were more instructive than the *Democracy*. Indeed, Tocqueville's appeal extended beyond West Germany. Wherever liberal democracy supplanted authoritarianism, that was where the *Democracy* was published and studied as a relevant and guiding text. For this reason, Italian scholars, who had engaged the idea of liberalism long before Mussolini's regime, resumed their engagement with it after his fall. And for this reason, too, editions of the *Democracy* have been appearing, in recent decades, in such countries as Spain and Portugal, in Latin America, and even in such a non-Western country as Japan.

Tocqueville captured the American mind in the years after the Second World War. It is really not hard to understand why he did so. He anticipated America's problems and world role with almost startling accuracy. He affirmed our institutions. And, in his analysis of our society, he appealed especially to our scholarly class.

It has impressed us as nothing short of remarkable that a man who spent no more than ten months on our shores, an alien to our language and our ways, should have been so capable of grasping our problems and anticipating what might come of them. *Democracy in America* went beyond being a book of anticipation: it was almost an eschatology. Tocqueville warned Americans about many components of their polity: the precariousness of liberty, the dangers of democracy, the threat of despotism, the fragility of federalism, the incontinence of an industrial aristocracy, the explosiveness of race relations—in sum, the tensions and contradictions that lay deeply embedded in the whole struture of our social and political institutions.

Many of the problems he foresaw have, to a lesser or greater degree, in fact been realized. He has in this way confirmed our sense of ourselves: both our sense of centrality in God's history and our apprehension about the role we are called on to play. We have long felt ourselves to be the people of the book; we resonate to the cry of prophetic warnings; we almost revel in jeremiads; and Tocqueville was surely the most cosmic of our Jeremiahs. He was in this way a latter-day Cotton Mather, with his own stupendous *Magnalia Democratiae Americana.*

Forecasting our problems alone would not have earned him our esteem. What fastened him in our mind was that he predicted our great prominence in world affairs. Working within the framework of his own providential dialectic, he underscored the antithesis of America and Russia, of liberal and despotic government. With remarkable insight, he factored out the element of democracy, which he regarded as universal and irresistible. In the coming democratic age, he said, men would insist on being equal, under a regime of liberty, if possible, or under a regime of despotism, if not. Perceiving the antipodes of Russia and America was hardly original with Tocqueville, but it satisfied exactly the way his mind formulated historical developments as the interplay of "pairs in tension," of forces that generated their own opposites, indeed their contradictions. His mind was never more alive than in contemplating history's paradoxes, ironies, and antitheses.[22] The discerning observer could find the working model of liberty by sailing due west, to the outermost reaches of the Western world. Where would he find the very opposite of the regime of freedom? By turning his eyes due east, to the Russia of Nicholas I, which learned Europeans took to be a regime of unqualified despotism. Posing the modular dyad of Russia and America was hardly the essence of Tocqueville's argument. But by making more of the antithesis than the *Democracy*'s principal theme warrants, Americans have converted his achievement from analysis to prediction. Over the business suit of the sober-minded Orleanist, they have, for their own reassurance, draped the mantle of a prophet.

Beyond predicting our role in the coming conflict between democracy and despotism, he affirmed our civilization. He balanced the valences and countervalences of our democracy and concluded that, on the whole, we had done a good job of it. It was the good fortune of the Americans, he said, that they had achieved liberty before democracy, that before the storm of equality swept across our polity, we had battened down the hatches of personal freedom. In sum, he put his stamp of approval on the American polity. Literally, he saw the democratic future in America, and, all in all, it was working. We were properly grateful for his favoring words in the 1830s, when European aristocracy everywhere condescended to us; we took affirmation wherever we could get it. But we clutched Tocqueville with an effusive zeal after the Second World War, when we suddenly found ourselves at the center of world politics. In the fearful struggle of ideology and power with the Soviet Union, where emblems and symbols counted as much as armaments, and precisely because they were themselves part of the armory, we scrounged the world for affidavits. Tocqueville's was one of the most important we found. In the age of disunited nations, he voted for America. In the age of conflicting ideologies, he bore witness for our democracy. He gave us a book of asseveration, a much-needed tonic for our troubled *crise de nerfs*. We were so flattered by his approval that we glossed over his reservations. It did not matter that he was not a Walt Whitman, or even a Ralph Waldo Emerson. However reservedly, he had said yes to us, and that was enough.

T O C Q U E V I L L E ' S current vogue rests, in no small measure, on his appeal to our intelligentsia, the men and women who run our colleges and universities, our learned journals, our reviews of politics and literature, indeed our popular presses. Seeking to comprehend all of American life, he postulated a usable hypothesis. He worked the highly complex terms of our political and social ways into a simple formula. He disclosed the touchstone of our institutions. In this sense, he was, for Americans trying to understand who they were and why they acted as they did, a brilliant discoverer: an estimable member of the company of Newton, Locke, Adam Smith, Darwin, Freud, Einstein. He was the unique founding father of the prodigious, amorphous undertaking of American Studies. The searching maxims of *Democracy in America* launched a thousand doctoral dissertations to sea. The new importance of the *Democracy* in the postwar decades may be ascribed not only to the quest for understanding America's idea and role in the new age of bipolar politics: it lay as well in the great growth, indeed the industrialization of the American scholarly enterprise. Here is why intellects everywhere were looking for a key. Tocqueville unlocked the door to the remarkable vista of American civilization, its contents and discontents. In stature and importance, only Karl Marx stood as his alternate in offering scholars a grand synthesis of the nature and prospects of American life.

For this reason, indeed, Tocqueville has appealed not only to American scholars but also to scholars throughout the democratic West. The new mandarins of a secular age, they have sought the guidance of Tocqueville's vast topography to understand and measure the contours of the Western polity. If they have not taken the *Democracy* as a book of holy writ, they have at least been engaged by its comprehending, predictive vision. As a professional class, scholars of the modern age are after all the keepers of the books, those select scriptures that are their polity's deposits of faith. And if they are not, in their studies and interpretations, looking for yet another heavenly city, they are withal inquiring about some social model for instruction and use. Tocqueville has therefore been enshrined by democratic scholars, who have made studying the *Democracy* an enterprise that underwrites both the importance of the book and of what they are saying about it. The Tocqueville revival in recent decades has generated a vast scholarly industry, whose manifold products may be found in books, articles, conferences, and a major transatlantic journal—*The Tocqueville Review/La Revue Tocqueville.*[23]

The publication of the master's writings is surely the most important sign of the Tocqueville renaissance. In France, under the superintendence of a specially designated national commission, the definitive edition of these writings has been appearing serially over the past few decades, as the *Oeuvres, papiers, et correspondances d'Alexis de Tocqueville (Oeuvres complètes).* Some fifteen volumes have thus far been published: the very first was *De la Démocratie en Amérique,* which appeared in 1951. Several books in the series have been translated into English. The English edition of the *Democracy,* edited by J. P. Mayer and Max Lerner, and translated by George Lawrence, came out in 1966. Most impressively, work on four major new editions of the *Democracy* is currently proceeding, each in a different language (French, English, Spanish, and Japanese) and all of them presenting, in varying degrees, important drafts the manuscript went through as well as the working papers Tocqueville used in writing his great book. The heavily annotated French edition of this *Democracy* in evolution, as it were, is being prepared by two of the foremost Tocqueville scholars of our day: the 1835 *Democracy* by James T. Schleifer; and the 1840 *Democracy* by Jean-Claude Lamberti. In tandem with these French volumes, Schleifer is editing an English edition of both volumes of the *Democracy,* which will similarly offer extensive annotation and commentary as well as a record of the variants and drafts of the ever-evolving book as Tocqueville kept working on it.

If publishing Tocqueville's works is a burgeoning enterprise, so too is writing about the man and the meaning of what he wrote. Lamberti, wondering whether Tocqueville was not in fact becoming an American author, has noted that American scholars have in recent years devoted considerable attention to his writings, and certainly to his *Democracy*.[24] Because of the extent of this scholarship, both in the form of monographs and articles, it would be infeasible to detail it here. But some note should be made of the fact that the whole venture of Tocqueville scholarship in America, started by Paul Lambert White at Yale, was effectively launched by George Wilson Pierson's magisterial volume, *Tocqueville and Beaumont in America* (New York, 1938). Tapping the vast resources of the Yale Tocqueville Manuscripts Collection, Pierson led successive generations of younger scholars into the Tocqueville adventure. Seymour Drescher's many works include two very important books on the great French master: *Tocqueville and England* (Cambridge, Mass., 1964), which closely analyzes the impact that his English visits and connections (apart from the obvious fact that his wife was English) had upon his evolving ideas about aristocracy, centralization, and the nature of free institutions; and *Dilemmas of Democracy: Tocqueville and Modernization* (Pittsburgh, 1968), which indicates how partial and ambivalent was his understanding of the transforming effect of industrialization in the three countries that figured principally in his political sociology—the United States, England, and France. Schleifer's *The Making of Tocqueville's Democracy in America* (Chapel Hill, 1980), a highly significant volume, perceptively discloses the remarkable intellectual journey the French political philosopher took in continuously shaping and reshaping the manuscript of his chef-d'oeuvre.

Recent French work on Tocqueville may be less extensive than American, but it is no less distinguished. Specific mention must be made here of two most impressive works. The first is the extensive and highly valuable biography of Tocqueville (Paris, 1984) by André Jardin, who is secretary of the French National Commission under whose supervision the definitive edition of Tocqueville's *Oeuvres complètes* is being published. The second is Lamberti's thought-provoking, profoundly analytical *Tocqueville et les deux démocraties* (Paris, 1983), which proceeds from the thesis (earlier argued by Seymour Drescher) that Tocqueville wrote what was, in effect, two books, and that he had envisaged two forms of democracy, their relevances, contrarieties, and ambivalences. To a lesser extent, but with hardly less significance for their respective polities, the study of Tocqueville is proceeding in the Federal Republic of Germany, Italy, Britain, the Iberian and Latin American countries, and Japan.

In the United States, in the years after the Second World War, Tocqueville's *Democracy* took on the quality of a major classic among the intelligentsia. We have already noted why: he had anticipated America's centrality in world politics; he had profoundly canvassed our major institutions and values; he had caught the essential nature of our society; he seemed on the whole disinterested, authoritative, and approving, and who would ask for anything more? It is beyond our scope here to explore the books on American history and life that owe much of their inspiration, even their ideas to the *Democracy*. Let it suffice to note only such highly influential volumes as Louis Hartz, *The Liberal Tradition in America* (New York, 1955); David Riesman and colleagues, *The Lonely Crowd* (New Haven, 1950); and *Max Lerner, America as a Civilization* (New York, 1957). Tocqueville was enshrined as one of the governing intelligences in the new discipline of American Studies. And his *Democracy* everywhere invaded the university, the virtually omnipresent emblem of the card-carrying intellectual. The more familiar of the two unabridged editions of Tocqueville's classic was the careful, indeed exemplary work of Phillips Bradley, which appeared in 1945 as the war ended and spread throughout undergraduate America in the paperbound Vintage Press format. Two decades later witnessed the publication of a second unabridged English-language edition of the

Democracy, edited by J. P. Mayer and Max Lerner, which we have already noted. As likely as not, university classes saw the *Democracy* in abridged versions, and of these the most widely used was the one prepared by Richard D. Heffner (New York, 1956). But there were also notable abridgments by Henry Steele Commager, Andrew Hacker, and Thomas Bender.[25]

The *Democracy* served in various ways as a commentary on American society and as a basis for contemplating it. Testimonies to its continuing relevance could everywhere be found. In *America Revisited: 150 Years after Tocqueville* (New York, 1978), Eugene McCarthy, a former United States Senator and a candidate for the presidency, retrospectively compared contemporary American problems with what Tocqueville had said about them. With something of a similar intent, Richard Reeves, a journalist, actually retraced Tocqueville's steps, looking for parallels and differences, in his *American Journey: Traveling with Tocqueville in Search of Democracy in America* (New York, 1982). With Tocqueville as their guiding intellect, Robert N. Bellah and his associates, in *Habits of the Heart* (Berkeley, Calif., 1985), studied the interplay of private and public life in America to understand its role in the survival of free institutions. In America's reviews of opinion and literature, it became fashionable to offer a quotation from the *Democracy* or to invoke its author as a sanctifying authority. And if one needed the assistance of a handy book of reference, one could readily consult *Tocqueville's America: The Great Quotations* (Athens, Ohio, 1983).

Contemporary scholarly interest in Tocqueville's *Democracy* in a Western polity arises from two sources: the particular nature and problems of the polity, and the special role of its scholarly class. For all that, merely adventitious events have stimulated the Tocqueville revival even further, as was evident from the major conferences that have recently been held to celebrate the sesquicentennial of the publication, in 1835, of the *Democracy*'s first part. *The Tocqueville Review*, which devoted an entire volume (number 7: 1985–1986) to these celebrations, listed three such meetings: in January 1985, sponsored by the Claremont Institute for the Study of Statesmanship and Political Philosophy; in August 1985, by the American Sociological Association; and in October 1985, by the Library of Congress and the Tocqueville Society.

There was in fact a fourth major American conference on Tocqueville's *Democracy*, held at Brooklyn College and at the Graduate Center of the City University of New York in October 1985, under the sponsorship of the Brooklyn College Humanities Institute and the C.U.N.Y. Academy for the Humanities and Sciences. It was at these meetings that most of the essays in this volume were, in variant forms, originally presented. Because the *Democracy* is a grand construct of ideas, the conference was (like the others) a ceremony of cerebration. And because Tocqueville explores issues that are perennially controversial and unsettled, the pronouncements of the assembled scholars were themselves very often matters of controversy and indeed of antithesis. Here it need be said only that a few of the contributors to this volume have done signal monographic studies of Tocqueville, that some others have written notable articles about him, and that in their diverse writings all have worked under his pervasive challenge. What binds them as participants in a valuable journey is that they have all taken the *Democracy* as a point of departure. From that point, each writer has undertaken to examine a significant problem posed by the *Democracy* and to answer the key questions that problem presents.

The principal subjects of the essays in this volume come under three larger rubrics: the sources of Tocqueville's basic ideas (his *idées-mères*, as he called them); the major themes he dealt with; and overall appraisals of the substance and importance of the *Democracy*. Rather than summarize the themes or arguments of the essays that follow, I considered it far more advantageous to pose the questions that each author has tried to

answer. It would surely be unprofitable to anticipate or distill
the argument the author sets forth. Posing each essay's key
questions, moreover, is very much in keeping both with the nature of the *Democracy*, which was animated by a spirit of inquiry, and the intellect of Tocqueville, who knew that to get
authentic answers one had to begin with authentic questions.

What were the origins of Tocqueville's grand ideas? This is
the large question considered by Gita May and Bernard E.
Brown. Napoleon, his unremitting nemesis, has been called a
son of the Enlightenment: how far may the same be said of
Tocqueville? And what in particular did he owe to Montesquieu, the founder of the modern school of political sociology,
in which the writer of the *Democracy* was surely one of the
most prominent members? To what extent did Tocqueville's
ideas about democracy originate with that special brand of pol-
itician-jurist that revolutionary and early republican America
had invented? Most significantly, what did the *Democracy* owe
to the most important single commentary on the constitution
and government of the United States: *The Federalist*?

What were the major themes of the *Democracy*? The question leads in turn to several others that are seriatim considered
by Seymour Drescher, Arthur M. Schlesinger, Jr., Melvin
Richter, and James T. Schleifer. That it appeared in two volumes, published at an interval of five years, has raised a besetting question: Is the *Democracy* one work or two? To what
extent did one mind unite both volumes, to what extent did the
passage of half a decade divide them? And, relatedly, how are
we to explain the variant portraits of democracy that we find in
the two volumes, with a spirited, active citizenry in the first,
and a self-involved, apathetic citizenry in the second? Constantly concerned as he was with the antimony of liberty and
authority in the democratic state, what did Tocqueville make of
France's recurrent drift toward her native brand of supervening
power: Bonapartism? And how far was despotism to be the
universal tendency of democracy? If every great work of politi-

cal theory offers a philosophy of history no less than an image
of its own time, what were the ideas about the past that informed Tocqueville's *Democracy*?

What appraisal have latter-day scholars, particularly those
of our own age, made of the *Democracy* as a commentary on
the larger lineaments of the American polity: the one that
Tocqueville saw and the one that has since evolved? This broad
problem is considered, from various perspectives, by Robert A.
Nisbet, Daniel T. Rodgers, Sean Wilentz, and Abraham S.
Eisenstadt. That Tocqueville was merely one of a distinguished
group of modern European social theorists has long been understood: but would it not richly enhance that understanding
to see his great work as presenting an ideal type of its essential
theme, the antithesis of democracy and aristocracy? In recent
decades, Americans have acclaimed the *Democracy* as a prevision of today's United States: but how far did Tocqueville, in
fact, err in his predictions and how far were these errors com-
pounded by his attempt to find a rationale for his predictions?
Despite its considerable range, how far was Tocqueville's understanding of the United States in the 1830s limited by his
underlying, essentially conservative premises? And, for this reason, did he not fail to see that, beyond that broad American
democracy on which he centered, there were in fact, in the
Jacksonian age, many democracies? The two most important
books ever written about the United States were written by two
foreign visitors: Alexis de Tocqueville and James Bryce. On
what grounds did Bryce find the *Democracy* seriously questionable, and what do his questions signify both for the *Democracy*
and his own distinguished companionate volume, *The American Commonwealth*?

T H E S E, then, are the subjects—and the questions they
elicit—which the contributors to this volume have sought to

address in their respective essays. The essays represent a collective effort in reconsidering Tocqueville's *Democracy in America*: its origins, themes, and meaning. The reading of the *Democracy* that each contributor offers is, so far as expertise is concerned, authoritative. But it is, for all that, provisional. That the *Democracy* is a book that invites reconsidering, indeed almost demands it, has been precisely the point of this introduction. Tocqueville offers us a double relevance. One is objective. There is much in what he says about our institutions, values, and role in world politics that accurately describes them and that yet retains an essential validity. But there is withal in the *Democracy* a subjective relevance. The book is important not merely for the light it throws upon the continuing actualities of American society but also for the way in which it serves as a mirror to our particular time. Is this not indeed the quality of a classic, that it lends itself to successive rereadings and reconsiderations? In this sense, wishing to find meaning for our own age, we shall continuously be looking for Tocqueville. In this sense, too, the essays in this volume are commentaries both on the *Democracy* and our generation. This is an aperçu that Tocqueville would very well have understood. In his masterpiece on America we see more than the image of democracy: we also see ourselves.

PART I
Origins

Tocqueville and the Enlightenment Legacy

GITA MAY

WHILE the centennial of the dedication of the French sculptor Bartholdi's Statue of Liberty in 1886 has been the object of great fanfare and popular rejoicing, as well as a much-publicized renewal of Franco-American relations, the sesquicentennial of the publication, in 1835, of Alexis de Tocqueville's *Democracy in America* was, by comparison, a rather quiet and subdued affair indeed, commemorated by a handful of historians and scholars and barely noted in the press and mass media. Perhaps the difference between the two celebrations has something to do with semiotics. The Statue of Liberty is a highly visible icon, sacralized by both history and popular myth. *Democracy in America*, on the other hand, is a far less tangible token of Franco-American friendship. The austere printed word has always had a hard time competing with the immediacy of the image. Yet both the statue and the book stand for the same ideas and ideals that were forged by the Enlightenment movement. Half a century before the French presented the Statue of Liberty to the American people, Tocqueville came to America, an experience that inspired a work that needs no renovation to show all its freshness and relevance.

As an adolescent, Tocqueville came upon the major works of the French Enlightenment in his father's library. It was a discovery that freed him of the conservative principles and religious orthodoxy inculcated in him by the family priest that had been entrusted with his education. All his life, Tocqueville would remain an avid reader and thoughtful disciple of the *philosophes.*

25

Tocqueville is a true son of the age of enlightenment and revolution in his political liberalism and in his passionate commitment to human freedom and democracy.

For Tocqueville, as for the eighteenth-century *philosophes*, politics and ethics are inextricably intertwined, and the aphoristic, pithy way in which he underscored this relationship brings to mind not only such brilliant practitioners of the terse, provocative phrase as Montesquieu and Voltaire, but also their seventeenth-century predecessors, notable La Rochefoucauld and La Bruyère. That Tocqueville belongs to this great French *moraliste* tradition has not, I think, been sufficiently acknowledged and would deserve a more detailed analysis. Examples of Tocqueville's fondness for the concisely expressed truth or principle, such as the following statement, "A man's admiration of absolute government is proportionate to the contempt he feels for those around him,"[1] abound in his writings.

He is also in the eighteenth-century tradition in his thorough engagement in his country's political life, in his willingness to risk official disfavor and even imprisonment for his principles. His cosmopolitism and cultural relativism are eminently eighteenth-century traits. So is his tirelessly analytic turn of mind. If some of the most striking, memorable passages of the *Journeys* are of a personal nature, the travel notebooks, diaries, and jottings primarily deal with the great themes of the formal works, especially *Democracy in America*, for which Tocqueville continues to be justly famous. As his correspondence also reveals, Tocqueville was wholeheartedly involved in the politics of his time.[2]

O N E has to go back to the age of enlightenment and revolution and its nineteenth-century aftermath to find the origins of the major modern political ideologies, notably liberalism, socialism, and fascism. There is no doubt that Tocqueville, by his

profound and passionate belief in individual freedom so fully
and clearly demonstrated in his writings as well as in his activities as a public servant, distinctly exemplifies political liberalism
at its best. In this respect, it is worth noting that his political
thinking, on the whole, is closer to that of Montesquieu than
that of Rousseau.

Both Montesquieu and Tocqueville, although they were privileged members of the aristocracy and aristocrats by personal
sensibility, wits by esthetic inclination, historians of ideas by intellectual choice, and travelers by predilection, became dedicated artisans of liberal reform by ideological conviction. Like
Montesquieu, Tocqueville looked upon the shortcomings of
contemporary French society with sharp eyes, and he had the
courage to voice his opinions with bold frankness. Like
Montesquieu, he acquired firsthand experience in the legal and
judicial system of his day, but he was too thoughtful and introspective to throw all his energies into a career, preferring to follow his calling as a writer and political theorist. Both
Montesquieu and Tocqueville were more interested in the great
principles of jurisprudence rather than in the practical, everyday side of legal or juridical work. It is also noteworthy that
Democracy in America, upon its publication in 1835, enjoyed
the kind of instantaneous popular success reminiscent of the
Spirit of Laws. And it is no mere coincidence that both works
are written in a clear, compact style that retains the informality
and directness of the spoken word, and that both are divided
into short chapters with helpful, descriptive headings to facili-
tate readability. In both works, furthermore, the author does
not hesitate to use the first person form to comment on an idea
or principle or to relate an anecdote. This use of a form characteristic of the memoir-novel endows the text with a continuous
narrative movement and flow that makes it strikingly vivid and
personal.

In this respect, *The Old Regime and the French Revolution*
is also particularly revealing, for Tocqueville specifically chose

as the model for this work Montesquieu's *Considerations on the Causes of the Greatness of the Romans and Their Decadence.* Tocqueville admired Montesquieu's ability to seek out the underlying, interconnected causes of historical events. He would approach history, and especially the French Revolution, its origins and aftermath, in the spirit of Montesquieu.

Like Montesquieu, Tocqueville would not be content to retell an already-familiar story. His narrative would offer a useful lesson to be drawn from the successes and failures of the past. Like Montesquieu, Tocqueville wished to use his study of history in order to illuminate contemporary events. He of course knew full well that he was not the first to undertake a history of the French Revolution, for he was well acquainted with Germaine de Staël's *Considerations on the Principal Events of the French Revolution* (1818), Adolphe Thiers's *History of the French Revolution* (1823–1837), Lamartine's *History of the Girondins* (1847), as well as with the studies on the same subject, either already in print or in the process of being published, by Carlyle, Mignet, Michelet, and Louis Blanc. Tocqueville, of course, could not be a mere compiler. He was an original thinker and writer, and his book bears the unmistakable stamp of his own thought and style. At the same time, however, his affinities with Montesquieu are quite striking, both in substance and style: notably the belief in the universality of law and justice, the preference for separation of powers through checks and balances, and the predilection for a clear, readable mode of expression.

Tocqueville was convinced that one could only gain a full understanding of present events and of their implications for the future if one first studied old regime France and the complex underlying causes of the Revolution, and he viewed the revolutions of 1830 and 1848 not as separate events but as part and parcel of a process that began in 1789.[3] In all his writings, Tocqueville stressed the continuity of the eighteenth and nineteenth centuries. For him there was no rupture between the two. Similarly, he viewed the American Revolution as a continuing process:

> The society of the modern world which I sought to delineate, and which I seek to judge, has but just come into existence. Time has not yet shaped it into perfect form: the great revolution by which it has been created is not yet over. . . . Although the revolution which is taking place in the social condition, the laws, the opinions and the feelings of men, is still very far from being terminated, yet its results already admit of no comparison with anything that the world has ever before witnessed.[4]

Tocqueville's correspondence with Arthur de Gobineau from 1843 to 1859 is emblematic of the growing opposition in the thinking of two men of fairly similar backgrounds and intellect; among other affinities, they both were greatly indebted to Montesquieu and to his notion of climate and geography as determining factors in history, both shared a fascination with the question of why civilizations rise and fall, and both were inveterate travelers. The estrangement between the two men became more sharply marked after the publication in 1853–1855 of Gobineau's *Essay on the Inequality of Human Races*, an enormously influential work closely identified with the beginnings of pseudoscientific racism and twentieth-century fascist anti-Semitic doctrine. While a gifted young man like Tocqueville threw himself wholeheartedly into the struggle for liberalism and reform in the tradition of the Enlightenment and Revolution, his somewhat younger contemporary and erstwhile friend committed his not-inconsiderable talents as a writer and polemicist to propagating a race theory of Aryan-Nordic supremacy based upon a grossly simplified and distorted notion of biological determinism.

Tocqueville's fame has long rested on his *Democracy in America*, on the finished part of *The Old Regime and the French Revolution*, and on his autobiography, *Recollections*.

Modern scholarship has greatly enriched our knowledge of Tocqueville through the publication of the political drafts, writings and discourse, the travel notebooks, and the correspondence. In this body of newly available material, one sees Tocqueville constantly analyzing and judging the industrial society taking shape under his eyes. His gift of prophecy has of course long been acknowledged, especially his uncanny ability to see in a United States of America slowly emerging from British colonial rule the makings of a modern, capitalistic superpower. These views are of course at the opposite pole of those that were being developed, almost during the same years, by Karl Marx and his associates and disciples.

It was Tocqueville's conviction that the exclusive quest for equality can only end up in servitude; that there is tension—and not a concordance—between liberty and equality, and that egalitarianism can all too easily lead to the worst kind of tyranny, for it can promote the concentration of all political power in the hands of one representative of the state and can lead to questioning of the legitimacy of private property, this last bulwark of the individual against the state. While Tocqueville could not help admiring the grandeur of equality as a revolutionary ideal, he was keenly aware of the dangers it presented to individual liberty:

> Of all the political effects produced by the equality of conditions, this love of independence is the first to strike the observing, and to alarm the timid; nor can it be said that their alarm is wholly misplaced, for anarchy has a more formidable aspect in democratic countries than elsewhere. . . . For the principle of equality begets two tendencies; the one leads men straight to independence, and may suddenly drive them into anarchy; the other conducts them by a longer, more secret, but more certain road, to servitude. Nations readily discern the former tendency, and are prepared to resist it; they are led away by the latter, without perceiving its drift; hence it is peculiarly important to point it out. (2: 345–346)

Tocqueville's uncanny prophetic gift has been borne out by the way in which he formulated the great political questions of his day, as he perceived them in his career as a public servant and as a writer, social observer and traveler, for the major modern political problems of our time are largely as he had predicted them. It is perhaps a paradox that this offspring of an aristocratic family, who had been imprisoned and had barely escaped the scaffold during the French Revolution, should have looked upon it as the fountainhead of modern democracy and that he should have rallied not only to the Revolution of 1830, but also to the more radical Revolution of 1848, despite private misgivings about some of its excesses. He paid for this and for his condemnation of the 2 December 1851 coup d'état by being briefly jailed and turned out of office by Napoleon III.

WHEN on the morrow of the 1830 Revolution, Tocqueville undertook to visit the United States, his primary goal was to observe at firsthand the workings of a democratic state, the way federalism operates, the penal system (the official goal of his trip), and, perhaps most importantly, the factors that had ensured the survival of the republic, a particularly crucial issue because such important eighteenth-century political writers as Montesquieu and Rousseau believed that a republic can subsist only in a small territory. He hoped that this visit would provide him with some of the answers to fundamental questions raised by recent political events in Europe, especially in France. Here he would glimpse what course one might expect not only France but other nations to follow as well, since America offered, he believed, a mirror image into the future:

It is not . . . merely to satisfy a legitimate curiosity that I have examined America; my wish has been to find instruction by which we may ourselves profit. . . . I confess that in America I saw more than America; I sought the image of democracy itself, with its inclinations, its character, its prejudices, and its passions, in order to learn what we have to fear or to hope from its progress. (1: lxxxi–lxxxii)

Tocqueville was not only intent upon seeing as much as possible of this vast land, he also wanted to meet as many Americans as possible. For nine months he kept up a feverish pace, meeting Indians, ordinary city dwellers and rural folks, as well as some of the leading political figures of the day (Andrew Jackson and John Quincy Adams, among others): "I have lived a great deal with the people in the United States, and I cannot express how much I admire their experience and their good sense" (1: 377). He was especially impressed by the dynamic nature of American society and by the apparent limitless possibilities afforded individual enterprise. That this fostered a spirit of restlessness, even among those who had everything to be content with their fate, did not escape him:

> America is a land of wonders, in which everything is in constant motion, and every movement seems an improvement. The idea of novelty is there indissolubly connected with the idea of amelioration. No natural boundary seems to be set to the efforts of man; and what is not yet done is only what he has not yet attempted to do. (1: 510–511)

To be sure, Tocqueville did not come away from his journey an entirely uncritical observer of American mores and social institutions. He denounced slavery with a vigor and indignation reminiscent of Montesquieu:

> The permanent evils to which mankind is subjected are usually produced by the vehement or the increasing efforts of men; but there is one calamity which penetrated furtively into the world, and which was at first scarcely distinguishable amidst the ordinary abuses of power: it originated with an individual whose name history has not

preserved; it was wafted like some accursed germ upon a portion of the soil, but it afterwards nurtured itself, grew without effort, and spreads naturally with the society to which it belongs. I need scarcely add that this calamity is slavery. (1: 424)

Tocqueville furthermore illustrated his thesis that "the more progress was made, the more was it shown that slavery, which is so cruel to the slave, is prejudicial to the master" (1: 430) by vividly contrasting the prosperity of Ohio, which had abolished slavery, with the economic stagnation of neighboring Kentucky, which still retained it (1: 430–434).

Acknowledging the powerful role played by religion in American society, he noted that "the sects which exist in the United States are innumerable" (1: 359), but that they agree with respect to civil freedom and to the duties and obligations due from one individual to another, and generally keep aloof from political parties and daily politics. That religion should exert such a strong hold on "the most enlightened and free nation of the earth" (1: 360) gave him pause, for such Enlightenment thinkers as Montesquieu and Voltaire had consistently stressed the relationship of religion to superstition, ignorance, and obscurantism. But his own antireligious bias shows in the remark that "hypocrisy must be common" (1: 359) in a country where religion is so dominant.

Tocqueville analyzed at considerable length the importance and power of the press in the United States and its great impact on public opinion as well as on laws, manners and mores: "The influence of the liberty of the press does not affect political opinions alone, but it extends to all the opinions of men, and it modifies customs as well as laws" (1: 204). At the same time, he was fully aware of the ways in which public opinion can be manipulated: "I shall not deny that in democratic countries newspapers frequently lead the citizens to launch together in very ill-digested schemes." (2: 134). But despite these reservations, he viewed freedom of the press as an absolute necessity in a democratic country, for the press is the best safeguard against abuses of power.

Tocqueville also noted, with an obvious lack of enthusiasm, the American love of physical comforts and prosperity and identified it as an essentially middle-class passion (2: 155), characteristic of a society that recognizes material success and wealth rather than privileges of birth and nobility:

> I never met in America with any citizen so poor as not to cast a glance of hope and envy on the enjoyments of the rich, or whose imagination did not possess itself by anticipation of those good things which fate still obstinately withheld from him. (2: 155)

The American frantic pursuit of pleasure and money elicited some of Tocqueville's most critical remarks:

> A native of the United States clings to this world's goods as if he were certain never to die; and he is so hasty in grasping at all within his reach, that one would suppose he was constantly afraid of not living long enough to enjoy them. He clutches everything, he holds nothing fast, but soon loosens his grasp to pursue fresh gratifications. (2: 160)

His journey to America led him to the conclusion that mores, beliefs and ways of thinking and feeling, more than written laws, determine the historical course of a democratic nation:

> The manners of the Americans of the United States are, then, the real cause which renders that people the only one of the American nations that is able to support a democratic Government; and it is the influence of manners which produces the different degrees of order and of prosperity. . . . Thus the effect which the geographical position of a country may have upon the duration of democratic institutions is exaggerated in Europe. Too much importance is attributed to legislation, too little to manners. (1: 383)

In this respect, Tocqueville, refining Montesquieu's theory of the impact of geography and climate upon civilization and culture, was one of the first to realize the importance of collective psychology, what the French call *mentalité*, a view of history fostered by such *Annales* School scholars as Fernand Braudel and Le Roy Ladurie. To understand a society, we must begin with its environment, climate, and resources, and then proceed to study its political and economic organization. It is this broad concept of *mentalité* that gave Tocqueville's idea of history a new depth and vitality that places him in a line that can be traced directly to Montesquieu.

Also uncannily relevant is Tocqueville's more than ever timely observation on the United States and Russia as the two new superpowers of the modern world:

> There are, at the present time, two great nations in the world, which seem to tend towards the same end, although they started from different points: I allude to the Russians and the Americans. Both of them have grown up unnoticed; and whilst the attention of mankind was directed elsewhere, they have suddenly assumed a most prominent place amongst the nations; and the world learned their existence and their greatness at almost the same time. (1:521)

Montesquieu, Diderot, and Rousseau had each written at some length about womanhood and the "woman question." Tocqueville remains faithful to the Enlightenment tradition by devoting four chapters (chapters 9, 10, 11 and 12 of Book Three) to a comprehensive survey of the impact of social and political changes in American society upon women, specifically their education (chapter 9), their marital status (chapter 10), their legal and moral status (chapter 11), and the way in which Americans understand the "Equality of the Sexes" (chapter 12).

Tocqueville must have realized that his analysis of the political, legal, and social stucture of American society would not be complete without an attempt to assess the role of women, and in this respect, his ideological stance is, on the whole, reminiscent of, yet more progressive than, Rousseau's in his fifth book of the *Emile*, devoted to the education of Sophie, the young woman destined to be Emile's lifelong companion. Present-day feminists have understandably balked at Rousseau's portrayal of Sophie as a rather pliable, docile, and passive creature, but earlier readers including such notable women as Madame Roland, Germaine de Staël, and George Sand, thought her an admirable, moving character, capable of ennobling life by endowing marriage and motherhood with a new moral seriousness and dignity. Similarly, Tocqueville approvingly notes the emphasis on those qualities of morality and character that make American women excellent wives and mothers. Yet at the same time, he underscores the remarkable independence and freedom of action enjoyed by women in the United States:

> Long before an American girl arrives at the age of marriage, her emancipation from maternal control begins: she has scarcely ceased to be a child, when she already thinks for herself, speaks with freedom, and acts on her own impulse. The great scene of the world is constantly open to her view: far from seeking concealment, it is every day disclosed to her more completely, and she is taught to survey it with a firm and calm gaze. Thus the vices and dangers of society are early revealed to her; as she sees them clearly, she views them without illusions, and braves them without fear; for she is full of reliance of her own strength, and her reliance seems to be shared by all who are about her. (2: 7–238)

Tocqueville could not help remarking that he was frequently "surprised, and almost frightened" at this "boldness" of thought, behavior, manner and even language (2: 238). But that he was basically sympathetic to the cause of women is made clear by the way he defined the problem:

I have shown how democracy destroys or modifies the different inequalities which originate in society: but is this all? or does it not ultimately affect that great inequality of man and woman which has seemed, up to the present day, to be eternally based in human nature? I believe that the social changes which bring nearer to the same level the father and son, the master and servant, and superiors and inferiors generally speaking, will raise woman and make her more and more the equal of man. (2: 251)

But like Rousseau, Tocqueville subscribed to the notion that is now generally characterized as "biological destiny," for he holds that nature has determined "wide differences between the physical and moral constitution of man and woman" (2: 252). Nature has fashioned woman to be dependent upon her male companion; hence the importance of those agreeable qualities in woman that will please man. Women who swerve from their essential calling as wives and mothers and strive to compete with men in the community and public affairs betray their very nature. Hence his approval that "in no country has such constant care been taken as in America to trace two clearly distinct lines of action for the two sexes, and to make them keep pace one with the other, but in two pathways which are always different" (2: 252).

Tocqueville's conclusion to the chapter once more underscores his ambivalent attitude toward women:

As for myself, I do not hesitate to avow that, although the women of the United States are confined within the narrow circle of domestic life, and their situation is in some respects one of extreme dependence, I have nowhere seen woman occupying a loftier position; and if I were asked, now that I am drawing to the close of this work, in which I have spoken of so many important things done by the Americans, to when the singular prosperity and growing strength of that people ought mainly to be attributed, I should reply,—to the superiority of their women. (2: 255)

Although Rousseau had hardly advocated equal rights for women, he had painted an extremely appealing picture of women as devoted wives and mothers. If nature did not destine women to be the intellectual equals of men, it conferred on them the more precious privilege of exerting a moral ascendancy over the family by their innate aptitude for love and unselfish devotion. In this way, their sphere of influence would be far greater than if they attempted to compete with men and to arrogate some of their authority. That they were necessary for the happiness of men made them their indispensable mates and trusted friends rather than their subservient vassals. A woman's fulfillment could only be found in her role as guardian of the home and hearth, since the natural order of things has preordained her, both physically and mentally, for this place in society.

THE AGE OF ENLIGHTENMENT was also the age of travel. But traveling was not enough. Eighteenth-century travelers were not only bent upon going to the outer reaches of the explored globe, they were also determined to share their experience with others by writing about it. This travel fever was bound to affect famous authors. Montesquieu, Voltaire, Johnson, Sterne, to cite only a few well-known names, explored geographical displacement as a major theme in essays, journals, and fiction. Certainly they recognized the powerful appeal of exotic new places as a way of stimulating the imagination and of escaping from the routine of everyday life.

But there was of course more to the eighteenth-century vogue for travel than mere escapism. In the ideological war that was being waged against ignorance, prejudice, and intolerance, the theme of travel became a wonderfully flexible tool, indeed a powerful weapon, for it enabled authors to question the very foundations of the sense of superiority that a western nation such as France or England might take for granted.

Eighteenth-century writers came to take great relish in pointing out differences and contrasts between nations, civilizations, cultures, and religions. The arbitrariness of particular customs and mores, both in the mother country and in the foreign land under scrutiny, could thus be highlighted, with entertaining comical and satirical effects. Such relentless, even obsessive inquisitiveness about the apparently most minute aspects of life of an alien people, the more exotic and alien the better, such a passionate desire to astonish the reader with strange customs and rituals were meant to erode his smug confidence in his own way of life. Thus eighteenth-century travel literature played a key role in laying the foundations of modern history and anthropology.

These are some of the reasons that induced authors to explore the globe, whether in actuality or vicariously through firsthand accounts, and to contrast cultures, civilizations, and nations in their essays, letters, and works of fiction. Eighteenth-century literature is replete with such confrontations between the French and English, the Persian and Parisian, the European and American, the Christian and Tahitian or Indian.

Tocqueville, as a relentless and tireless traveler with a sharply inquiring mind, perpetuates a tradition brilliantly exemplified by the whole eighteenth century. He had long been an avid reader and great admirer of travel accounts, and one of his favorite works was the *Letters from Italy*, by Charles de Brosses, a friend of Buffon and contributor to the *Encyclopedia*.

What is it that attracted Tocqueville so strongly and consistently to the travel journal or travel account as a literary genre? His own restlessness and love of travel, the delight he took in comparing cultures and civilizations, and the personal pleasure he derived from discovering new places and customs certainly had a great deal to do with this fascination. But Tocqueville was of course no mere hedonist seeking novel sensations and pleasurable impressions. His quest was of a more profound nature. He sensed intuitively that one of the deepest yearnings of the human spirit is for the unknown, the strange, and the exotic. Travel satisfies this need for change, for to move from city to city, to discover new places and to behold unaccustomed sights is fully to experience one's own freedom.

Tocqueville's *Journeys* continue to be highly readable and informative works to this day because of their wealth of perspicuous observations on political and social institutions, highly personal views on local traditions and customs, and their vivid picturesque sketches, vignettes, and scenes. The tone is genial and informal and is further enlivened by well-placed dialogues and anecdotes; the descriptions are pithy and pungent, the overall pace is brisk. Here again Tocqueville's style and manner are closer to the eighteenth century than to the high-flown prose and lyrical outbursts of Chateaubriand's travel accounts. Humor, nimbleness of thought, lightness of touch, and wariness of any kind of posturing characterize Tocqueville the traveler and tourist. His outlook is remarkably close to eighteenth-century cosmopolitanism, relativism, and humorous irreverence.

Despite the inconveniences and discomforts of travel in his time, Tocqueville obviously enjoyed his journeys. His insatiable curiosity, his love of adventure, his good-natured willingness to cope with, even welcome, the unexpected, his affability and sociability with both travel companions and strangers, his perceptiveness as a political observer, his skill as a narrator and storyteller, all these qualities endow his *Journeys* with an enduring charm and appeal. And in these lively pages and informal notes, the twentieth-century reader can glimpse towns and landscapes the contours of which have by now all but vanished. In this largely rural and pastoral America, Tocqueville moved tirelessly from town to town, making most of the opportunities of meeting and chatting with people in coaches and inns, and disregarding exhaustion in order to set down his thoughts and impressions.

AS A POLITICAL libertarian and dauntless opponent of all forms of sham and hypocrisy, Tocqueville is a worthy heir of the age of enlightenment and revolution. He remained a devoted student of the literature and thought of the eighteenth century, and Montesquieu, probably more than any other author, had a profound and lasting impact on his political, ethical, and esthetic outlook.

Tocqueville's style, which generally steers clear of the more sumptuous rhetorical effects of poetic imagery and metaphor, and, as has already been suggested, consistently remains faithful to the classical model of clarity and readability, could, when the author deemed that a more romantic flourish was in order, rise to lofty levels of oratory and summon the richer orchestration of poetical similes. Nothing demonstrates more vividly this rhetorical virtuosity than the way in which Tocqueville bids a fond farewell to the vast, new land to which he had devoted so much thought and energy in his epoch-making journey:

> A traveller, who has just left the walls of an immense city, climbs the neighbouring hills; as he goes further off he loses sight of the men whom he has recently quitted; their dwellings are confused in a dense mass; he can no longer distinguish the public squares, and he can scarcely trace out the great thoroughfares; but his eye has less difficulty in following the boundaries of the city, and for the first time he sees the shape of the vast world. (1: 515)

Tocqueville returned to France convinced that the United States represented a precious symbol of hope for humankind and living, enduring proof that the eighteenth-century belief in

the feasibility of human, moral betterment and social perfecti-
bility had not been a merely utopian dream:

> In that land the great experiment was to be made, by civilized man,
> of the attempt to construct society upon a new basis; and it was
> there, for the first time, that theories hitherto unknown, or deemed
> impracticable, were to exhibit a spectacle for which the world had
> not been prepared by the history of the past. (1: 11)

Tocqueville and Publius

BERNARD E. BROWN

HAROLD LASKI once observed that *Democracy in America* is probably the greatest work ever written on one country by the citizen of another. It is also generally agreed that *The Federalist* is the greatest work of political science (if not of political theory) ever written by Americans. What is the relationship between these two classics? Or rather, since *The Federalist* was written almost half a century earlier, to what extent were Tocqueville's ideas shaped by his reading of James Madison, Alexander Hamilton, and John Jay?

Tocqueville refers frequently to *The Federalist* throughout the 1835 volume of *Democracy*. The first of many citations is to Hamilton's paper number 45 on the federal system. In a long footnote, Tocqueville says: "I shall often have the occasion to cite *The Federalist* in this work," going on to describe the circumstances under which Jay, Hamilton, and Madison—under the collective signature of Publius—wrote the articles that now comprise the complete treatise. There follows an enthusiastic commendation: "The Federalist is a great book which, although uniquely American, should be known to the statesmen of all countries."[1]

Tocqueville's debt to *The Federalist* appeared obvious to many Americans at the time. In 1840 Joseph Story complained in a letter to Francis Lieber: "The work of de Tocqueville has a great reputation abroad, partly founded on their ignorance that he has borrowed the greater part of his reflections from American works, and little from his own observations. The main body of his materials will be found in *The Federalist*, and in Story's *Commentaries on the Constitution*. . . . You know ten times as much as he does of the actual workings of our system and of its true theory."[2]

43

We know that Tocqueville read Story's *Commentaries* (presented to him by the author) with care. Tocqueville thereby received a double dose of *The Federalist*. Story himself declared in the preface that he was greatly influenced by the work of Hamilton, Madison, and Jay, as well as by the ideas of Thomas Jefferson and John Marshall. Much of Story's *Commentaries* are little more than a gloss on *The Federalist*. Page upon page from Hamilton and Madison (including Number 10 in its entirety) were reproduced in order to illuminate the meaning of certain passages in the Constitution. Tocqueville also had Story as a guide to the very "great book" he read on his own and so frequently cited.

Most students of Tocqueville have paid no attention to Joseph Story's complaint, or have dismissed it out of hand. It is rare to find any reference among French critics to the possible influence of *The Federalist* upon Tocqueville. Perhaps the foremost American authority on Tocqueville, George W. Pierson, mentions Story's claim only in order to refute it—though his reasoning is flawed by glaring contradictions. Pierson first assures us that any influence of Publius on Tocqueville was indirect. He explains that Tocqueville had hired two young Americans (Theodore Sedgwick and Francis J. Lippit) in Paris to assist him with the task of amassing and translating materials. Inasmuch as both Sedgwick and Lippit were educated in America, comments Pierson, it is natural that Tocqueville was exposed to the ideas of both Story and Publius. Nonetheless, he argues, the Frenchman reworked these ideas in the light of his own larger theoretical and political concerns. Secondly, Pierson points out that Tocqueville cited both Story and *The Federalist*, thereby publicly acknowledging their direct influence! Pierson compounds the confusion by mentioning that Tocqueville copied many pages from *The Federalist* into one of his notebooks (the "cahier E").[3] One is reminded of the vaudeville routine: "I never borrowed your pot; and besides, there was a hole in it."

Whether Tocqueville was influenced directly or indirectly by Publius is no longer a matter of speculation or dubious logic, thanks to the fine detective work done recently by James T. Schleifer. Tocqueville purchased a copy of *The Federalist*, Schleifer reports, during his trip to the United States. Apparently he had not read and did not subsequently make use of the French translation. His copy was the single-volume edition published in Washington, D.C. in 1831 with "the Numbers Written by Mr. Madison Corrected by Himself." From 27 to 29 December 1831 Tocqueville read *The Federalist* with extreme care, and he took copious notes—arranged under the headings: "Union: Central Government" and "Sovereignty of the People." Schleifer argues that Tocqueville absorbed the ideas of *The Federalist* so thoroughly that he could no longer distinguish between those ideas and his own. Many of the specific points Tocqueville copied into his notebooks were used in the *Democracy* without any indication of their source. The uncovering of these unacknowledged debts, concludes Schleifer, "makes his reliance seem even more substantial than perhaps he himself realized." He goes on to assert that Tocqueville reflected *The Federalist* "probably more than he realized and certainly more than the *Democracy* would disclose."[4]

What was borrowed, how much of that was changed, and how much rejected? In raising these questions I do not wish to suggest that Tocqueville was a plagiarist, or that his work is merely derivative. That would be absurd. We rightly celebrate Tocqueville as one of the most creative thinkers of the nineteenth century. But Tocqueville drew many of his *"idées-mères"* (as he put it) from *The Federalist*; recognition of that influence is necessary in order to arrive at a proper appreciation of Tocqueville's own contribution. The analytic current runs in the reverse direction as well. *Democracy in America* is an interpretation of *The Federalist* by a master theorist. Tocqueville's view is in refreshing contrast to that of some twentieth-century political scientists seeking to demonstrate that *The Federalist* is merely the ideology of a wealthy and advantaged elite.[5] Tocqueville rather saw *The Federalist* as a seminal work of political science, one that offered a key to an understanding of the process whereby orderly freedom may come out of revolution.

THE FIRST extensive citation of *The Federalist* by Tocqueville—and the point where he graciously acknowledges his intellectual debt to Publius—occurs during his discussion of federalism. It is a measure of Tocqueville's brilliance that, from his first reading of *The Federalist* (as is evident from his notes in the "cahier E"), he could grasp the central meaning of federalism and its import for France. One of the causes of the French Revolution, according to Tocqueville, was a hypercentralized administration that extinguished the spirit of enterprise. But how could the integrity of the French nation be maintained if provinces and localities enjoyed autonomy?

The American solution, he saw, was to divide responsibilities between states and the national government by giving each the power to enforce decisions against individuals, and by giving the national government all the power it needed to meet its obligations of defense and the maintenance of national unity. A vast territory could be governed, as Tocqueville understood the American experience with the aid of Publius, by combining vibrant local with strong national government through the federal principle. Tocqueville considered this "wholly novel theory" to be a "great discovery of contemporary political science."[6]

He immediately understood the implications of that theory for France. It could be demonstrated that the centralized administration fashioned by the old regime and further developed under the Revolution and Bonaparte was *not* essential to secure the interests of the nation; rather, a decentralized administration and polity could be even more effective in reconciling local

initiatives with central direction. "The Union is free and happy
like a small nation," Tocqueville pointed out, "and glorious
and strong like a large nation." The *loi Defferre* (instituting decentralization) adopted by the Mitterrand government in 1982
was modeled on Tocqueville's vision of diversity within unity,
which in turn derived from his meditation upon the principles
of federalism as set forth by Publius.[7]

The section of the *Democracy* that caused the greatest stir
when the book appeared in 1835, and which most observers
believe is Tocqueville's most original contribution, is on the
"omnipotence of the Majority in the United States and Its
Effects." It is here that Tocqueville develops his striking argument: a powerful democratic revolution is taking place everywhere; it is irresistible; but the majority is tyrannical. What an
arresting paradox! Is there any way out for those who want
both democracy and freedom? Few students of Tocqueville are
aware of the inspiration he drew from Madison in both stating
and analyzing the problem.

In an early draft of the *Democracy*, Schleifer reports,
Tocqueville wrote: "How *démocratie* leads to tyranny and will
happen to destroy liberty in America. See the beautiful theory
on this point exposed in *The Federalist*. It is not because powers are not concentrated; it is because they are too much so that
the American Republics will perish."[8] The reference to Madison's "beautiful theory" (better translated as "great theory," in
my opinion) disappeared in the final version of the *Democracy*
—thus obscuring a vital link between Publius and Tocqueville.
If we reestablish that link, Tocqueville's thought appears in a
new light.

The key to Tocqueville's theory of majority tyranny is to be
found in the last three pages of chapter 7 of the 1835 *Democracy*. After leading us through a complex argument in which
paradoxes are stated, taken apart, and replaced by solutions,
Tocqueville declares his satisfaction that "President Madison
expressed the same thoughts," particularly in Number 51.

Inasmuch as Tocqueville actually started out with Madison's "great theory" on majority rule and tyranny, the observation is disingenuous. Tocqueville then quotes a long passage from Number 51 that American readers are tempted to skip over because of its familiarity. But it deserves the same careful scrutiny by us that the young French liberal gave it; it contains the essential elements of his theory.

Madison here asserts that, in a republic, not only must society be guarded against the oppression of its rulers, but one part of society must be guarded against the injustice of the other part. "Justice is the end of government" and the civil society. Madison then sums up the basic argument of Number 10. He postulates a critical difference between faction (even when it is embodied by a majority) on the one hand and justice or the public good on the other. Throughout *The Federalist* the warning is sounded that the immediate interests of individuals as well as of majorities may not further the long-term good of the collectivity. As one example (cited many times by Publius): debtors may gain temporary relief through the issuance of cheap paper money; but in the long run, they and everyone else will suffer from the lack of a sound currency. The distinction is reminiscent of the one made by Rousseau between the "will of all" and the "general will."[9]

Tocqueville's citation from Number 51 continues, hammering home the point that a majority can be either oppressive or just, depending upon how it is consulted and the role it plays in governance. If the stronger faction can unite and oppress the weaker, Madison argues, "anarchy may as truly be said to reign as in a state of nature, where the weaker individual is not secured against the violence of the stronger." Now comes the crucial step, which anticipates the last phase of the French Revolution and the emergence of Bonaparte.

And, as in the latter state [of nature], even the stronger individuals are prompted by the uncertainty of their condition to submit to a government which may protect the weak as well as themselves, so, in the former state [of oppressive majority rule], will the more powerful factions be gradually induced by a like motive to wish for a government which will protect all parties, the weaker as well as the more powerful. It can be little doubted, that, if the State of Rhode Island was separated from the Confederacy and left to itself, the insecurity of right under the popular form of government within such narrow limits would be displayed by such reiterated oppressions of the factious majorities, that some power altogether independent of the people would soon be called for by the voice of the very faction whose misrule had proved the necessity of it.[10]

Tocqueville, obsessed by the link between the Revolution and Bonapartism, at once grasped the central teaching of Publius: that oppression of minorities is unjust, even for the majority. Out of majority omnipotence comes one form of anarchy and a cry for a power "altogether independent of the people"—the dictator (to use the term current in America at the time).

Madison derived his theory from Jefferson's reflections upon his experience as wartime governor of Virginia. As governor, Jefferson was saddled with a council of state (one of whose members for a period was none other than James Madison), which hampered him at every turn. The assembly gathered most power in its own hands. But no assembly can actually govern; the result was that power concentrated in the legislature led to chaos, in turn producing profound dissatisfaction on the part of the people and even among the delegates—the situation described by Madison in Number 51. In the last days of Jefferson's term, a motion to appoint a dictator narrowly failed of adoption. The incident outraged Jefferson, who blamed it on the lack of separation of powers in the Virginia constitution.[11]

For Madison, the instrument of majority tyranny in a republic is the legislature, cited throughout *The Federalist* as the expansive force that must be countered by the other powers of government. Tocqueville chose to close his argument by citing Jefferson on the "tyranny of legislatures," rather than Madison, "because I consider him the most powerful apostle that democracy ever had."[12] Tocqueville thought he was forcing an admission even from Jefferson that the all-powerful legislature, as the preferred instrument of majority factions, was the major threat to the public good. He did not connect the thinker he admired (Madison) with the democrat he distrusted (Jefferson), unaware that the former got his major principles from the latter!

Let us now go back to the beginning of chapter 7 to see how Tocqueville applied Madison's "great theory." One shudders at the thought that generations of scholars and students in the English-speaking world have expended their energies trying to make sense of the Henry Reeve translation, as revised by Francis Bowen, and continued in the popular Phillips Bradley edition: "I hold it to be an impious and detestable maxim that, politically speaking, the *people* have a right to do anything; and yet I have asserted that all authority originates in the *will of the majority*. Am I, then, in contradiction with myself? [my italics][13] It takes Hegelian gymnastics to find a contradiction between "the people" and "the will of the majority" (which presumably is less than the whole people). What Tocqueville actually said is not tortuous dialectics, but straightforward Madisonianism: "Je regarde comme impie et détestable cette maxime, qu'en matière de gouvernement *la majorité d'un peuple* a le droit de tout faire, et pourtant je place dans *les volontés de la majorité* l'origine de tous les pouvoirs. Suis-je en contradiction avec moi-même?" The correct translation: I hold detestable the doctrine that "the *majority of a people* has the right to do anything; and yet I have asserted that all authority originates in the *will of the majority*."[14] *That* is an apparent contradiction.

How to defend against the inexorable logic of democracy? By whom can limits be imposed upon majorities? The answer is implicit in the enterprise undertaken by Publius—to secure the ratification of a constitution by a majority of the people that would impose limits upon themselves and future majorities. How can one majority limit another? By positing a difference between a majority that creates a fundamental law and a majority that then makes decisions according to that fundamental law. Drawing up and ratifying a constitution is considered by any people to be a solemn and binding act, quite different from a change of legislation. It calls for a "judicious choice," as Hamilton put it in Number 1, based on our "true interests, unperplexed and unbiased by considerations not connected with the common good." The problem is thus solved: the people can be made to realize that, in their own interests, they should place limits on their sovereign power.

Tocqueville's development of this theme follows in the footsteps of Publius. Above the factional struggle, above even the majority, is justice—termed a general law of mankind, not merely that of a majority. When Tocqueville proclaims that in refusing to obey an unjust law he appeals from the sovereignty of the people to the sovereignty of mankind, he is repeating one of Madison's favorite dicta. The Athenian majority had the power to condemn Socrates to death, Madison pointed out several times, but it thereby committed an act of injustice. Tocqueville likewise denounced the doctrine of majority rule as fit only for a slave, declaring: "the power to do everything, which I should refuse to one of my equals, I will never grant to any number of them."[15] French readers would immediately sense a repudiation of the Terror.

Tocqueville's condemnation of unlimited power as evil, whether concentrated in the hands of people or king, aristocracy or democracy, monarchy or republic, is a direct echo of doctrines of Madison and Jefferson. In criticizing the first Virginia constitution in *Notes on Virginia*, cited extensively by Madison in Number 48, Jefferson stated:

> All the powers of government, legislative, executive, and judiciary, result to the legislative body. The concentrating these in the same hands is precisely the definition of despotic government. It will be no alleviation that these powers will be exercised by a plurality of hands, and not by a single one. One hundred and seventy three despots [the number of delegates in the Virginia Assembly] would surely be as oppressive as one.

The logic of *The Federalist* and, later, of the *Democracy* unfolds in parallel fashion. In a popular government (Publius) or democracy (Tocqueville) the greatest danger is the accumulation of power in the legislature. Why? Drawing upon Jefferson, Madison argued that a legislature is unable to govern because of the very nature of a large group—its diversity of interests, tendency to quarrel, and inability to arrive at consistent decisions. Hence, assembly government would inevitably lead to disorder and anarchy, out of which would come the cry for a dictator. Tocqueville, on the basis of the experience of revolutionary France, shared Madison's horror of assembly government, and for the same reasons. We have already noted Jefferson's furious reaction to the call for a dictator by the Virginia assembly during the American Revolution; and Madison and Hamilton predicted the emergence of a dictator (identified as in all probability a military demagogue) if the Constitution were not ratified. Similarly, Tocqueville was witness to the cycle of anarchy and terror in France, which culminated in the rule of Napoleon Bonaparte. Just as Publius had argued, a theoretically all-powerful assembly eventually would wish to be delivered of its impossible burden by turning to the providential man on horseback.

What is the solution? Publius argued for the extended republic and a proper distribution of power among the several branches. As Jefferson put it in the same passage cited at length in Number 48: "An *elective despotism* was not the government we fought for; but one which should not only be founded on free principles but in which the powers of government should be so divided and balanced among several bodies of magistracy as that no one could transcend their legal limits without being effectually checked and restrained by the others." Similarly, Tocqueville: "Suppose a legislative body so constituted as to represent the majority without necessarily being the slave of its passions; an executive power that has strength of its own; and a judicial power independent of the other two powers; then you would still have a democratic government, but there would be hardly any risk of tyranny."[16]

In his conclusion to the 1835 *Democracy*, Tocqueville characterizes the republic in the United States in terms drawn straight from Madisonian theory. The republic is based on the "enlightened will of the people"; it is the "tranquil rule of the majority." After it has time to reflect and find itself, the majority is the source of all power. "But the majority is not all powerful. Above it, in the moral world, there is humanity, justice and reason; in the political world, established rights. The majority respects these barriers and, if it happens to break through them, it is because it has passions like any man, and like any men, it can do evil in aiming at the good."[17]

Tocqueville was in complete agreement with Publius over another great advantage of representative government. According to Madison, it offered the possibility of vesting power in virtuous men, who know the difference between factionalism and the public good or justice. The people had sufficient virtue, Madison believed, to select men of virtue for public office; if not, then the republic would be a lost cause. And men of virtue would filter the raw passions and demands of the people, "refining" their views in the interest of the nation as a whole. Tocqueville conceptualized this distinction by contrasting "égoisme" and "individualisme" on the one side with "la force individuelle" or "l'intérêt bien entendu" on the other. Liberty would be safeguarded in a democracy only if an aristocracy of merit and virtue could temper popular demands, Tocqueville argued, and lead the people rather than merely following them. Thus would egoistic individualism (Madison's factionalism) be transcended and an era of enlightened self-interest (Madison's public good) ushered in.

Some of Tocqueville's strictures on the danger of popular tyranny in the United States are confusing at first sight. Readers might well wonder why that danger still exists after the adoption of the new Constitution. Tocqueville declared: "The government of the American republics seems to me as centralized and more energetic than that of the absolute monarchies of Europe. I do not, therefore, believe that it will perish from weakness." If the free institutions of America are ever destroyed, it will be due to the omnipotence of the majority, which will provoke minorities to desperation and recourse to force. "Anarchy will then be the result, but it will have been brought about by despotism"—a central theme in *The Federalist* as well.

But in a footnote (all too easy to overlook), Tocqueville adds that he is speaking "not of the federal government, but of the individual governments of each state that the majority directs despotically."[18] That is exactly the point made by Madison: a majority in a state like Rhode Island can adopt measures that oppress a minority (by printing paper money, for example), creating economic chaos, and a demand by that very majority for order—imposed by a dictator if need be. Tocqueville's condemnation of majority tyranny is directed at the states where separation of powers does not (in his opinion) exist. Hence, he shared the fury of Publius over the anarchy created by Shays' Rebellion, and by Rhode Island's all-powerful legislature. The solution of Tocqueville is exactly the same as that proposed by Publius: adoption of a fundamental law with a proper separation of powers, including a role for leadership by the more enlightened members of society. However, Tocqueville and Publius had somewhat different notions of the people who fit that description.

IT COMES as no surprise that a French aristocrat, profoundly shocked by the terror of the Revolution and scornful of the up-start Bonapartist rule it spawned, should have political differ-ences with a member of the Virginia planter class, a New York lawyer and banker of uncertain lineage, and a prominent New York jurist—all active participants in a revolution. Tocqueville parted company with Publius on a number of important points, especially as regards the nature of executive leadership and of freedom of opinion.

In the *Democracy* of 1835 Tocqueville shared with Publius a concern that in a republic the greatest threat of accumulation of power comes from the legislature, the only branch directly elected by the people. If anything, the French have been more sensitive to the dangers of assembly government than the Amer-icans. Tocqueville was impressed, indeed overly impressed, with one of the checks on legislative power described by Publius: an independent judiciary. By training a lawyer and magistrate, Tocqueville was favorably disposed toward the le-gal profession and judges. He accorded the Supreme Court a far greater role in maintaining separation of powers than did Madison or even Hamilton.

The most important check on the legislature, according to Publius, was an independent and energetic executive. From his reading of *The Federalist* (in particular numbers 66 through 77, cited extensively in the *Democracy*), Tocqueville assimilated a major point Madison derived from Jefferson's *Notes on Vir-ginia*, one that was repeated by Hamilton. Care must be taken not to render the president's decisions subordinate to a council, Tocqueville said, which would weaken the government and

diminish its responsibility.[19] Tocqueville also agreed with
Publius that there are no absolute guarantees. In the long run
we must depend upon the good sense and virtue of the citizens.
"There is no country where the law can foresee everything, and
when institutions can take the place of reason and mores."[20]
Compare this with Number 43, where Madison asks what can
be done about an insurrection pervading all the states. "The
answer must be that such a case, as it would be without the
compass of human remedies, so it is fortunately not within the
compass of human probability; and that it is a sufficient recom-
mendation of the federal Constitution that it diminishes the
risk of a calamity for which no possible constitution can provide a cure."

The enthusiasm with which Hamilton described the power
and potential of the presidency is missing in Tocqueville. The
office of the presidency had indeed suffered a decline after
Jefferson's retirement and up to Jackson's election. Nonetheless, Tocqueville did not sufficiently appreciate the leadership
roles of Washington, Jefferson, and Jackson. He mentioned a
possible future expansion of presidential power in the event
of a threat to the union or due to an increased importance of
foreign affairs, but he pointedly omitted domestic policy. Hamilton proved to be a far better prophet of presidential government than Tocqueville.

Consider Tocqueville's characterization of the presidential
office. "The president is placed besides the legislature," he asserted, "as an inferior and dependent power." Because the veto
can be overridden, for Tocqueville, the president is not part
of the sovereign power, but merely its agent. The argument
becomes confused when Tocqueville attributes almost royal
prerogatives to the president, only to declare that he has no occasion to use them and that the rights that he can use are circumscribed. "The laws allow him to be strong; circumstances
keep him weak." Writing when Andrew Jackson was in office,
he allowed himself to say that the president cannot prevent

laws from being passed, that his enthusiastic and sincere cooperation is undoubtedly useful, but is not necessary to the operation of government.[21] The statement is technically correct in that a veto may be overridden; it is politically inaccurate.

Tocqueville endorsed popular supremacy in the abstract, but he could not accept its political consequences. A president, he said, becomes obsessed with the desire to be reelected; every action is subordinated to that goal; and as the crisis of election approaches, the "individual interest takes the place of the general interest." He saw the president as prostrating himself before the majority in order to secure reelection. "Instead of resisting its pressure, as his duties oblige him, he caters to its caprices." He described Andrew Jackson (whom he considered a vulgar demagogue) as an instrument of the "blind democratic instinct of the country." General Jackson, he continued, is the "slave of the majority"; he follows its will, desires its barely veiled instincts, or rather he anticipates it and runs to place himself at its head. He treats the representatives of the national will with disdain by exercising the veto; the power of General Jackson increases, that of the presidency decreases. He even dismissed Jackson's victory at New Orleans as a mere bagatelle—though not all French generals of aristocratic origins could claim victories against English armies under any circumstances.[22]

How could such a "mediocre talent," opposed by the "enlightened classes," rise to a position of supreme power? Because the natural instincts of democracy induce the people to reject distinguished citizens as their rulers; an equally strong instinct induces able men to retire from the political arena. Tocqueville referred specifically to the new southwestern states that are a conglomeration of "adventurers and speculators." How can the state be protected and the society be made to flourish, he asked, when such people are invested with public authority? In his travel journal, Tocqueville recounts with disbelief the story of his encounter with an apparent scoundrel—a former governor of Tennessee who left his family, lived with an Indian woman for a time, and now sought to make his fortune elsewhere. How could such a character ever have received the votes of his fellow citizens, Tocqueville asked the passengers on the river boat—as if the phenomenon were beyond rational explanation. It turned out that the adventurer was none other than Sam Houston—whose future exploits as a general and founder of the Republic of Texas could hardly have been imagined by the young French aristocrat.[23]

Tocqueville sought support for his views on the political incapacity of the electorate by selective quotations from *The Federalist*. He cited Hamilton to the effect that the inconstancy and mutability of laws is a blemish on the character and genius of American government. And he reproduced a long passage from Hamilton purporting to demonstrate that the people are loathe to tax themselves, from which Tocqueville deduced that a democracy will find it difficult to raise armies, create navies, or defend itself against an absolute monarchy. In both cases Hamilton's thought was taken out of context. The New Yorker blamed the mutability of laws on assembly government, not on popular elections. Secondly, Hamilton was arguing in favor of the union, which would stimulate commerce; and commerce, he believed, is a more regular source of revenue and taxes than excises upon goods or taxes upon land. He certainly believed that a popular government could raise revenues—most effectively by levying taxes upon trade and commerce. Tocqueville's pessimistic conclusions about the viability of democracy were not shared by Publius.[24]

Tocqueville could not accept the implications of the argument developed by Publius: that the people must elect their chief magistrate (in a manner, it is true, that affords as "little opportunity as possible to tumult and disorder"); and that the chief magistrate is expected to lead, not merely to carry out the will of Congress. According to Hamilton, the executive generates the "energy" that activates government; while the legisla-

ture is best adapted to "deliberation and wisdom" and to the
defense of the privileges and interests of the people. The notion
that the president innovates while the legislature reacts and
controls is central to an understanding of the American political system. What Tocqueville thought to be presumptuous on
the part of the president (a refusal to carry out the will of the
legislature by exercising the veto) was considered by the founders as the sheet anchor of the system, a solid barrier to pernicious assembly government.

According to Tocqueville, the Americans went too far in
relying upon the people to restrain themselves by electing leaders who would "refine and enlarge" upon their views and who
would agree to have their powers held in mutual check. His
ideal remained a government founded on the "real wishes" of
the majority, but where the majority, "overcoming its natural
egalitarian instincts, in order to favor the order and stability of
the State, consents to invest with all the attributes of the executive power *a family* or an individual."[25]

Here Tocqueville reveals a crucial difference between himself
and Publius. The authors of *The Federalist* had ruled out monarchy (despite Hamilton's lingering nostalgia for the British
model); republican government was the only form of government they considered. For Tocqueville, constitutional monarchy offered the best chance to preserve a role for aristocrats,
who were far more likely than merchants or industrialists in his
view to place the national interest above self-interest. His preference for monarchy, mentioned only incidentally (even fur-
tively) in the *Democracy*, was clearly stated elsewhere. In his
thoughtful address to the voters of Valognes in 1837, candidate
Tocqueville began by affirming that absolute power in France
had created an eternal cycle of servitude and anarchy, and he
elaborated on the need for an enlarged liberty. The now-
famous author then presented his book's thesis: "The study of
the United States showed me that republican institutions absolutely did not suit us" (*ne nous convenaient point*), though it

offered a glimpse of how free institutions could increase the power, wealth, and glory of a people.[26]

Reflecting many years later upon his experience as a minister under President Louis Napoleon, Tocqueville first commented specifically on the choice of a republic or a monarchy for his own country. "I did not believe then, any more than I do now, that the republican form of government is best suited to the needs of France. What I mean exactly by republican government, is an elected executive power. With a people among whom habit, tradition, custom have assured so vast a place to the executive power, its instability will always be, in exciting times, a cause of revolution; and, in peaceful times, a cause of great uneasiness." His concluding remarks have universal application. "Moreover, I have always considered that the Republic was a government without counterbalance, which always promised more, but always gave less liberty than constitutional monarchy."[27]

Publius accepted the American Revolution's stubborn logic of political responsibility and sought to create order within that logic. Tocqueville could not see leadership coming from any source other than an aristocracy (of birth or of the judicial robe). He sought to salvage what was valid in the aristocratic ideal and to place it in the service of democracy. This French aristocrat found inspiration and strong leads in *The Federalist* but not a satisfactory definition of the political role he envisaged for his class and for himself.

"I know of no country," declared Tocqueville in the *Democracy* of 1835, "in which there is in general so little independence of mind and real freedom of discussion as in America."[28] Taken literally, we are asked to believe that there was less independence of mind and freedom of discussion in America than in, not only England and France, but Russia and China, Prussia and Japan, or anywhere else. The formula has shock value that serves at the very least to concentrate the attention of the reader.

On this point Tocqueville differs sharply from Publius. Madison also denounced the tendency of democracy to oppress minorities and individuals. But he was careful to point out in Number 10 that he was referring to a "pure democracy," where a small number of citizens assemble and administer the government in person. "A common passion or interest will, in almost every case, be felt by a majority of the whole; a communication and concert results from the form of government itself; and there is nothing to check the inducements to sacrifice the weaker party or an obnoxious individual." Those democracies, he continued, have ever been "spectacles of turbulence and contention." The key point here is that the evil flows from the form of government itself. There are no checks on the sovereign people, no possibility of recourse to higher or even to other authorities. Hence, a philosopher accused of corrupting the youth of Athens may be judged and condemned to death without any appeal. As Madison put it in Number 55: "Had every Athenian citizen been a Socrates, every Athenian assembly would still have been a mob."

Hamilton and Madison were concerned that majority rule in individual states (their constant example was Rhode Island) would approach the model of pure democracy and hence lead to majority oppression. But the whole purpose of adopting the Constitution was to institute a republic with a proper separation of powers, which would safeguard minority and individual rights. "As long as the reason of man continues fallible," said Madison in Number 10, "and he is at liberty to exercise it, different opinions will be formed." The problem for him was not an alleged absence of free thought, but rather "a factious spirit" that threatened to poison the wellsprings of government. The raging debate over the Constitution, followed by the rivalry between Federalists and Democrats, hardly suggested to Publius a lack of free discussion.

To better appreciate Tocqueville's position, it would be useful to keep in mind what he did *not* mean. He did not

mean—as his French readers might naturally have assumed—that the press was censored, or that political opposition was stifled. In Tocqueville's America it could hardly be
said that the Whig opposition was reluctant to complain about
the alleged despotism of "King Andrew." Indeed, Tocqueville
goes out of his way, in a chapter on freedom of the press in
America, to cite extensively a violent partisan attack on President Jackson in the first newspaper he read upon his arrival. He
wanted to show his compatriots that a lively and free press
would not necessarily undermine the stability of a political
system.[29]

Tocqueville also admired American education, which he said
was based on experience and common sense, serving admirably
the purpose of self-government.[30] In the opening chapter of the
Democracy of 1840, he paid tribute to the "philosophical
method" of Americans, which is to challenge received traditions and established opinions, to constantly seek the reasons
for things as they are, to search for the meaning behind the
forms, and thereby to escape from the yoke of habit, family
maxims, class opinions, and national prejudices.

Tocqueville did not look with favor upon the questioning of
fundamental religious beliefs by rationalist thinkers. On the
contrary, he believed that religion acts as a check on impulses
toward instability and anarchy. If religion is too weak to per-
form that task, then freedom becomes license, and the way is
open to disorder and despotism. For him, religion is more necessary in democratic republics than anywhere else, because it
helps to create a moral unity.[31]

What, then, was behind Tocqueville's sweeping assertion
about the lack of "real" (véritable) freedom of discussion in
America? His most recent biographer, André Jardin, suggests
that the young French traveler was struck by the sensitivity of
Americans to criticism by foreigners.[32] Tocqueville argued
that, in the "proudest nations of the old world," books have
been published that satirize or criticize the vices and vanities of

rulers. He mentioned specifically La Bruyère residing in the court of Louis XIV when he wrote his chapter on great men, and Molière criticizing the court in plays performed before it. But the sovereign in America, the people, will not tolerate any questioning of its capacity to govern; it is wounded by the slightest criticism, and demands praise instead. "The majority, then, lives in a state of perpetual adoration of itself; only foreigners or bitter experience can bring some hard truths home to American ears." And hence his startling conclusion: there are no great writers in America because there can be no literary genius without freedom of mind; and "there is no freedom of mind in America."[33]

As Jardin points out, some of the Americans Tocqueville and Beaumont met in 1831 were profoundly irritated by Captain Basil Hall's *Travels in North America in the Years 1827 and 1828*. The English author had been graciously received everywhere; but to the consternation of his former hosts, he lambasted every aspect of American society, culture, and politics—not omitting speech and posture. Captain Hall was an especially arrogant Tory; his offensive remarks reopened wounds from the revolution and the recent War of 1812.

That Americans resented the comments made by Captain Hall—along with those of other European writers, including notably Mrs. Trollope—was probably true, though Francis Lieber thought otherwise. Writing in 1835, the German liberal who had settled in America had an impression exactly contrary to that of Tocqueville. He found his hosts to be eminently "good-natured." The Americans, he reported, "will allow you freely to make your remarks upon this country, laugh heartily with you, and never get angry on account of your free remarks. I have found this so constantly and in so striking instances, that I do not hesitate to state it as a fact."[34]

Whatever the case, the sensitivity of individuals to harsh criticism of their own country is hardly the same as lack of freedom of mind. Tocqueville remarked elsewhere that Americans

should not be brought to speak of Europe, because of their pre-
sumptions and pride, but they were extremely well-informed
about their own country.[35] It worked the other way, too. Europeans expressed presumptuous and prideful views concerning America; that Americans (or some of them) consequently
were irritated would be understandable.

Tocqueville's bill of indictment, it may be suggested, is best
seen as an integral part of his comparison of republics and
monarchies. Mention has already been made of his observation
in the *Recollections* that republics promise more but allow less
liberty than monarchies. There must always be a superior social
power in a nation, he contended in the *Democracy*, but liberty
is endangered when that power has no obstacle before it. A
monarch can be opposed in the name of the people; but in
whose name can the people be opposed? The most absolute
sovereigns in Europe cannot prevent certain hostile ideas from
circulating. But in America, once the majority makes up its
mind, everyone must acquiesce and be silent. "The reason for
this is simple: there is no monarch so absolute that he can concentrate in his hands all the forces of society, and overcome resistance, as can a majority endowed with the right to make and
execute the laws."[36]

Tocqueville's litany of monarchical virtues and republican
deficiencies continues. In monarchies there is always one social
element prepared to champion or propagate dissenting views.
In an absolute monarchy, the critic has the people behind him;
and in Tocqueville's idealized version of the constitutional
monarchy, the critic "can, if need be, take shelter behind royal
authority." In contrast, the critic in America, though legally
free to speak up, is deprived of the will to do so. In democratic
republics, tyranny "leaves the body free, and goes straight to
the soul."[37]

The evidence marshalled by the French aristocrat in support
of monarchy is far from compelling, as was noted at the time
by John Stuart Mill. "It is perhaps the greatest defect of M. de

Tocqueville's book," Mill wrote in his 1840 review, "that from the scarcity of examples, his propositions, even when derived from observation, have the air of abstract speculations. He speaks of the tyranny of the majority in general phrases, but gives hardly any instances of it, nor much information as to the mode in which it is practically exemplified."[38]

Tocqueville selected two examples of critical expression under European monarchies, conveniently omitting the myriad instances of censorship, arbitrary arrest of opposition leaders, and repression that were regular occurrences in such regimes. The only proof of majority tyranny in America he cited was an attack by a mob on an antiwar newspaper in Baltimore in 1812; and the pressure brought to bear on free blacks not to vote in Pennsylvania. The first was an explosion of nationalist sentiment in wartime, a phenomenon not unknown in monarchies. Slavery did indeed call American democracy into question. But voting by free blacks in the North was a minor facet of that problem. The contention that there are no great writers in America scarcely stands up in view of the emergence in Tocqueville's own lifetime of such literary figures as Ralph Waldo Emerson, Henry Thoreau, Nathaniel Hawthorne, Herman Melville, Henry Wadsworth Longfellow, Edgar Allen Poe, Walt Whitman, and James Fenimore Cooper.

When Tocqueville declared that the people would not tolerate any criticism of their capacity to govern, he was basically expressing his disappointment that there was in America no serious public consideration of his own preferred political system—constitutional monarchy. Those best able to govern, he asserted, were being driven out of politics because they could not bring themselves to flatter the people, whom they were beginning to fear and despise. "If the misgovernment of democracy leads one day to a political crisis, *if monarchy ever presented itself in the United States as a practicable alternative*, one will soon discover the truth of the proposition I am advancing [my italics]."[39]

But no one in Jackson's America even entertained the idea of monarchy. James Fenimore Cooper was as severe a critic of majority tyranny as Tocqueville was; but for him the solution was to go back to the first principles of the founders, to block majority tyranny through the separation of powers, and to motivate a new class of "American gentlemen" to participate in politics and lead the people. Similarly, Francis Lieber (who met Tocqueville in 1831 and remained in contact afterward) denounced the "divine right" and absolutism of the people, but did so as a "true and staunch republican." The real rule of the people, he held, is the institutionally organized country as distinguished from the mere mob.[40] In short, Publius rather than Tocqueville.

In the *Democracy* of 1840, Tocqueville retreated to a more defensible position. Here he noted a tendency in democracy that favored intellectual curiosity, because citizens were constantly questioning received opinion as well as the social establishment. On the other hand, wherever the majority rules, there is a danger of imposed intellectual conformity. His preference is again clearly stated: " . . . the intellectual empire of the greatest number will be less absolute among a democratic people *subject to a king*, than in a pure democracy. . . ."[41] To speak of a favorable tendency and a possible danger is a far cry from the dogmatic assertions of the first volume.

Tocqueville's ambiguous remarks about majority tyranny underline a general weakness of his analytic method. All too often he identified a possible danger, then converted that possibility into a present reality, which, in a burst of rhetoric, became an inescapable future. Because the majority rules in a democratic republic, it may be tyrannical; therefore, it is tyrannical; and it will always be thus. Similarly, he warned that the Europeans driven to America by misfortune or misbehavior were bringing with them "our greatest vices"; he predicted that democracy in America would perish at the hands of these rootless and ungrateful European wretches, unless the government created an armed force capable of suppressing urban unrest. In later years, he made equally disparaging comments about Irish and German immigrants. He also glimpsed the coming of modern despotism, in which an all-powerful state would take on the responsibility for the welfare of its citizens, who would thereby lose their freedom.[42]

Tocqueville did not admit of other possible lines of development: that democratic republics might protect freedom of mind, nurture literary talent, and generate great political leaders; that a massive immigration of European peoples could strengthen American democracy; and that a welfare state could be made compatible with individual freedoms under appropriate conditions. Like *The Federalist*, the *Democracy* is an extraordinary mix of careful observation and brilliant insights. But Tocqueville, more than Publius, has caught our imagination with rhetorical flourishes and general theory—much of which calls for modification in the light of actual historical developments.

TOCQUEVILLE and Publius were concerned above all with the postrevolutionary moment: the critical period when authority must be reestablished. Revolutions let loose anarchic impulses that may make it impossible to maintain authority, even that based on revolutionary principles. Disorder and violence make people long for the good old days when they at least felt secure in their everyday lives. Out of revolution in the name of freedom there may come an even greater despotism than the one that was overthrown. According to Tocqueville, that is precisely what happened in France. As he put it in the foreword to *The Old Regime and the French Revolution*, the French abandoned their original revolutionary ideals, turned their backs on freedom, and acquiesced in "an equality of servitude under the master of all Europe."

Tocqueville's supreme goal as an analyst—which drove him to study America in the first place—was to explain why the American and French revolutions had had such different outcomes. In the new world, revolution had led, after a short period of instability and near anarchy, to a free constitutional order. In his own country, revolution had been followed by terror and anarchy, and then by Bonaparte. He also felt a personal responsibility for helping his country break out of the infernal cycle. In defining and analyzing the problem, and in making a political commitment, Tocqueville was following in the footsteps of Hamilton, Madison, and Jay. They, too, wished to ensure that a democratic revolution should not degenerate into despotism by way of anarchy. They, too, made political analysis the basis of political action, by campaigning for ratification of the Constitution, and then by assuming major responsibilities in the new system.

Tocqueville was well aware that he was dealing with the very same theoretical problems that concerned the founders of the American republic. In a striking passage on the character of the founders, Tocqueville surely hoped that the American example might be understood and followed in France. In the time of crisis, Tocqueville wrote, the American people chose not the men they loved but those they most respected. The founders, he said, were remarkable for their enlightenment and patriotism.

They all emerged in the middle of a social crisis, during which the spirit of liberty had continually to struggle against a strong and domineering authority. When the struggle was over, and while as usual the excited passions of the mob were directed still at dangers that had long ceased to exist, these men paused. They cast a calmer and more penetrating look at their country; *they saw that a definitive revolution had been carried out; and that henceforth the only perils hanging over the people could only come from the abuses of liberty.* What they thought, they had the courage to say, because they felt in their hearts a sincere and ardent love for that very liberty; *they dared to speak of restraining that liberty because they were resolved not to wish to destroy it* [my italics].[43]

This is how Tocqueville saw his own role in France: through analysis of the postrevolutionary moment to help the people rise above petty concerns, and to accept limits on their own power in the higher interest of preserving freedom. The founding of the American republic offered a lesson to the French. What is new in history, said Tocqueville, "is to see a great people, warned by its leaders that the wheels of government were blocked, examine itself without undue haste and without fear, to probe the extent of the disease, restrain itself for two whole years in order to discuss the remedy at leisure, and when the remedy is pointed out, to accept it voluntarily, without its costing neither a tear nor a drop of blood to humanity."[44]

Tocqueville had one opportunity to follow in the footsteps of the American founders, when he was elected to the committee charged with drafting a new constitution for France after the revolution of 1848. To his eternal disappointment, the committee worked under great pressure and never discussed first principles. "All this bore very little resemblance to those men, so certain of their goal and so well acquainted with the means required to attain it, who, under Washington's presidency sixty years before, drew up the American Constitution."[45]

In committee deliberations, Tocqueville supported a republic as the only feasible alternative at the time. As he explained later, the Legitimists were despised, the Orleanists discredited by their exclusive identification with the middle class, and a seizure of power by Louis Napoleon would be a reversion to despotism. But what kind of republic? Tocqueville wished to apply the lessons drawn from the American Constitution: that popular power should be held in check in order to maintain liberty. He put the issue as follows:

> Did we wish to persevere in the artful and somewhat complicated system of counterbalances, and place powers held in check, and consequently prudent and moderate, at the head of the Republic? Or did we have to start out in the opposite direction and adopt the simpler theory, according to which affairs are turned over to a single power, homogeneous in all its parts, without barriers, and consequently impetuous in its movements, and irresistible?

The committee disregarded Tocqueville's advice; it accorded vast powers to a president who would be popularly elected. His prediction came true: in a country with a strong monarchical tradition, such a president could not be anything but "a pretender to the Crown."[46]

In the revolutionary turmoil of 1848, Tocqueville reflected bitterly on the course of French historical development. "I had spent the best years of my youth amid a society which seemed to become prosperous and great again in becoming free again; I had conceived there the idea of a moderate, orderly liberty, held in check by faith, custom and law; the attractions of this liberty had touched me; it had become the passion of my entire life." In his last years he feared that the French would have to drag on miserably "amid alternate reactions of license and oppression."[47]

The main elements of Tocqueville's analysis may be found in the very first number of *The Federalist*, written by Hamilton. He posed the question immediately: "It has been frequently remarked that it seems to have been reserved to the people of this country, by their conduct and example, to decide the important question, whether societies of men are really capable or not of establishing good government from reflection and choice, or whether they are forever destined to depend for their political constitutions on accident and force."

Hamilton goes on to stress the need to rise above the passions of the moment (so difficult to do, in Tocqueville's opinion, in France). "Happy will it be if our choice should be directed by a judicious estimate of our true interests, unperplexed and unbiased by considerations not connected with the public good." And Tocqueville must have been impressed by Hamilton's perceptive anticipation in Number 1 of revolutionary terror and Bonapartist impulses:

> a dangerous ambition more often lurks behind the specious mask of zeal for the rights of the people than under the forbidding appearance of zeal for the firmness and efficiency of government. History will teach us that the former has been found a much more certain road to the introduction of despotism than the latter, and that of those men who have overturned the liberties of republics, the greatest number have begun their career by paying an obsequious court to the people, commencing demagogues and ending tyrants.

Most striking from the point of view of a French observer is the warning made by Hamilton in Number 85 against the dangers of anarchy and "perhaps the military despotism of a victorious demagogue."

Tocqueville also shared with Publius a certain conception of political science. Throughout *The Federalist* there are references to the "principles of political science"—not put forward as immutable laws (which would be contrary to the spirit of science) but rather as hypotheses, derived from careful study of history, to be further appraised or tested in the light of unfolding political experience. For example, Publius suggested that representative government was a great advance, making possible geographically extensive republics and a separation of branches of government that protects the people from abuse of power. One special advantage of a republic, said Madison in Number 10: "it may well happen that the public voice, pronounced by the representatives of the people, will be more consonant to the public good than if pronounced by the people themselves, convened for the purpose." Hamilton added in Number 71: "The republican principle demands that the deliberate sense of the community should govern the conduct of those to whom they intrust the management of their affairs; but it does not require an unqualified complaisance to every sudden breeze of passion, or to every transient impulse which the people may receive from the arts of men, who flatter their prejudices to betray their interests."

The idea of representative government was central to the *Democracy*, John Stuart Mill wrote in his review of the first volume, and Tocqueville agreed. In a letter to Mill of 5 December 1835 acknowledging his review, the author further developed his position:

> For friends of Democracy it matters less to find the means of enabling the people to govern, than to get them to choose those most capable of governing, and to give the people in addition sufficient sway over their rulers so that they can direct the conduct of the latter as a whole, but not the details of their action nor the means of execution. That is the problem. I am fully convinced that upon its solution depends the fate of modern nations.[48]

Publius and Tocqueville are founders and exemplars of the liberal tradition in social science—what Max Weber would later call the "ethic of responsibility," as opposed to the "ethic of ultimate ends" characteristic of authoritarian leaders and their admirers. Publius and Tocqueville had a passion for politics, and certainly they did not conceal their political values. But, unlike those devoted to an ethic of ultimate ends, they were able to put distance between themselves and their passions, and to assess objectively the consequences of their own actions. Publius was suspicious of abstractions and generalities, turning instead to the study of real nations and peoples. Similarly, in his study of the French Revolution, Tocqueville voiced his distrust of intellectuals who were completely divorced from power. They tended, because of their lack of knowledge of the real problems of governance, to engage in wild flights of fancy.

It was on the basis of their studies of history and politics that Publius and Tocqueville proposed to *do* something to help resolve political problems and change the course of history.

Publius and Tocqueville also struck the same balance between determinism and free will—the kind of balance characteristic of the ethic of responsibility. Hamilton and Madison insisted that people have a choice. It is up to them whether popular government will lead to tyranny (by permitting the weak Articles of Confederation to continue) or to liberty (by approving a Constitution that creates effective government and separation of powers). "The establishment of a Constitution," said Hamilton in Number 85, "in time of profound peace, by the voluntary consent of a whole people, is a PRODIGY, to the completion of which I look forward with trembling anxiety." In the magistral conclusion of the 1840 *Democracy*, Tocqueville said in the same vein: "Men and peoples are neither enslaved nor completely free. Within the limits set by God, men and nations are powerful and free. Nations can no longer choose social inequality; but it depends upon them whether equality shall lead to servitude or liberty, barbarism or civilization."

It may be difficult to make democracy work; but the obstacles can be overcome if the people have the knowledge and the will to do so. Hence, the need for a science of politics infused by a preference for freedom and democracy. As Hamilton observed in Number 9, the advocates of despotism constantly point to the tendency of popular government to degenerate into factionalism and insurrection. "If it had been found impracticable to have devised models of a more perfect structure, the enlightened friends to liberty would have been obliged to abandon the cause of that species of government as indefensible. The science of politics, however, like most other sciences, has received great improvement."

Tocqueville echoed Publius's belief that principles of political science may help a nation protect freedom within a democracy. Those who direct society have the duty to educate the people, Tocqueville contended in the introduction to *Democracy*, to assist them in overcoming blind instinct and seeing their true interests through the acquisition of knowledge. "Il faut une science politique nouvelle à un monde tout nouveau."[49] A new political science is needed not just for the new world, but for the whole world as transformed by the American and French revolutions.

PART II
Major Themes

More than America:
Comparison and Synthesis
in *Democracy in America*

SEYMOUR DRESCHER

Democracy in America is clearly among those stimulating writings that raise important questions about their meaning in direct proportion to the care with which they are read. Take, for example, a question that for most other books would seem to have a straightforward answer. Is *Democracy in America* one work or two? Despite the fact that it was published in two parts, in 1835 and in 1840, the presumption has generally been that the reader is being offered a single organic study.[1] Both parts were published under a single title. Tocqueville, in his preface to the second volume, explicitly stated that it was to be regarded as complementary to the first and part of "single work." Volume one, Tocqueville explained, dealt with the American "political world" and volume two with "civil society."[2]

During the past century-and-a-half most American scholars have accepted the author's statement at face value. They have then gone about their business, whether in order to apply Tocqueville's insights to Jacksonian American democracy as in John Diggins's *Lost Soul of American Politics,* or in order to treat his study as a portent of the contemporary American condition, as do Robert N. Bellah and his colleagues in *Habits of the Heart.* Even those who question Tocqueville's reading of America begin with the presumption that his central and persistent focus was indeed on democracy in America. When American scholars acknowledge differences between the 1835 and 1840 publications, they tend to emphasize the overriding continuity of the two volumes. Max Lerner's long introduction to

77

the most recent translation of *Democracy in America* attributes
the difference in scope and style of the 1840 volume to the
more philosophical approach of an older, wiser, and sadder
Tocqueville.[3] At most, it is argued, Tocqueville was general-
izing more about democratic mass society and speaking less
empirically of America.

In the richest and most detailed study of the making of
Tocqueville's *Democracy,* James Schleifer comes to the same
general conclusion. He explicitly recognizes the expanded scope
and altered focus of the volume of 1840. But Schleifer insists
that the later study reflects a slowly evolving process of rumina-
tion. He ascribes the contradictory implications of many of the
Democracy's statements to a long list of peculiar psychological
habits: Tocqueville's comparative perspective, his tendency to
think in terms of "pairs in tension," his excessive theoretical
boldness, or simply to forgetfulness and the "sheer passage of
time." The reader is even warned against imposing "too much
consistency" or straining overmuch toward unity in relation to
Tocqueville's work.

Schleifer insists throughout his analysis on both the organic
integrity of the argument of *Democracy in America* and on the
entirely "evolutionary" quality of its conclusions. Significant
shifts in the 1840 volume are to be seen as either the result of a
gradual maturation, a fleshing out of "germs" already embedded in the 1835 volume, or as a new area of exploration. So,
even though the *Democracy* of 1840 became, in Tocqueville's
own estimation, less American and more democratic, Schleifer
boldly begins his study of the gestation of the *Democracy* with
a section entitled "Tocqueville's Second Voyage to America,
1832–1840." He emphatically closes his book with another
chapter called "Tocqueville's return to America." Schleifer
therefore remains entirely faithful to the tradition that runs
from Tocqueville's preface of 1840 to George Wilson Pierson's
"Le 'second voyage' de Tocqueville en Amérique."[4]

Two decades ago I proposed that there was considerable

heuristic value in distinguishing the publications of 1835 and 1840 as "Tocqueville's Two *Démocraties*⁵—as substantially independent works written by an author with certain enduring concerns but with a dramatically altered perspective on his subject. Recent French scholars have also found a similar approach to be fruitful as a mode of understanding the development of Tocqueville's *Democracy*. Jean-Claude Lamberti entitles his major recent study *Tocqueville et les deux démocraties*, and he devotes a section of his analysis to the "Genesis of the second *'démocratie.'*" André Jardin, in the first full-length biography of Tocqueville published in almost half a century, also devotes a chapter to what he calls "The second *'Démocratie.'*" Most significantly, the most recent edition of Tocqueville's major works contains for the first time separate editorial introductions to the "first" and "second" *Democracies*.⁶

Should one consider this merely a quibble among Tocqueville scholars? Not even the most unequivocal American "lumper" denies that Tocqueville substantially altered his views on at least one major prognosis. And none of the French "splitters" would assert that Tocqueville altered his basic premises about the inevitability of democracy or the value of political liberty. It can easily be shown, however, that a number of Tocqueville's central themes are clarified when viewed as having emerged in two independent stages.

First let me offer some *prima facie* evidence, both quantitative and qualitative, for thinking in terms of two democracies. In the 1835 volume, Tocqueville devoted most of his study to democracy in *America,* with a long final section on things "American" but not democratic: race relations, the survival of the federal union, and the implications of American economic growth. If we consider only the "democratic" portions, content analysis shows that at least three-quarters of the 1835 volume was specifically devoted to American democracy, with the remaining quarter divided between democracy in France, or in Latin America, or democracy "in general." On the other hand,

André Jardin, more precisely quantifying my earlier analysis,
finds that America occupies only about 20 percent of the first
three parts of the 1840 volume and only 2 percent of its final
part. And Françoise Mélonio notes that while a majority of the
chapter titles of the second *Démocratie* refer to America, less
than a quarter of the work really deals with it. The conclusion
seems inescapable: the second *Democracy* registers a dramatic
decline of American focus, ending in its virtual abandonment. It
will become equally clear that America as a subject of the work
not only declined in salience but in significance. Having been
the normatively democratic society in the 1835 volume, it had
become the most exceptional of democracies by the close of the
1840 volume.

For the diehard skeptic, Tocqueville even offers us a "smok-
ing gun." In November of 1838 he took note of the fact that he
had altered his views on subjects already raised in 1835, and he
decided to mention the fact in his second preface: "Point out—
to myself as well—that I was led in the second work to take up
once again some subjects already *touched upon* in the first, or
to modify some opinions expressed there. Necessary result of
so large a work done in two parts [Tocqueville's emphasis]."[7]
While Tocqueville took deliberate note of his altered second
work, he did not indicate this perception in the published
version of his preface. Nor did he emphasize the shift of his
analysis from what he privately considered as a book "more
American than democratic" to one "more democratic than
American."[8] Instead, Tocqueville directed attention only to the
complementarity of the two parts.

In fact, much of the 1840 volume was not only more democratic than American but European-democratic rather than
American-democratic. America was quite obviously irrelevant
for entire chapters covering such subjects as pantheism, science,
the arts, literary characteristics, theater, historiography, rents,
leases, wages, place-hunting, revolutions, armies, warfare, and
bureaucratization.

Is the general difference between the two volumes to be explained by the passage of time, the size of the work, or by a "speculative" shift from comparative analysis to synthesis, i.e., to statements about democracy in general? We can easily dismiss any simple "time" theory. The "sheer passage of time" — three years between the *Democracy* of 1835 and the completion of the 1840 draft—by itself signifies nothing.[9] It certainly does not tell us why Tocqueville's ideas shifted in a given direction, or why his speculations about "generic" democracy should have changed from one volume to the other.

Nor are the changes between the two *Democracies* to be explained by the fact that Tocqueville moved from an empirical analysis of democracy in America and France in 1835 to more comparatively based statements about democracy in general. The very first page of the 1835 volume was as comparative as any of those of the 1840 volume. If anything, Tocqueville's introduction immediately drew attention to both the comparative and French dimensions of his study of democracy in America. What made America interesting to him, as a European, was the transatlantic analogy of social equality on the one hand and the different degrees of political liberty in America and France on the other.

From the very outset, however, Tocqueville was not just comparing two democracies (America and France), but formulating a generic conception of the nature and future of democracy in general: "I admit," he wrote in his introduction of 1835, "that I saw in America more than America; it was the shape of democracy itself which I sought, its inclinations, character, prejudices and passions."[10] Tocqueville was already seeking to fathom the full theoretical consequences of his observations, even at the cost of going to the verge of the false and the impracticable in pursuit of that objective. And he wished thereby to capture not only the shape of democracy but its future. The Tocqueville of 1835 was therefore just as comparative, synthetic, speculative, and prognostic as the Tocqueville of 1840. Nor was he holding his full speculative fire for the second volume. In 1835 he had no plans for a sequel to his study.[11]

Thus built into the original project of the *Democracy* were a variety of goals that were conceptually quite distinct. Comparative social analysis, contrasting two different entities, demands that clear distinctions be maintained between internally coherent paradigms: America versus France, or America versus England, or Anglo-America versus Latin America. In the 1835 study, Tocqueville continually compared such geopolitical alternatives. The 1840 volume also contained many distinctively comparative statements. The difference between them lay in the fact that, in 1840, overt comparisons were relatively fewer in relation to synthetic statements about democracy in general.

What changed most between the two years were Tocqueville's ideas about the whole "democratic" future.[12] This change can be clearly traced in both his published thoughts and his notes. It was based, I would contend, on his new evaluation of one of the two major empirical bases of his comparison. The difficulty was that this reevaluation was never made as clear to the reader as it was to Tocqueville himself. Therefore neither the degree of change nor the precise reasons for his rethinking the probable future of democracy was explicit in 1840.

The changes in some of Tocqueville's major ideas about the democratic future brought some of his most fundamental conclusions in the first volume into latent or overt contradiction with those of 1840. And it was because he made a decisive shift in the relative prognostic significance of his two major comparative examples (America and France) that the *Democracy* of 1840 is so different from that of 1835. If, as Schleifer contends, Tocqueville thought frequently in terms of "pairs in tension,"[13] the most fundamental of these "pairs in tension" are Tocqueville's two *Democracies* themselves.

TO DEMONSTRATE the validity of this hypothesis, one needs to look at two of the most famous concepts in *Democracy in America*: "centralization" and "individualism."

In 1835 Tocqueville used the concept of centralization in almost exclusively comparative terms in relation to democracy. His two empirical examples in dealing with centralization were administratively decentralized America and administratively centralized France. Tocqueville emphasized and reemphasized this dichotomy and its implications for the political habits of the world's two most democratic societies.[14] The most startling feature of the American polity was its striking decentralization.[15] So far was Tocqueville from considering centralization a threat to American democracy that he explicitly located his fears for its future in the excessive instability and mutability of American public administration.[16]

But what of democracy in general? What weight did these two democratic societies, which were polar opposites on the spectrum of centralization, carry into the future? In one sentence, in 1835, Tocqueville seemed to point to a correlation between administrative centralization and democracy in general: "I am convinced that no nations are more liable to fall under the yoke of administrative centralization than those with a democratic social condition."[17] And the explicit, empirical source offered for this conclusion was France. By itself, however, the statement implied no more than that democratic nations were more prone than others to centralize, just as certain age groups today are more prone than others to be involved in serious automobile accidents—not that most members of those groups at risk actually do so.

Tocqueville did not even imply that the democratic future lay with state centralization. The same section in which his observation on the risk of centralization appeared ended on an unqualifiedly optimistic note. In both America and England, he concluded, all men, whether democratic or antidemocratic, regarded institutional centralization as a great blessing. Only people who were ignorant of the political effects of provincial institutions disparaged them.[18]

What then of the whole future, including that of democratic France? Tocqueville himself provided an optimistic general prognosis in his first published analysis of France, written late in 1835 and published in John Stuart Mill's *London and Westminster Review* in 1836:

> Thus nations whose social condition is becoming democratic almost always begin by centralizing power in the prince alone; later, when they have accumulated the necessary strength and energy, they break the *instrument,* and transport the same prerogatives into the hands of an authority responsible to themselves; [when they have become] still more powerful, better organized and more enlightened, they make a new effort, and, taking back some portions of administrative power from their general representatives, they allocate them to secondary representatives. Such appears to be the natural, instinctive, and one could say compulsory course followed by societies which are pulled towards democracy by their social condition, their ideas and their habits.[19]

Administrative centralization was therefore only the second stage of a transitional movement toward democracy. Societies moved from a condition of aristocratic decentralization through periods of autocratic and democratic centralization to a final state of democratic decentralization. A condition of decentralization was ultimately linked to an equality of social conditions.

The concluding section of *Democracy in America,* in 1835 (on the implications of American democracy for Europe), pointed in the same direction. It did not emphasize the dangers of democratic centralization.[20] The lack of concern for administrative centralization was perfectly congruent with Tocqueville's general perspective in the *Westminster Review* essay.

In the *Democracy* of 1840, we enter another world. Rather than being transitional, state centralization comes close to achieving full parity with democracy as an "irreversible" fact of both the present and the future. In 1835, only democracy was accorded the following attributes: it was said to be universal, permanent, and beyond human control. Every event, every person, every group helped it along. In 1840, centralization was endowed with every one of these secular historical characteristics: it was increasing everywhere, in a thousand different ways. Wars, revolutions, conquests, peace, tranquility, and prosperity all nurtured it. As with "democracy" in 1835, citizens were led, day in and day out, willingly, insensibly, or even against their wills, to surrender fresh portions of their individual independence to the government. Those very same men, brooded Tocqueville, "who . . . trampled kings . . . [now] bend without resistance to the slightest wishes of some clerk."[21] What had begun in 1835 as an awesome and deliberate choice between the dangers of a tyrannical majority and the unlimited tyranny of a Caesar, had crumbled by 1840 into a host of petty submissions to bureaucratic centralization.[22] It is clear that the "comparative" choice of 1835 had become transformed into a generic statement about the whole future.

THE OTHER striking feature of the *Democracy* of 1840 was Tocqueville's new emphasis on "individualism." In the second work, the reader is introduced to a major concept that had not even appeared in the *Democracy* of 1835, although the word was already current in France.[23] I would argue that Tocqueville did not use the term in 1835 because his idea of American social relationships simply did not fit the French meaning he gave to the term in 1840. Only in 1838 did he begin to introduce the word into his notes for the sequel, applying it to individuals who were politically turned in upon themselves, who deliberately withdrew into private circles of family and friends, leaving society to look after itself. "Individualism" was the rational choice of men who cultivated the private virtues at the expense of the public ones. Tocqueville had unearthed this pattern of democratic behavior, not from his memories of America but among his own countrymen. The real significance of the introduction of the concept of "individualism" in 1840 is that it was used to describe democracy generally, not just its continental European variant. Indeed, the French connection was not so much as mentioned in the *Democracy* of 1840. The two chapters that introduce the concept contain no European referent whatever.[24]

From Schleifer's research, moreover, we know that Tocqueville had a clear idea of this kind of "individualism" even before 1835. He discussed it extensively in his American notes, in his correspondence, and in his drafts for the first *Democracy,* denoting it by such terms as *égoisme imbecile* and "political atheism."[25] The phenomenon, if not the term, briefly surfaced even in the *Democracy* of 1835. There Tocqueville referred to the inhabitants of some (unnamed) countries who showed a repugnance to accept political responsibilities and communal participation. They shut themselves up within a "narrow egoism," bounded by the hedges of their fields. To his dismay, Tocqueville encountered this behavior among some of his own closest friends.[26]

In 1835, however, Tocqueville was more preoccupied in his *Democracy* with a quite different kind of "individualism." Tocqueville's new science of politics unveiled an "egoism" of a new kind in America, a kind where rational self-interest was intimately bound to public participation. The *Democracy* of 1835 brims with descriptions of activist American democrats. It was they who caused Tocqueville to write that one could imagine American freedom or American equality from afar, but that the political activity of individual Americans had to be experienced to be truly understood.[27] The *Democracy* of 1835 repeatedly paused to wonder at the energy with which a people in perpetual interaction built churches and schools, chose representatives, planned economic improvements, and reformed alcoholics. It was the hyperactivity of these ordinary individuals that spread upward, by contagion, to their representatives. Public activism literally spilled over into American economic, social, and intellectual life. There was more intellectual activity, wrote Tocqueville, even at the edge of the American frontier, than in most enlightened and populous districts of France.[28] The *Democracy* even found something heroic in the entrepreneurial adventurousness and multidimensionality of Americans. In other words, the citizens of the United States had uncovered a new formula for linking public and private interests: American democracy not only expanded public life, but created a social symphony of "tumultuous agitation." It had thereby dissolved or at least finessed the classical political antagonism between public and private virtue.[29]

At only one point in the 1835 volume did Tocqueville pause to describe the phenomenon of political withdrawal in the United States. He discovered it not among the democrats of America but among the remnants of its old aristocratic and wealthy families. In 1835, withdrawal and political apathy in both America and France were characteristic of the fading world of aristocracy.

As in the case of centralization, the shift of "individualism" to the democratic future in 1840 was not the result of a simple maturation or evolution of Tocqueville's 1835 portrait of democracy in general.[30] As we have seen, the comparative polarities of activism and withdrawal had been delineated well before the composition of the first *Democracy,* but in 1835, Tocqueville had accentuated the activist "American" individualism and had relegated the "political atheism" of his French friends to the past.

HOW, THEN, did Tocqueville come to decide what temporal "weight" to give each type of individual behavior in looking toward the future? Why was so much space devoted to the "benign" egoism of the participatory citizens in 1835 and so little to the pathological egoism of retreat that dominates the second *Democracy?* For the very same reason I submit, which underlay his choice about the relative significance of centralization between 1835 and 1840. In 1835, for the individual as for the state, Tocqueville posited a three-stage theory, going from the primitive "instinctive" patriotism of aristocracies to the enlightened self-interested patriotism (*égoisme éclairé*) of democracies, after passing through a transitory phase of withdrawal.[31] Tocqueville's analysis of France in the *Westminster Review* laid great stress on the gradual growth of assertive individualistic liberty even during the old regime.[32]

What held for the presentation of the concepts of "centralization" and "individualism" characterized the whole shift of historical prognosis between the two *Democracies.* The hyper-associational democrat of 1835 is sociologically connected to the "tryanny of the majority." The apathetic individualism of 1840 is sociologically linked to the paternalistic state. The first *Democracy* was as disproportionately saturated with allusions to public activism as the second was to public apathy.

The fact that one can indeed locate "germs" of synthetic 1840 chapters in isolated 1835 sentences therefore deepens the problem of Tocqueville's shift, rather than offering an explanation. It does not bring one to grips with the problem, because it minimizes the change of direction that Tocqueville painfully underwent. How did the activist-democratic future so dramatically metamorphose into a passive bureaucratic future?

Tocqueville's new ideas on the democratic model almost certainly reflected the development of his extra-American experiences. Shortly after the publication of the 1835 *Democracy,* Tocqueville was startled by signs of centralization in England.[33] It suggested to him that centralization, French-style, was not just an alternative path to the future but the most likely pattern of democratization. His subsequent observations of parallel trends on the continent, and especially in France, seem to have played a major role in bringing about a reformulation of his synthetic prognosis. Viewing public policy toward one social and economic problem after another, Tocqueville detected the unrelenting intrusion of an ever-expanding state: in public welfare schemes, in banking reform, in mining legislation, in prison reform, and in railroad building schemes.[34] The politicians seemed to anticipate and to welcome governmental intrusion. In his notebooks of 1837 and 1838, Tocqueville recorded cases of what he began to call the "ultra-centralizing tendencies of our day." If most of the cited instances were French, his own inference was both unequivocal ("ultra") and general ("of our day").[35]

Equally significant, the "ultra-centralizing tendencies" of socioeconomic development were not counterbalanced by any French movement toward institutional decentralization or revived political life.[36] The "transitions" to decentralization and to enlightened or patriotic egoism anticipated in the *Westminster Review* essay simply failed to materalize. Until 1835, Tocqueville's anxiety about apolitical symptoms in France had been tempered by allowances for the threat of popular insurrection. Despite the stabilization of the regime after 1835, however, nonviolent public activity did not reemerge. To Tocqueville's dismay, indifference remained the governing mood among the electorate.[37] French individualism seemed to be as contented with bureaucratic authority in tranquility as it had been in turbulence, and centralization was as compatible with the quest for economic prosperity as it was with the search for public security.

The extraordinary degree to which Tocqueville's frame of reference changed by 1840 may be gauged by those societies whose experiences were deemed most relevant to predicting the democratic future. In 1835, when he began to construct his new science of politics for a new world, the examples he cited were the newly independent republics of the Americas and postrevolutionary France. By the 1840 volume, not only all of the monarchies of Europe but the bureaucratic empires of China and Egypt were considered as normative for the future as was the United States. Indeed, in some ways, imperial China was regarded as more typical than republican America.[38]

In 1840 the extent to which the Old World was allowed to overbalance the New can be seen in Tocqueville's occasional recharacterizations of democratic America itself. At one point, in the concluding section of the *Democracy,* Tocqueville seemed to assimilate even decentralized America to his correlation between democracy and the omnipotence of the administrative state.[39] Even more crucial perhaps was Tocqueville's rewording of the relationship between democracy and liberty. In 1835, Tocqueville's principal hope for the future lay in the fact that democratic liberty continuously showed its advantages to every citizen. Public participation afforded each citizen daily experience of democracy's material benefits and thereby generated public pride and patriotism. The power of the American experience caused Tocqueville to regard much of the French experience as temporary and transitory. In the *Democracy* of 1840, "liberty" was articulated within an older, more classical, and more elitist mold. Liberty involved activity that "occasionally gives sublime pleasure" to a restricted number of citizens.[40] In 1840, the eastern hemisphere, from France to China, was the wave of the future. The new science of politics was now drawing its conclusions from deep wells of old world experience.

HOW MAY such a reinterpretation bear on the contemporary reading of *Democracy in America*? In the first place, it alerts us to the fact that Tocqueville's generic statements were often derived from only one of his comparative models, and that the prognostic weight given to one or another society varied over time. This is of little significance when all of Tocqueville's major variants of democracy pointed in the same direction. An example of such convergence may be observed in the weight accorded to public opinion or in the passion for material well-being in democratic societies. The picture becomes more equivocal, however, when the implications of different examples diverge—as in the cases of centralization and decentralization. This is the more so because Tocqueville failed to indicate when he was using one variant rather than another as the basis for a synthetic statement. He may have subtly avoided discussing his increasing dependency on continental models, but this strategy shifted the burden of distinguishing between comparative and synthetic statements to future generations of readers.

A vision of two *Democracies* should at the very least give pause to those who treat the entire work as a study on *Democracy in America*. In some cases, this can lead to a good deal of secondary finessing. John Diggins, in his stimulating *Lost Soul,* has "the once-conscious and freely determining individuals" (of the 1835 volume) simply "drift" into the collective stupor of mass society (of the 1840 volume).[41] They certainly do have to "drift" from one condition into its opposite, because there is no sociological way for Diggins to get them from one state to the other. If there is, it is certainly not from using the dichotomous logic of Tocqueville's two democracies.

A second kind of confusion derives from the application of Tocqueville's diagnosis of "French" democratic individualism of the late 1830s to the Americas of the mid-1830s or of the mid-1980s. Robert Bellah, et al., like Diggins, assume that Tocqueville derived his vision of individualist withdrawal from his synthesis of the American democratic experience, and that the validity of that synthesis is demonstrated by the history of the last century-and-a-half.[42] Considering the source of Tocqueville's observations on individualism, however, the thrust of the *Democracy*'s observations concerning democratic America point to an opposite set of "participatory" linkages between public and private behavior. In fact, there seems to be a dearth of historical studies that actually demonstrate that Tocqueville's "associational Americans" of the 1830s have become proportionately less participatory in the 1980s, despite the enormously increased power of the central government. In any event this is a question that is better decided by detailed comparisons between America in 1835 and 1985 than by extrapolating from Tocqueville's American experience of the early 1830s to his European experience of the late 1830s. It is just possible that a geographical contrast has been metamorphosed into a historical development.

It is equally possible that historical continuities have been obfuscated by Tocqueville's ambiguity. Stanley Hoffman is dismayed to discover that late twentieth-century Europe, in a sharp break with its own variegated past, has become even more deeply enmeshed in "Tocqueville's nightmare of disconnected individuals under a tutelary state" than America has been.[43] It might be less dismaying, and it certainly would be less shocking, to realize that Tocqueville's own model of democratic individualism was directly distilled from continental experience a century-and-a-half ago. Europe best anticipated Tocqueville's "nightmare" because it already filled his waking hours.

I therefore conclude that just as there are Rousseau and Adam Smith "problems" regarding divergent texts, there is also a "Tocqueville problem." The great difference lies in the fact that in the case of Tocqueville, the problem lies within the confines of a single title. Provided, however, that one keeps clear the ever-shifting ground between comparative analysis and synthetic projection in *Democracy in America*, there is ample room for deriving both historical and political insights from Tocqueville's separate but equally perceptive studies.

Individualism and Apathy in Tocqueville's *Democracy*

ARTHUR SCHLESINGER, JR.

A S ALEXIS DE TOCQUEVILLE interpreted the modern world, history had confronted western civilization with a momentous choice. The revolution of equality, he believed, was irresistible. The question now was whether equality of legal conditions would lead on to free institutions or to despotism; whether the democratic revolution would end in liberty or in servitude. It was this underlying drama of choice that gives his vision of society its coherence and its troubled intensity.

Tocqueville's consuming passion was liberty; and the challenge before western man in his mind was to devise ways of securing liberty in the era of equality. He was vividly aware of perils in the new dispensation. It was no simple thing to reconcile liberty and equality. Still he could not accept, as he wrote in 1835, "that God has been pushing two or three million men for several centuries toward equality of conditions in order to have them end in the despotism of Tiberius and Claudius."[1] Within the fatal circle of necessity, men and communities retained a wide verge in which they could shape their own destiny — or at least this was the conviction that animated and inspired Tocqueville's message to his age.

In working out the means of salvation, Tocqueville drew much, but not all, from the social philosopher whom he had read longest and with the greatest sympathy—Montesquieu. For Montesquieu, virtue was the essential principle of republics, and virtue meant the renunciation of self for the sake of the public good. But Montesquieu's scheme did not quite fit Tocqueville's world. The republics Montesquieu had in mind were the ancient Greek city-states—polities limited in size and dedicated to husbandry and war. The pure principle of republican virtue seemed archaic among the bustling capitalist nation-states of the nineteenth century.

Montesquieu himself, however, had already somewhat modified that principle. For he was also the proponent of what Albert Hirschman calls the *"doux-commerce"* thesis—the contention that the rise of commerce would soften manners, tame passions, enlarge the mind, confer reciprocal benefits, reduce prejudice, and diffuse enlightenment.[2] The *doux-commerce* thesis thus qualified the commitment to republican virtue by providing an opening for self-interest. Commerce assumed a double aspect: on the one hand, it was the carrier of modern civilization; on the other, it remained, as it had been under the civic republican ethos, a potential source of luxury, egoism, and decay. The hope was that enough republican virtue could survive to check the excesses of self-interest and thereby gain the benefits of commerce without the risks of corruption.

According to Tocqueville, self-interest was inherent in democracy; perhaps in all societies. At one point he spoke of "private interest" as "the only immutable point in the human heart."[3] His American journey gave this immutable point new salience. Soon after his arrival in 1831, he asked himself what held together this dizzying miscellany of languages, beliefs, opinions mingled in a society without roots and without memories. "What serves as the link among such diverse elements? What makes all of this one people? Interest. That is the secret. . . . In this, we are quite far from the ancient republics, it must be admitted, and nonetheless this people is republican."[4]

The American experiment, Tocqueville thought, demonstrated the possibility of reconciling public virtue and private interest, and therefore the possibility of reconciling liberty and equality. He first explained the reconciliation by claiming that "in a physical situation so fortunate . . . the private interest is never contrary to the general interest, which is certainly not the case in Europe."[5] As he elaborated his understanding, he began to revise and amend Montesquieu. "The Americans are not a virtuous people," he wrote in a note "Concerning Virtue in Republics," "and yet they are free. . . . It is not necessary to take Montesquieu's idea in a narrow sense. What this great man meant is that republics can survive only by the action of the society on itself. What he understood by virtue is the moral power that each individual exercises over himself and that prevents him from violating the rights of others." That power of self-discipline, when it results from the weakness of the temptation or from calculations of personal interest, may "not constitute virtue in the eyes of the moralist; but it is included in the idea of Montesquieu who spoke much more of the result than of the cause. In America it is not virtue which is great, it is temptation which is small, which amounts to the same thing. It is not disinterestedness which is great, it is interest which is rightly understood, which again almost amounts to the same thing."[6]

The great distinction, in short, between the classical republics and modern democracies lay in the insertion of the commercial motive. The city-state was founded on virtue, the nation-state on interest. The problem was to make private interest the moral equivalent of public virtue. This could be achieved through the disciplinary influence exerted by society on its members—an influence embodied in the mores and in laws and institutions. *Self-interest rightly understood*: this Tocqueville saw as the key to the balance between virtue and interest in commercial democracies.

In another note, indited at all places up the river at Sing-Sing, he enlarged on the difference between "the republics of antiquity," whose principle was to sacrifice private interests to the general good, and the United States, where the principle was "to make private interests harmonize with the general interest. A sort of refined and intelligent selfishness seems to be the pivot on which the whole machine turns." But the balance was precarious, and Tocqueville could not but wonder whether it could be maintained. "Up to what extent," he asked himself, "can the two principles of individual well-being and the general good in fact be merged? How far can a conscience, which one might say was based on reflection and calculation, master those political passions which are not yet born, but which certainly will be born? That is something which only the future can show."[7]

L O O K I N G at America in the 1835 *Democracy,* Tocqueville returned a rather hopeful answer. Religion, voluntary associations, local government, federalism, the free press, the machinery of justice, the traditions of the people, the absence both of feudal system to overthrow and a violent revolution to overthrow it—all held out the prospect of keeping private interest under social control.

Above all, he was impressed and reassured by the national ardor for civic participation. "In no country in the world," he remarked, "do the citizens make such exertions for the common weal."[8] Participation was both stimulated and guaranteed by political freedom. "Civic zeal," as Tocqueville put it, "seems to me to be inseparable from the exercise of political rights."[9]

Yet the balance between virtue and self-interest remained precarious, and he identified an array of dangers. Aggressive participation in the life of society, so valuable within limits, threatened if carried too far to enforce a tyranny of the majority —so heavy a pressure against the dissenter "that one must give up one's rights as a citizen and almost abjure one's qualities as a man if one intends to stray from the track" the majority prescribes.[10] Equally threatening to self-interest rightly understood was the "love of money." Tocqueville said he knew of no country where the acquisitive drive had "taken a stronger hold on the affections of men."[11] Still he left the United States reasonably optimistic about the American capacity to transmute private interest into a facsimile of public virtue and thereby to preserve the balance.

The 1840 *Democracy,* as we all know, presented a less
cheering picture. Here Tocqueville introduced his theory of
individualism. By individualism Tocqueville meant something
very different from Emersonian self-reliance or Darwinian
rugged individualism. He meant something close to the modern sociological concept of "privatization." For Tocqueville individualism meant not self-assertion but self-withdrawal—the
disposition of each member of the community "to sever himself
from the mass of his fellows, and to draw apart with his family
and friends, so that after he has thus formed a little circle of his
own, he willingly leaves society at large to itself."[12]

What was the source of this absorption in the democratic
self? As Tocqueville explained it, individualism sprang from a
"crude" interpretation of self-interest—that is, from self-
interest wrongly understood.[13] This wrong understanding, he
thought, resulted from the love of money and material
gratification characteristic of democratic society. "The effort to
satisfy the least wants of the body and to provide the conve-
niences of life," he wrote, "is uppermost in every mind."[14]
This acquisitive compulsion, he feared, originated in the principle of equality itself; that principle "makes the passion for
physical gratification and the exclusive love of the present pre-
dominate in the human heart."[15] As he put it more flatly a
quarter century later in his foreword to *The Old Regime and
the French Revolution,* when the aristocratic ties of family, of
caste, of class, and of craft disappear, people tend "to think exclusively of their own interests, to become self-seekers practis-
ing a narrow individualism and caring nothing for the public
good."[16]

Self-interest wrongly understood thereby upset the balance
between virtue and interest. The outcome was "that *general apathy* which is the consequence of individualism."[17] By apathy,
he meant civic apathy. Individualism fosters the isolation of
people from one another, "saps the virtues of public life," and

makes it "difficult to draw a man out of his own circle to interest him in the destiny of the state."[18] People begin to see their public obligations as a vexatious distraction from the scramble for money. Public purpose is displaced by private interest. People, their lives defined by the marketplace and the family, lose their concern for the long run. "The better to look after their own business, they neglect their chief business, which is to remain their own masters."[19]

In retrospect, one wonders whether Tocqueville did not go astray in linking civic apathy so definitively to the acquisitive drive. With the benefit of another century-and-a-half of history, we recognize that civic apathy is even more marked in nations that seek to abolish the acquisitive impulse than it is in capitalist nations. He would have done better to see his recessive individualism as a function of mass society in general than of capitalist society in particular.

Individualism, in any case, was bad news, though Tocqueville was never quite sure what form the dénouement would take. Apathy, he said at one point, could "almost indifferently" beget either anarchy or tyranny.[20] But, since anarchy was classically the prelude to tyranny, they amounted to the same thing in the end. If tyranny came, he no longer expected it in the guise of the specters haunting the 1835 *Democracy*—the uninstitutionalized tyranny of the majority, or the tyranny of legislative encroachment on the executive, or the tyranny of the Caesars. He anticipated rather the tyranny of the bureaucratic state—an "immense and tutelary power . . . absolute, regular, provident, and mild," covering society with "a network of small complicated rules" and reducing a nation to "a flock of timid and industrious animals, of which the government is the shepherd."[21]

Tyranny, in whatever form, would end in stagnation. When "men continue to shut themselves more closely within the narrow circle of domestic interests," when citizens grow "inaccessible to those great and powerful public emotions which perturb nations, but which develop them," then Tocqueville said, in a startlingly personal outburst:

> I cannot but fear that men may arrive at such a state as to regard every new theory as a peril, every innovation as an irksome toil, every social improvement as a stepping-stone to revolution, and so refuse to move altogether for fear of being moved too far. I dread, and I confess it, lest they should at last so entirely give way to a cowardly love of present enjoyment as to lose sight of the interests of their future selves and those of their descendants and prefer to glide along the easy current of life rather than to make, when it is necessary, a strong and sudden effort to a higher purpose.[22]

In a curious digression in the 1840 *Democracy,* Tocqueville warned against supposing that, because Rome fell under the barbarian onslaughts, civilization could perish in no other way. His mind drifted to China, which, he said, had "lost the power of change" for entirely internal reasons and had sunk into a "strange immobility." Egalitarian society, he suggested, might follow the course of China rather than that of Rome. "If the light by which we are guided is ever extinguished," he observed, "it will dwindle by degrees and expire of itself." Some nations "allow civilization to be torn from their grasp"; others "allow themselves to trample it underfoot."[23]

It is an instructive coincidence that, at the very time Tocqueville was penning such sentiments at his brother's chateau in Baugy, the only other nineteenth-century mind to rival him in the profundity of his meditations on democracy was pondering the threat to the American experiment in a similar spirit and language. "At what point," Abraham Lincoln asked the Young Men's Lyceum of Springfield, Illinois, in January 1838, "is the approach of danger to be expected? I answer, if it ever reach us, it must spring up amongst us. It cannot come from abroad. If destruction be our lot, we must ourselves be its author and finisher. As a nation of freemen, we must live through all time, or die by suicide."[24]

The 1840 *Democracy* has a brooding, at times melancholy, cast; and ever since Seymour Drescher's notable essay twenty years ago,[25] commentators have wondered about the shift from the pervading optimism of 1835 to the pervading pessimism of 1840. Between the two works, the democratic distemper changes from mob rule to mass apathy, from activism to anomie. Plainly exposure to French politics after his return from America gave Tocqueville a new sense of the perils of privatization. He was struck by the "universal pettiness" of political life in his native land, by "the astonishing absence of disinterestedness," by the domination of "miserable day-to-day interests."[26] He began to fear that, once political liberty was "well established, and exercised in a peaceable milieu, it impels men to the practice and the taste of well-being, to the care and passion for making fortunes; and, as a repercussion, its tastes, its needs, its cares" extinguish political as well as religious passions.[27] His reentry into French politics thus persuaded him that self-interest could all too easily be wrongly understood.

At the same time, his visits in these years to England made him aware, as the American tour never had, of the potential impact of industrialism on democracy. He had taken from Montesquieu the idea that the spirit of commerce was favorable to liberty. But Montesquieu knew nothing of the spirit of industry; and this was another matter. Tocqueville's visit to Manchester left him with a horrified impression of the contrast between the "huge palaces of industry" and the homes "of vice and poverty . . . the last refuge a man might find between poverty and death. . . . Here is the slave, there the master; there the wealth of some, here the poverty of most; there the organised effort of thousands produce, to the profit of one man, what society has not yet learnt to give. Here the weakness of the individual seems more feeble and helpless even than in the middle of a wilderness; here the effect, there the causes."[28]

The forebodings generated by his visit to Manchester poured into his brilliant chapter in the 1840 *Democracy* on "How an Aristocracy May Be Created by Manufacturers." Where commerce was benign in its social effects, industry required a division of labor that divorced the worker from his product and deprived him of "the general faculty of applying his mind to the direction of the work. . . . What can be expected of a man who has spent twenty years of his life in making heads for pins?" At the same time that manufacturing degraded the class of workers, it elevated the class of masters. "This man," Tocqueville wrote, "resembles more and more the administrator of a vast empire; that man, a brute . . . and their differences increase every day."[29] Democratic freedom was compatible with a commercial destiny. But the *doux-commerce* thesis hardly applied to the industrial age.

LET US recapitulate the train of Tocqueville's thought. Where the republics of antiquity beloved by Montesquieu were founded on the principle of public virtue, modern democracy rested on private interest; and the hope for liberal institutions relied on a precarious balance between virtue and self-interest, rightly understood. But self-interest lends itself to being wrongly understood, especially after an established democracy begins to surrender to acquisitive passions and after commerce gives way to industry. Self-interest wrongly understood tilts the balance away from republican virtue and from public purpose. The individual withdraws from the public sphere, becomes isolated, weak, docile, powerless. Individualism in the Tocquevillian sense leads on to apathy, apathy to despotism, despotism to stagnation, stagnation to extinction. The light dwindles by degrees and expires of itself.

Now it is often asserted that Tocqueville, after writing about America in the 1835 *Democracy,* was really writing about Europe in the 1840 *Democracy*. Nor can anyone doubt that his confrontation with apathy in France and industrialism in England shaped the second treatise. Yet his ultimate concern was not to describe one side or the other of the Atlantic, but to set out the structural characteristics and tendencies of democracy as a new stage in the history of humanity. Although the time-frames might be different, although the law of uneven development might apply, America like France displayed a proclivity toward universal pettiness in public affairs; America, like England, was heading into the industrial age. The digression on China did not occur in the last third of the 1840 *Democracy*, where America was hardly mentioned; it occurred in the early chapter entitled "Why the Americans Are More Addicted to Practical than to Theoretical Science." Temporarily protected by geographic and political circumstance, America could not expect to remain forever immune to the maladies of egalitarian democracy.

Tocqueville saw the problem of reconciling equality and liberty as in a special sense a European problem. In meeting the problem, Americans had the advantage of having been born equal instead of having had to endure a democratic revolution. Nonetheless, it was an American problem too, and, as Tocqueville formulated it, a deeper and more subtle problem in 1840 than he had thought in 1836, rendered so by the discovery of individualism. In 1835 he had casually spoken of the irresistible movement of equality that "shatters and reduces to powder every obstacle, until we can no longer see anything but a moving and impalpable cloud of dust, which signals the coming of the Democracy."[30] But in 1835 he saw the cloud of dust seized and molded by powerful individuals and associations. By 1840, society itself appeared to be whirling away in the cloud of dust.

Individualism was the extension, at once logical and pernicious, of self-interest, even when rightly understood. How, Tocqueville asked in 1840, "to ward off a disorder at once so natural to the frame of democratic society and so fatal?"[31] He had at hand the pharmacopeia of institutional remedies prescribed in 1835 — the collection of democratic expedients, from the town meeting through the free press to the jury system, which, he thought, could do the work done by intermediate powers in an aristocracy. But, more urgently than ever, he gave fundamental emphasis to civic participation and above all to direct participation in the political process. "In order to combat the evils which equality may produce," he wrote in the 1840 *Democracy*, "there is only one effectual remedy: namely political freedom."[32]

He had none of the patrician disdain for the political arena that he had encountered among the respectable conservatives he interviewed on the American journey. As scandal sheets seemed a not unreasonable price to pay for a free press, so party politics seemed a not unreasonable price to pay for political freedom. He briskly dismissed the objections "derived from electioneering intrigues, the meanness of candidates, and the calumnies of their opponents. . . . Such evils are doubtless great, but they are transient; whereas the benefits that attend them remain." Election quarrels might break up friendships; but "the electoral system brings a multitude of citizens permanently together who would otherwise always have remained unknown to one another. Freedom produces private animosities, but despotism gives birth to general indifference."[33]

His approval extended to political parties; for parties drew individuals out of their own circles. However much individuals might be kept apart by age, mind, and fortune, the party "places them nearer together and brings them into contact. Once met, they can always meet again." He likened the parties to "large free schools, where all the members of the community go to learn the general theory of association"; and the art of association, as he often said, was the "mother of action."[34]

Political participation and public action, he said, force individuals to recognize that they live not just for themselves but in society. "Men attend to the interests of the public, first by necessity, afterwards by choice; what was intentional becomes an instinct, and by dint of working for the good of one's fellow citizens, the habit and taste for serving them are at length acquired."[35] The object, he once told John Stuart Mill, was "to put the majority of citizens in a fit state for governing."[36] Politics, in short, was the great means of counteracting private interest, of reviving public virtue, and of overcoming the apathy that invited despotism. "Governments," Tocqueville concluded, "must apply themselves to restore to men that love of the future with which religion and the state of society no longer inspire them."[37]

YET AN anomaly still lingers in Tocqueville's portrait of democratic man. The essence in 1835, as we have noted, was activism—the ardent, committed citizen, establishing schools, repairing roads, forming associations, reading newspapers, electioneering, and voting. "To take a hand in the regulation of society and to discuss it," he wrote then, "is his biggest concern and, so to speak, the only pleasure an American knows. . . . If an American were condemned to confine his activity to his own affairs, he would be robbed of one half of his existence; he would feel an immense void in the life which he is accustomed to lead; and his wretchedness would be unbearable."[38]

By 1840, the essence was no longer activism, but apathy. Tocqueville's democratic man now confined his activity to his own affairs, not because he was condemned to do so and was wretched doing it, but because it was his dearest wish. The 1840 American could not wait to shuck off the public world and to withdraw into a circle of his own. What had happened? Tocqueville, having portrayed in successive volumes the American as activist and the American as solipsist, was puzzled. "An American," he wrote in 1840, "attends to his private concerns as if he were alone in the world, and the next minute he gives

himself to the common welfare as if he had forgotten them. At
one time he seems animated by the most selfish cupidity; at another, by the most lively patriotism." It was indeed a puzzle.
"The human heart," Tocqueville thought, "cannot be thus divided"; and he rather lamely recurred to his early notion of the
mysterious reconciliation of public virtue and private interest.
Americans, he said, "alternately display so strong and so similar a passion for their own welfare and for their freedom that it
may be supposed that these passions are united and mingled in
some part of their character."[39]

With his marvelous antennae, Tocqueville perceived that
American democracy comprehended both the public-spirited
citizens of his first volume and the self-centered apathetic ones
of his second. If he had reflected more on his own passing
observation that Americans "alternately display" those contradictory qualities, he might have perceived further that public
purpose and private interest succeed each other in cyclical se-
quences. He had perhaps too linear a view of the democratic
process in America. Virtue and self-interest were not, as he
sometimes seemed to think, in a condition of steady or un-
steady balance. They were rather in dynamic equilibrium, first
one prevailing, then the other, as the excesses of each phase
regularly produced frustration, disenchantment, boredom, and
the desire for change. It is an odd coincidence that Tocqueville
saw democratic man as activist at the height of the age of
Jackson and as apathetic in the year the voters terminated the
Jacksonian phase and elected a Whig president.

Wise men have long remarked on patterns of alternation, of
ebb and of flow, in human history. "The two parties which divide the state, the party of Conservatism and that of Innovation," wrote Emerson in 1841,

> are very old, and have disputed the possession of the world ever
> since it was made. . . . Now one, now the other gets the day, and

still the fight renews itself as if for the first time, under new names and hot personalities. Innovation presses ever forward; Conservatism holds ever back. We are reformers spring and summer, in autumn and winter we stand by the old; reformers in the morning, conservers at night. Innovation is the salient energy; Conservatism the pause on the last movement.[40]

Half a century later, Henry Adams applied a more precise version of the cyclical thesis to the first years of the American republic. "Experience seemed to show," he wrote in the sixth volume of his great *History of the United States of America During the Administrations of Thomas Jefferson and James Madison,* "that a period of about twelve years measured the beat of the pendulum. After the Declaration of Independence, twelve years had been needed to create an efficient Constitution; another twelve years of energy brought a reaction against the government then created; a third period of twelve years was ending in a sweep toward still greater energy; and already a child could calculate the result of a few more such returns."[41]

Henry Adams's pendulum swung back and forth between the centralization and the diffusion of national energy. There have been subsequent interpretations of the cyclical phenomenon. My father half a century ago defined the swing as between conservatism and liberalism, between seasons of concern for the rights of the few and seasons of concern for the wrongs of the many. Albert Hirschman has recently reformulated the cycle in terms especially pertinent to the discussion of Tocqueville. In an extension of consumption theory to politics, Hirschman argued in *Shifting Involvements* (1982) that western society since the industrial revolution passes back and forth between times when citizens become wholly absorbed in the pursuit of private affairs and times of intense preoccupation with public issues; a regular alternation, in his words, between "private interest" and "public action."[42]

For people can be wholly fulfilled neither in the public nor in the private sphere. We try one, then the other, and the disappointments of the quest account for the shifts in involvement. Hirschman quotes Kant's remark to Karamzin, the Russian historian: "Give a man everything he desires and yet at this very moment he will feel that this *everything* is not *everything*." Tocqueville was aware of the strain of insatiability in modern man, though he tied it, too narrowly perhaps, to the search for equality. "They can never attain as much as they desire," he wrote in the 1840 *Democracy*. "It perpetually retires from before them, yet without hiding itself from their sight, and in retiring draws them on. At every moment they think they are about to grasp it; it escapes at every moment from their hold. They are near enough to see its charms, but too far off to enjoy them; and before they have fully tasted its delights, they die." This permanent frustration, Tocqueville thought, accounted for the perpetual restlessness of Americans, for the "strange melancholy" that haunted inhabitants of democratic countries in the midst of their abundance and the "disgust of life" that seized them in the midst of calm and easy circumstances.[43]

Also, in looking at the history of his own country, Tocqueville had a sense of the cyclical effect. "On several occasions during the period extending from the outbreak of the Revolution up to our time," he wrote in *The Old Regime and the French Revolution*, "we find the desire for freedom reviving, succumbing, then returning, only to die out once more and presently blaze up again."[44] The French dialectic, as he saw it, was between freedom and equality, but it could as easily have been, in the terms he inherited from Montesquieu, between public virtue and private interest. He arrived in New York only forty-two years and twelve days after George Washington's first inauguration, and his American experience was too brief to enable him to discern cyclical rhythms in the American democracy. Yet his observations support the cyclical hypothesis; and the cyclical context completes his diagnosis by resolving the apparent contradictions between 1835 and 1840, between involvement and individualism, between activism and apathy. The struggle between public purpose and private interest continues to be the essence of American democracy. It is likely that in the future, as in the past, this struggle will work itself out in the cyclical mode.

Tocqueville, Napoleon, and Bonapartism

MELVIN RICHTER

If an absolute government were ever established in a country as democratic in its state of society [*état social*] and as demoralized as France, there would be no conceivable limits upon tyranny. Under Bonaparte we have already seen one excellent specimen of such a regime.

Tocqueville to Kergolay, January 1835

To snow men, if possible, how to escape tyranny and degradation [*l'abâtardissement*] during the period when they are becoming democratic. This, I believe, is the general idea that sums up my book [the 1835 *Démocratie en Amérique*], and which will appear on every page of what I am now writing [the 1840 *Démocratie*].

Tocqueville to Kergolay, 26 December 1836

In societies with religious faith, or little knowledge, absolute power often constrains men without degrading them. This is because such power is acknowledged as legitimate. . . . In our time, this cannot be the case. The eighteenth century and the French Revolution have not left us any moral or honorable ways of submitting to despotism. . . . Thus . . . when men submit to its laws, they can only despise it and themselves.

Tocqueville's 1842 address to the *l'Académie française*

When I come to the Empire, analyze thoroughly its composition: the despotism of a single person raising himself upon a democratic base; the combination best suited for producing . . . the most unlimited despotism, the one best supported by the appearance of being derived from right and sacred interest, that is, of the greatest number; and at the same time, the least responsible.

Tocqueville [c. 1853] on the First Empire

NAPOLEON BONAPARTE, First Empire, and Bonapartism were among Tocqueville's earliest interests in political theory and history. Prominent among Tocqueville's concerns in the *Democracy* were determining the relationship of Bonapartism to democracy and revolution, and by referring to American counterexamples, to dispute earlier French liberal claims that democracy led to Bonapartist dictatorship. Some recent interpreters of the *Democracy* claim to have detected a decisive shift in Tocqueville's thought between 1835 and 1840. They allege that by 1840 Tocqueville no longer perceived Napoleon's form of rule as a major threat to liberty in democratic societies. I shall argue in this paper that Tocqueville's writings in the 1840s contradict such interpretations. In fact, Tocqueville's concern with Napoleon and Bonapartism continued to grow, even before the coup d'état of 1851, preliminary to the Second Empire. As late as 1856, three years before his death, Tocqueville was still planning to complete his study of the old regime and the French Revolution by a volume focused on Napoleon and his empire.

Born in 1805 during the First Empire, Tocqueville died in 1859 during the Second, which he regarded as the most degrading political experience of his adult life. Ten years old at the time of Waterloo, Tocqueville's political consciousness was shaped initially not so much by the ancien régime as by the experience of a disastrous national defeat under the first emperor and his empire. Many years later, Tocqueville remarked not without irony that Napoleon was the only great general, perhaps the only general, ever to have lost four armies.[1] When, during the Restoration Tocqueville first began to reflect on politics, it was inevitable that he would inquire just how Napoleon and Bonapartism were related to those concepts that already dominated his thought: democracy, revolution, centralization, liberty, and equality.

A number of details, a set of significant repetitions indicate how vivid were Tocqueville's memories, how deep his antipathy to Napoleon. In 1833 while visiting England, Tocqueville was in the House of Lords when Wellington rose to put a question. In his travel notes Tocqueville recorded: "So great was his glory, so singular his prestige . . . that I felt as though my blood had begun to foam in my veins."[2] Twenty years later, during the Second Empire, Tocqueville wrote a friend: "Tomorrow is the anniversary of the evening before the battle of Waterloo. How many somersaults and backflips we have taken since that time only to fall flat once again back into the same gutter."[3] Thus four decades after the event, Tocqueville recalled the exact date of Waterloo, which he linked to the equally degrading regime created by Napoleon's nephew. As late as 1856, Tocqueville still considered the First Empire as contemporary history and himself as a surviving witness with insight into its general causes.[4]

What was there about democratic society, about democratic theory, that had facilitated the rise of Napoleon? Did he fulfill and consolidate the French Revolution, or did he betray and pervert it? Was Napoleon able to seize and hold power only because of conditions peculiar to France at a time of revolution and war? Or could the military do likewise in any democratic society? Because of Napoleon's extraordinary personal qualities, Tocqueville perceived him as presenting formidable problems for historical as well as political and social explanation. What was Napoleon's part in determining the great events with which he was associated? Had his own abilities and character been decisive? Or had it been great general causes and trends that brought about and explain those opportunities Napoleon adroitly exploited but did not create?

Tocqueville's analysis of Bonapartism merits careful attention. One leading authority has called Tocqueville's treatment of it in the *Democracy* the first sustained political sociology of that phenomenon.[5] "Bonapartism" as I use it here, refers to that concept or regime type designating dictatorships, which after seizing power by force, then claim to be both democratic and legitimate because of public approval gained after the fact by plebiscites.[6] Thus by "Bonapartism," I mean neither the theoretical programs and actual policies of Napoleon Bonaparte and Louis Napoleon during the First and Second Empires, nor the French political movements that supported them.[7] Both Bonapartes executed military coups that overthrew republican governments, themselves created after the revolutions of 1789 and 1848. Both Bonapartes used plebiscites to register ostensible popular approval, first of their dictatorships, and then of their empires. Because so many political theorists, analysts, and actors believed that a new phenomenon had appeared, a new but contested concept came into use. Even its name as an "ism" provoked controversy: contemporaries had to choose among such neologisms as "Bonapartism," "Caesarism," "Napoleonism," and "imperialism."[8]

Practicing politicians such as Bismarck, theorists such as Tocqueville, Marx and Engels, Bagehot, Lorenz von Stein, Donoso Cortes, Jacob Burckhardt, and Max Weber—all sought to analyze, explain, and explore the implications for the future of this postrevolutionary form of rule, unanticipated and undesired by any of those originally involved in the two major revolutions that transformed Europe. In the second half of the nineteenth century and well into the twentieth, theoretical speculations about Bonapartism were an integral part of political discourse. As a regime type, Bonapartism, during that period was almost as prominent in the discussion as "absolute monarchy" had been in the sixteenth and seventeenth centuries, and as debates about "totalitarianism" would be in the twentieth century.

Tocqueville wished to describe, explain, and condemn the long-term effects of Bonapartism upon French political life.[9] In what sense were Bonapartist regimes democratic? How did they affect democracy in France? In Tocqueville's view, the French Revolution had left an ambiguous heritage, two traditions of democracy: one compatible with citizens ruling themselves, while enjoying liberty, the rule of law, and individual rights; the other, where there was rule in the name of the people by individuals, groups, or parties openly contemptuous of any limitations on popular sovereignty, the ostensible source of the power they exercised. Prominent among the significant contributions to the Revolution's illiberal legacy were those Tocqueville attributed in large part to Napoleon: the perfection of a centralized administrative machinery; the codification of a civil law that encouraged individualist self-enrichment but limited freedoms of the press and association; the launching of theoretical justifications and actual precedents for seizing power by force from constitutional governments; the invention of plebiscitary dictatorship as a pseudo-democratic alternative to representative government; and among those who regarded themselves as revolutionary, the creation of a tradition of disregard for individual rights and constitutional government.

All these aspects of Bonapartism reinforced tendencies developed earlier in what Tocqueville considered the most violent and least defensible periods of the revolution. As a result of the series of revolutions it had undergone, in which Tocqueville included the Eighteenth Brumaire, the Consulate, and the First Empire, France now had a distinctive set of postrevolutionary political *moeurs* [operative practices or political culture]. Many Frenchmen accepted the assumptions that violence is normal and acceptable in politics, that the state may as a matter of course set aside individual or group rights whenever they are found to conflict with the general or national interest; that strong leadership is incompatible with representative institutions. Napoleon had instilled the taste for decisive action and perfected the machinery for executing national policy without genuine consultation of the citizens. Thus to these existing postrevolutionary political *moeurs,* Napoleon added the empire's bureaucratic and legal structures, which effectively excluded citizens and their representatives from deliberating together and from making decisions on any level. Once in power, all successor regimes not only used, but expanded the machinery put into place by the first emperor.

Tocqueville's concern with such questions was more than purely theoretical. By the time Tocqueville's political career began, the Napoleonic legend was being created. This could not but affect Tocqueville's judgments in the 1840s about Napoleon, the First Empire, and Bonapartism. Nor did he fail to connect what he found most menacing in the July Monarchy to Thiers, a political rival, and a historian who had written more than twenty volumes on the Revolution as a preparation for a work of equal length on the empire. Thiers tried to justify Napoleon's role in centralizing French administration, applaud his amoralism in international politics, and center attention on Napoleon's military victories. Along with Guizot, Thiers played an important part in the July Monarchy's attempt to turn the Napoleonic legend to its advantage.

Napoleon both implicitly and explicitly was a prominent concern during the 1840s, Tocqueville's second decade as author and politician. In the 1830s he had visited the United States, established his reputation through the *Democracy,* and begun his parliamentary career. In the 1840s Tocqueville wrote no great book, but devoted himself to his political career. The Revolution of 1848 prepared the way for his elevation to the highest position in politics he ever attained, that of foreign minister in the Barrot government of the Second Republic. But even before Louis Napoleon's coup in December 1851, Tocqueville knew that his political career was over. He realized that he would leave his mark on posterity by what he wrote rather than by any further political activity. It was in 1850 that he first conceived his project for a work he even then considered to be on the same scale and having the same degree of importance as the *Démocratie*. From 1850 to his death in 1859, Tocqueville was engaged in writing the work now known as *The Old Regime and the Revolution*. His career as theorist and historian falls into three decades: the 1830s, 1840s, and 1850s. Throughout all three decades, Tocqueville's views of Napoleon and Bonapartism did not change significantly from those expressed in the 1835 *Democracy*. Tocqueville always considered Napoleon Bonaparte, the First Empire, and Bonapartism as among the most sinister outcomes of the French Revolution. The ten years between 1789 and 1799 had combined on an unprecedented scale democracy, revolution, and war. The emergence of Napoleon and the creation of the First Empire was viewed by Tocqueville neither as the end of the Revolution, nor as isolated episodes, but rather as phases of a continuing revolutionary process. Already in 1836 Tocqueville noted the presence in the French political scene of Louis Napoleon. His failed coup in Strasbourg elicited Tocqueville's first conjectures about the relationship of the military to democracy, as well as the possibility of a recurrence of revolution in the Bonapartist mode.

This essay has several purposes: 1) to demonstrate how central to Tocqueville's thought were his ideas on Napoleon and Louis Bonaparte, their two empires, and Bonapartism, which Tocqueville treated as a perverted form of democracy and democratic theory as well as a misappropriation of the original aims of the French Revolution; 2) by examining Tocqueville's treatment of Napoleon and Bonapartism after the *Democracy*, to test a major reinterpretation of Tocqueville: this posits a disjunction between Tocqueville's positions in the 1835 and 1840 parts of *Democracy in America* on the subject of Bonapartism; 3) to establish in fact that after finishing the *Democracy*, Tocqueville was so far from abandoning the interest he had taken in Bonapartism in the *Democracy* of 1835 that he continued to emphasize this subject in the 1840s; 4) that his inaugural address as a member of the French Academy in 1842 constitutes the link between the *Democracy* and *The Old Regime*. Three-quarters of that address was devoted to the long-term effects of Napoleon and the Empire upon French political *moeurs*.

T O C Q U E V I L L E very early took an important step in his use of the concept of Bonapartism. French liberals had from the beginning linked Napoleon Bonaparte to the Revolution. Madame de Staël, Benjamin Constant, Guizot, Royer-Collard had all asserted that because Napoleon came to power in the wake of the Revolution, this proved that democracy and equality were incompatible with an ordered liberty guaranteeing individual political and civil rights. Tocqueville was the first French liberal to argue that the only alternative to Bonapartism was an ordered, constitutional, and self-limiting democracy, along the lines of the United States as he described it.[10] In the 1835 *Democracy,* Tocqueville made this point as he concluded two of his most important chapters.[11] His most notable statement reads:

> [I]f democratic institutions are not introduced gradually among us, and if all citizens are not provided with those ideas and sentiments that first prepare them for liberty, and then allow them to apply such ideas and sentiments, there will be no independence for anyone, not the bourgeois, not the noble, not the poor, not the rich, but an equal tyranny for all. And I foresee that if in time we do not succeed in establishing the peaceful rule of the greater number, we shall end up sooner or later under the *unlimited* power of a single person.[12]

In a book that combines detailed textual analysis with a consideration of Tocqueville's political concerns in France, Jean-Claude Lamberti has recently offered a brilliant reinterpretation

of the *Democracy*.[13] Lamberti's interpretative strategy resembles but is not identical to that of Seymour Drescher, who
first argued the thesis of the incompatibility between the 1835
and 1840 parts of the *Democracy*, and who restates his case in
the essay in this volume.[14] Although differing in their emphases and explanations of the reasons for Tocqueville's alleged
shifts, Drescher and Lamberti agree in rejecting Tocqueville's
own assertions about the continuity between the two parts of
the *Democracy*, and his reaffirmation throughout his life that
he had never abandoned the positions he had taken in what he
regarded as one rather than two works.[15] Both contend that
Tocqueville's favorable initial assessment of the United States in
1835 was by 1840 superseded by a new and lasting pessimism
about the future of French politics. This in turn led to a decline
in Tocqueville's belief that the United States could provide a
significant alternative to the forms of European democratic society and politics. Both Drescher and Lamberti hold that after
1840 Tocqueville stressed the dangers to democracy, not of
"the despotism of a single person," but rather the graver threat
of that "democratic despotism" that is depicted in the closing
pages of the 1840 *Democracy*.

A complex dispute on the unity of *Democracy in America*
now divides Tocqueville scholars. In his own invaluable book,
James Schleifer defends Tocqueville's claim for the continuity
between the 1835 and 1840 parts of the *Democracy*.[16] François Furet also stresses the unity of Tocqueville's thought,
which he argues took shape remarkably early in his development.[17]

All these studies have revitalized discussion of the *Democracy* by the suggestiveness of their hypotheses and by the novelty of their evidence, which includes the unpublished notes,
drafts, and working manuscript of the *Democracy*. That these
interpreters bring together Tocqueville's French and American
concerns is also among their contributions. Tocqueville's books
were directed to a French audience; his work always depended

upon proof by the comparative method.[18] Many American readers have exaggerated Tocqueville's interest in the United States as an object of study. They forget Tocqueville's warning: "In the final analysis, this work is written principally for France, or if you prefer modern jargon, from a French point of view."[19]

Except on the one point crucial to my own argument, I shall not review in detail the cases for and against these revisionist reinterpretations. Rather I shall confine myself to asking whether fundamental shifts occurred in Tocqueville's view of the dangers to liberty posed by the political and social characteristics of democracy as he defined it. Bonapartism ranked high among these dangers, as diagnosed in the 1835 *Democracy*.

Drescher claims that by 1840 Tocqueville's conception of tyranny had undergone a basic alteration: instead of offering his readers, as he had in 1835, the choice between democratic liberty and the boundless power of a single man, Tocqueville by 1840 believed that despotism in democracies would take the form of centralized bureaucratic government: "Its locus was no longer in the majority of acting unthinking citizens, because Tocqueville's democratic citizens no longer acted or thought. An excessive sense of impotence rather than arrogant pride would be the view of the democratic age."[20]

Lamberti is even more emphatic. In the 1840 *Democracy*, he claims, Tocqueville abandoned the notion that "democratic despotism," the greatest single danger to liberty connected with democracy, had anything to do with "the despotism of the Terror and the Empire."[21] Lamberti argues further that Tocqueville transcended the liberals preceding him, for they could see despotism only as excessive domination by the state, imposed by force upon society.[22] Tocqueville, in his first phase as of 1835, assimilated despotism to the revolution and empire; in his second phase, that of 1840, he distinguished revolutionary elements peculiar to the history of France from the permanent tendencies of democratic societies. He discovered in centralization the true nature of "democratic despotism."[23]

This theory of centralization as the greatest danger democratic nations have to fear is the pessimistic conclusion to Tocqueville's 1840 *Democracy*. Lamberti holds that this view permanently overrides Tocqueville's qualified optimism (based on American ways of mitigating the perils to liberty inherent in democracy), with which he closes the 1835 work.

Although Schleifer on the whole argues that the 1835 and 1840 parts are basically at one, he agrees with Drescher and Lamberti on this one point: Tocqueville abandoned his theory of Bonapartism as a great danger to liberty and individual autonomy in democratic societies. In Schleifer's view, after 1835 Tocqueville abandoned his model of a democratic regime taken over by "a military tyrant like Napoleon or Caesar" for that vision of "administrative despotism" described in the 1840 chapter on what sort of despotism democratic nations have to fear.[24]

I cannot present here a complete version of my own alternative reading of how Tocqueville treats Napoleon and Bonapartism in the *Democracy*. But in short, my view is that although Tocqueville created an arresting new vision of "administrative" or "democratic despotism" in 1840, he never stopped thinking about the dangers of another Bonapartist seizure of power, legitimated by a pseudodemocratic argument justifying plebiscitary dictatorship. Because Tocqueville in 1840 found the greatest threat to liberty in this new type of despotism, it does not follow that he thought that Bonapartism had ceased to be a danger to democracies.

Clearly, excessive centralization of administration was part of Tocqueville's critique of French political development. But centralization had always figured prominently in Tocqueville's definition of problems growing out of the historical development of democratic society and politics. In a passage often ignored because it occurs within a footnote printed at the end of

the 1835 *Democracy,* Tocqueville rejected the prevalent view
that centralization had been produced by the revolution. Instead, Tocqueville identified centralization as the longstanding
policy of all who have held central power in France, and he
equated Louis XIV and Bonaparte in their contributions to an
indefensible degree of administrative centralization.[25] How
much of an alteration from this early image is involved in
Tocqueville's famous chapter in the 1840 volume on "What
Species [*Espèce*] of Despotism Democratic Nations Have to
Fear."

After analyzing references to Napoleon in both the 1835 and
1840 parts of the *Democracy,* I have found no diminution of
Tocqueville's interest in the man and in the form of rule he had
created out of revolution and democracy. Although Tocqueville
in the 1840 text created a new model of that type of despotism
most likely to menace liberty in democratic societies, he did not
discard the possibility of a Bonapartist seizure of power on the
basis of a pseudo-democratic legitimation, which he had first
identified in the 1835 volumes. The rule of a single person re-
curs as a possibility, although not as the greatest peril.

Indeed, in the 1840 chapters on the military, Tocqueville
added to his previous analysis another structural conflict in
democratic societies exemplified by Napoleon: that between the
majority of civilians and the professional army. During an
extended war, desired by soldiers to promote their special interests, there are almost irresistible pressures to increase governmental centralization, that is, central control over persons and
resources. As for administrative centralization, which precludes
citizens' self-government of their own local affairs, nowhere in
the 1840 text was there any repudiation of the point made in
1835: that administrative centralization was begun under the
old regime, extended by the Revolution, and completed by Napoleon. Thus much of the controversy about the novelties and
changes imported into the 1840 text may be reduced to the
question of whether Tocqueville believed that the machinery

finally put in place by Napoleon could function without him and the Empire. This Tocqueville believed to be the case.

The striking vision of democratic despotism introduced into the printed text of 1840 incorporates a number of features later identified by Tocqueville as having characterized Napoleon's mode of rule under the First Empire. These include: the characterization of democratic despotism as mild [*doux*] rather than violent; as degrading because of the degree of knowledge and morality attained in the society; as covering all of social and individual life with a network of detailed regulations, and hence the studied creation of a legal system encouraging individualist desires for material well-being; the denial of any rights (freedom of the press, of association, of citizen participation in the political process) that might call into question the ruler's monopoly; and Napoleon's claim to represent the interests of the nation, and thus to be its permanent guardian or tutor without ever setting a time when it might be recognized as sufficiently developed to handle its own business. And what Tocqueville had written in 1840 about Bonaparte in terms of general and particular causes as constituting a crucial phase of the Revolution would in another form become the project for the great work, of which he completed only the beginning. This work began with his consideration of Napoleon and the empire and their relationship to the French experience with democracy and revolution.

Despite the alterations Tocqueville specifically acknowledged in this chapter, he never abandoned the model of Bonapartism developed in the 1835 *Democracy*. When they are examined within the context of Tocqueville's whole life as a political theorist and actor, Napoleon Bonaparte and Bonapartism turn out to have been among Tocqueville's most durable concerns. This is not to say that on these subjects Tocqueville never altered his views. Indeed, references to the first Bonaparte and to the First Empire can and should serve as one marker for tracing Tocqueville's political and historical theories. While he was consistent in his repertoire of themes and concepts, Tocqueville's use of even the same details could vary greatly, depending upon the problems that most concerned him at any particular point in his argument or as a political actor.

But the unity of the *Democracy* is not all that is at issue. There remains the question of the relationship of that work or works to Tocqueville's subsequent thought in the 1840s and 1850s, most notably to his lamentably unfinished study of the old regime and the Revolution, including the Empire, and the emperor.

There is much incontrovertible evidence indicating that Tocqueville never abandoned his original intention to make Napoleon Bonaparte and the First Empire into the climax of what would probably have been a three-volume work, had he lived to fulfill his design. For that reason, I attribute considerably more continuity to Tocqueville's thought and historiography than do those recent analyses that cut off their discussion of Tocqueville's thought with the completion of the *Democracy* in 1840. Surely it is unsatisfactory for interpreters to make so drastic a cut-off. Less than two years after the publication of the second part of the *Democracy,* Tocqueville was once again developing theories now alleged to have been abandoned definitively at that time.

D I D A basic change in Tocqueville's political theory occur in the late 1830s? Did Tocqueville in fact abandon the notion that in modern democracies there is a persisting danger of repeating the precedents set by the first Bonaparte in his mode of seizing power, in the pseudodemocratic legitimation he constructed for himself and his state, and in the political and administrative centralization he perfected in the Empire? Did Tocqueville ever abandon his disposition to treat Napoleon Bonaparte's performances in the Directory, Consulate, and Empire as phases of the Revolution, which contributed to consolidating both a despotic tendency in the revolutionary political tradition and the Revolution's obsession with foreign conquests? If dramatic changes in Tocqueville's thought are registered in the 1840 *Democracy,* then these shifts ought to be manifest in his works during the 1840s. What did he write about Napoleon and the empire during that period?

In 1842, Tocqueville was inducted into the French Academy. Its protocol called for the new member to deliver a eulogy of his predecessor's life and work. Tocqueville's address was thus bound to address the career of M. de Cessac, who had contributed to the *l'Encyclopédie,* served the old regime, the Revolution, and had held high administrative office under the Empire. The occasion of this address was not regarded as trivial by the young and ambitious writer turned politician:

> My reception is . . . to take place on Thursday. . . . This speech is a great occasion. . . . I am putting into relief more than ever the keen and tenacious love I have for free institutions, a love that forms the essence of my politics. I will also be forced to speak of the Empire. . . . I reproach it for the illiberal side of its institutions, but at the same time I do full justice to the personal grandeur of Napoleon, the most extraordinary being, I say, who has appeared in the world for many centuries. I even enhance him at the expense of his work, since I say that the grandeur of the Empire is due to his person alone. I learned yesterday that the Queen had asked that a seat in the gallery be kept for her.[26]

In this 1842 address, Tocqueville both summarized arguments he had made in the *Democracy,* and went on to develop and illustrate some of its key passages, the original meaning of which had not been at all clear. Above all, he made the most sustained assessment of Napoleon he had written up to this point. Only after 1850 did Tocqueville analyze Bonaparte and Bonapartism at comparable length. And when he did so, it followed in large part the indications he had provided in 1842. In his address, Tocqueville continued to employ that mode of historical explanation prominent in the 1840 *Democracy*.[27] Again we encounter Tocqueville's distinction between general causes and those he called secondary or accidental; the pointed inquiry as to how many of the effects produced by Napoleon are attributable to his own abilities, and how many to opportunities provided by the circumstances of his period, nation, and revolution.

Yet there were also some important changes from what Tocqueville had written about Napoleon in the *Democracy*. In 1840, Tocqueville, absorbed in detailing the reasons why democratic societies favor centralization, virtually absolved Bonaparte of responsibility for perfecting the already strong administrative machinery of France.[28] In 1842, Tocqueville accused him of having deliberately rejected the one real opportunity in French history to break with the tendencies begun by the old regime and continued by the Revolution. The crises of the Directory marked this critical point when it might have been possible to establish new political *moeurs*, which could have introduced into French politics and administration a version of democracy compatible with liberty. This interpretation first offered in 1842 was maintained by Tocqueville when he wrote his drafts of the two chapters dealing with the Directory for his unfinished work on Napoleon and the First Empire.[29]

Here is Tocqueville summarizing in 1842 what he had asserted in the 1835 *Democracy*:

> Once the powers of directing and administering the nation were no longer considered the privileges of certain men or families, such powers began to appear as the product and agent of the will of all [*la volonté de tous*].
>
> It was then generally recognized that this will ought to be subject to no other limits than those it imposed upon itself. After the destruction of classes, corporations, and castes, this will appeared to be the

necessary and natural heir of all secondary powers. Nothing was left so great that it was inaccessible; nothing so small that it could not be reached. The ideas of centralization and popular sovereignty were born on the same day.

Although these ideas originated in [demands for] liberty, they could easily lead to servitude.

Those unlimited powers that had been rightly refused to a king [*prince*] . . . now were conceded to an individual ostensibly representing the nation's sovereignty. Thus Napoleon could say, without much offending public opinion, that he had the right of command over everything because he alone spoke in the name of the people.[30]

What Tocqueville stressed in this passage are the dangers to liberty from a leader who uses pseudodemocratic theories to legitimate the seizure and exercise of power in a democratic society. Such an abuse of democratic theory is explicitly attributed to Napoleon, who had not been identified by name in the 1835 text. There Tocqueville had written about the strange discovery by modern demagogues that there can be legitimate tyrannies, provided only that they are exercised in the people's name.[31]

Most significant for the argument being made here are two facts: first, Tocqueville was presenting in 1842 theories about Bonapartism that he is alleged to have abandoned in 1840; second, Tocqueville returned in this 1842 text to political participation by citizens [the thesis so prominent in the 1835 volumes] as the only antidote for those dispositions of democratic society he had identified as peculiarly dangerous to liberty [in 1840]. These dangers included individualism, as well as the preferences for equality over liberty, for centralization over local self-government, and the passion for material well-being. What is new is Tocqueville's suggestion that Bonaparte arrived on the French scene at the only time when it might have been possible to alter significantly the mores [*moeurs*] or political culture that had been created by the long-term trend toward ever greater administrative centralization. Napoleon used all the means at his disposal, including the recodification of the civil law, to encourage concern with private well-being. Thus citizens could be distracted from participating in politics.

In both the 1835 and 1840 texts, Tocqueville had analyzed two tendencies in the French Revolution: one claiming liberty for all citizens; the other despotic in its willingness to sacrifice liberty to equality or to some other overriding value, such as the common interest or general will. While in 1840 Tocqueville had suggested only that Napoleon had contributed to such democratic despotic tendencies, by 1842 Tocqueville had assigned to Napoleon the primary responsibility for having instituted absolute power upon a democratic base. No one before Napoleon had so well understood that the principal ideas of the Enlightenment and the French Revolution could lead either to a free regime or to an absolute power, which because of its capacity to manipulate its democratic constituency, exceeded in its control over the population any form of domination previously known. With his extraordinary intelligence, Napoleon was the first to perceive the opportunities provided by the Enlightenment and the Revolution for establishing such power:

> He saw that his contemporaries were closer to submission than they knew. He saw that it was far from madness to aspire to a new throne and a new dynasty. . . . Carried away by Napoleon, the French soon found themselves further away from liberty than ever before in their history. . . .
>
> The emperor without difficulty executed an extraordinary project. At one stroke and on a single plan, he rebuilt the entire fabric of society. He did so in order to make it accommodate absolute power without strain. Those who have legislated for societies coming into existence were not themselves sufficiently civilized to conceive of

such a project. Those who have legislated for aging societies could not have executed this task, for in the debris of ancient institutions, they confronted insurmountable obstacles. Napoleon had at his disposal the knowledge attained by the nineteenth century. The nation, upon which he acted was almost as bereft of law, customs, and *moeurs* as if it had just been created. This permitted Napoleon to construct a despotism far more rational and skillfully articulated than any previously attempted. After having promulgated with the same unitary spirit all those laws regulating the relations of citizens with one another and to the state, he was able to create at a single stroke all the powers charged with executing those laws. Thus he could structure all of them so as to constitute a great but simple machine of government. Napoleon alone was its motor.

Nothing comparable had ever been created anywhere. . . . The formidable unity of the system, the powerful logic that linked all its parts, left no refuge for liberty.

Absolute government is endowed with a special and pernicious capacity to nourish and develop all the bad instincts of the new society; such government at once depends upon these instincts and allows them to develop without limit.[32]

These passages are among Tocqueville's most important contributions to the concept of Bonapartism. Whether or not he was correct in his characterization of the Bonapartist system, he here created a stunning image of a new form of total domination based on an unprecedented organization of government and society. It is striking that Tocqueville still used the term "absolute government," for what he had in mind was an image that eclipsed anything even aspired to by absolute monarchs.

When Tocqueville referred to France as being almost totally bereft of laws, customs, and established *moeurs,* as if it had just been created, he was referring to conditions during the Directory when Napoleon first seized power. In the draft chapters on that period, which Tocqueville wrote in the 1850s for his unfinished work on Napoleon, this point is considerably developed and documented.

In both places, Tocqueville was using his theory of historical explanation to make two points: first, Napoleon was enabled to create the structures that he did because of antecedent conditions created by both the kings of the old regime and by the policies of the French Revolution up to the point when he became an actor in it; second, that these conditions of breakdown under the Directory in no way necessitated what Napoleon in fact did. Had he been concerned to break with the tradition of administrative centralization, he would have had a better chance of bringing this off than any French statesman before or after him. Such was the imaginative general conception, what Tocqueville called his *idée-mère*, that he first stated in this text of 1842. What was most striking about its use came in Tocqueville's description of the Directory as offering a unique opportunity for introducing into France some equivalent of the liberal democracy on the American model he had described in 1835. Then he had attributed to the general political participation in public affairs, made possible by American administrative decentralization, the effective limitation of dangers to liberty inherent in democracy. Such common deliberations and participatory political action by persons and associations were emphasized by Tocqueville in 1835 as among the ways Americans mitigated the individualism and materialism of democratic society.

It has been alleged that the 1840 volume registers Tocqueville's loss of faith in the possibility of countering individualism and materialism, his recognition that political apathy could not be overcome. This is said to have been due to his experiences upon returning to a France that was fatigued and disillusioned by its revolutionary struggles, incurably addicted to placing all political and administrative powers in the same set of hands, that of the central government.

How were these subjects treated in Tocqueville's French

Academy address? First, he repeated his 1835 formula of granting rights to all and encouraging public participation in order
to counter the dangers to liberty created by the isolation,
selfishness, and materialism endemic to democratic or egalitarian society, as he defined it. Second, he provided his own
diagnosis of the blow dealt to liberty in France by Napoleon,
his place in the historiography of the French Revolution. By
recreating and perfecting the centralized state machinery,
Napoleon had come closer to total domination of French
society than anyone before him. He perceived with great clarity
the opportunities for such domination that had been created by
a democratic revolution, the possibilities offered by an individualistic, materialist, and egalitarian society for a more complete
denial of liberty than had been available to past despots. In
Tocqueville's draft chapters on Napoleon and the Empire,
written ten years later, there was a considerable convergence
between the administrative or democratic despotism depicted
in the final pages of the 1840 *Democracy* and Tocqueville's
portrait of the First Empire.

In still another application of his philosophy of history,
Tocqueville gave his reasons for believing that in the long run,
France could not and would not acquiesce permanently in
regimes denying it political liberty. Later he would reject the
judgment that in the First and Second Empires, France had
found governments appropriate to its passions and needs.

> The diffusion of knowledge [*des lumières*] and the division of
> property has made each of us independent and isolated from the
> rest. Only interest in public affairs can temporarily unite our minds,
> and on occasion, our wills. But absolute power would deprive us of
> this unique setting for deliberating together and acting in common.
> It chooses to enclose us in that narrow individualism, to which we
> are already over inclined.[33]

Appealing to his audience's political imagination, Tocqueville asked his audience to consider what the world might have

been like had Napoleon and his empire been succeeded by a regime, which unlike the Restoration, had believed in extending political liberties. Such liberty to participate in public affairs presupposes other liberties as well: freedom of thought and discussion, freedom of the press, freedom of association. All these points had been made in both parts of the book that had brought Tocqueville election to the French Academy at so early an age; they would be reaffirmed many years later in *The Old Regime*, when Tocqueville referred with great bitterness to Napoleon's cynical violations of these liberties.[34]

> Who can predict what would have happened to the human spirit, if the exciting drama of attempting to conquer the world had been replaced by the prospect of establishing liberty? Who can predict what would have occurred, if after all the noise and glamour [of the Empire], everyone had not been obliged to return to silence and to their undistinguished conditions, where they could think only of how best to conduct their private affairs.

> I believe firmly that our contemporaries can make us great as well as prosperous, but only on the condition that we remain free. Only under liberty can we share those powerful emotions which raise and sustain us above our individual selves. Only liberty can bring variety to our otherwise uniform conditions; only liberty can raise the level of our aspirations, relieve us from the domination of petty thoughts.[35]

Tocqueville now had to assess Napoleon's legacy, and this could be done only by viewing against the backdrop of the French Revolution those institutions, legal systems, and administrative machinery left behind by Napoleon. Here Tocqueville's theory of historical explanation reappeared. Bonaparte as an individual must be related to the general causes operative in the circumstances he first found and then profoundly affected. The balance sheet of the First Empire, in Tocqueville's view, had been a series of unprecedented disasters for France. Napoleon had used his genius to restore and to perfect despotism, thus defeating the generous purposes of the Revolution at its inception. As for the project of conquering Europe, this had led to no ordinary defeat in battle, but to the ignominious occupation of France by its foreign enemies. However extraordinary Napoleon's abilities, ultimately he was responsible for ruining himself and the nation. No one else had been in a position to dislodge him from power. This only he could do, and in fact he destroyed himself. Napoleon's most durable achievement had proved permanently harmful to France, for he had completed the machinery of administrative centralization. His dazzling personal qualities had facilitated the acceptance of the system he had perfected. But it was independent of its creator.[36]

> His singular genius justified and in a sense legitimated [*légitimait*] the extreme dependence of his contemporaries in their own eyes. The hero concealed the despot. It seemed plausible that in obeying him, submission was rendered not to his power, but to the man. Yet after Napoleon ceased to light up and animate the new world he had created, nothing was left of him except his despotism. This was the most perfect ever exercised over this nation.[37]

In weighing what Napoleon had achieved in the First Empire, Tocqueville returned to the historiographical issues raised in the *Democracy*. How much should be attributed to the exceptional individual, how much to the general causes at work in his time and society? This issue, originally derived from Montesquieu's *Considérations,* was brilliantly applied by Tocqueville to French history. No case was more challenging in this context than that of Napoleon. His character and fate fascinated the nineteenth century, much as Hitler's and Stalin's fates have fascinated our own. For at first view, there is a tendency to attribute to such individuals powers almost as superhuman as they themselves believed they possessed. And at the time Tocqueville was speaking, the Napoleonic legend was becoming a potent force.

Tocqueville's reaction, as in his earlier comment in the *Democracy*, was to deflate such claims.[38] Tocqueville always conceded Napoleon's extraordinary intelligence, his capacity to plan and to organize his grandiose projects; and above all, his ability to mobilize national energies and loyalties in the service of his own interests. But from the beginning to the end of his career, Tocqueville considered Napoleon to have been the most dangerous enemy of liberty yet to have appeared. Nevertheless, even when it came to administrative centralization, Tocqueville assigned to Napoleon the place of an astute exploiter of forces already at work, the masterly coordinator of a scheme already in place. This analysis was already highly developed in the 1840s and did not await that chapter of *The Old Regime* entitled, "Administrative Centralization was an Institution of the Old Regime, not the Work of the Revolution or the Empire."[39] Tocqueville invariably used his own scheme of historical explanation to deny Napoleon the decisive role in any of the great achievements attributed to him.

> Although the Empire's achievements were surprising, it was not itself the real source of this grandeur. It owed its *éclat* to accidents rather than to any intrinsic merits of its own.

> The Revolution had brought France to its feet; Napoleon ordered it to march. The Revolution had amassed enormous and unprecedented forces; these he organized and utilized. He produced prodigies, but in an age of prodigies. The person who founded and maintained this Empire was the most extraordinary phenomenon to appear for many centuries. Napoleon was as great as a man without virtue can be.[40]

Tocqueville used Napoleon and the Empire as examples when in 1842 he returned to themes he had treated as history in both the 1835 and 1840 parts of his *Democracy*. Although irreversible trends operated upon the modern world, yet there were all-important choices remaining to be made. As he had

written in the closing paragraphs of his 1840 text, which he repeated almost verbatim in 1842, for democratic nations to be
virtuous and prosperous, they need only to will it.[41] Again, in
his Introduction to the text of 1835 and in the final paragraphs
of 1840, Tocqueville reiterated the belief that in democracy
there were mighty dangers that it is possible to ward off,
mighty evils that may be avoided or alleviated. His philosophy
of history remained consistent: he denied historical inevitability
when it was carried to a point that left no room for either individual choice or collective deliberation and action:

> Providence has not created mankind either entirely free. It is true
> that around every man a fatal circle is traced beyond which he can-
> not pass. But within those vast limits, man is powerful and free.
> The same is true of peoples. The nations of our time cannot prevent
> conditions from becoming equal. But it depends upon themselves
> whether equality is to lead to servitude or liberty; to knowledge
> [*lumières*] or to barbarism; to prosperity or to wretchedness.[42]

Napoleon, Tocqueville remarked in 1842, had not been able
to direct history, despite periods when it seemed as though he
was doing precisely that. This man who believed himself to be
greater than human [*plus grand que l'humanité*], succeeded in
ruining himself.[43]

In his introduction to the 1835 text, Tocqueville had addressed the question of the conditions of legitimacy in the modern age in some striking sentences, the precise meaning of
which remained unclear. Tocqueville seemed to be contrasting
obedience to legitimate authority in aristocratic or feudal ages
to obedience to illegitimate authority in democratic ages. But
while Tocqueville's point was clear in relation to feudal society—such authority and obedience was not degrading—it
was not clear which case of degrading obedience to illegitimate
authority in a democratic age Tocqueville had in mind:

> While the power of the crown, supported by the aristocracy, peaceably governed the nations of Europe . . . the people, never having conceived the idea of a social condition different from their own, and never expecting to become equal to their leaders, received benefits from them without discussing their rights. They became attached to them when they were clement and just, and submitted to their exactions without resistance or servility, as to the inevitable visitations of the Deity. . . . Inequality and wretchedness were then to be found in society, but the souls of neither rank of men were degraded.

> Men are not corrupted by the exercise of power or degraded by the habit of obedience, but by the exercise of a power they believe to be illegitimate, and by obedience to a rule which they consider to be usurped and oppressive.[44]

In his French Academy address, Tocqueville made it clear that he had been referring to obedience to Napoleon's illegitimate, usurped power. The conditions of legitimate authority had been permanently altered. Citizens could not without degradation obey the commands of absolute rulers. For after the Enlightenment and the Declaration of 1789, obedience to an absolute ruler cannot be compatible with either individual morality or national honor:

> In societies that either possess faith, or else possess little knowledge, absolute power often constrains men's souls, but without in the least degrading them. This is because such power is acknowledged as a legitimate state of affairs [*comme un fait légitime*]. Then the rigors of absolute power are suffered unnoticed; endured, with no consciousness of its exercise. In our time, this cannot be the case. The eighteenth century and the French Revolution have not left us with any moral or honorable ways of submitting to despotism. Human beings have become too independent, too disrespectful, too sceptical to believe sincerely in the rights of absolute power. This they perceive only as a dishonorable escape from that anarchy they

themselves were not brave enough to oppose, as a shameful protection necessitated by the vices and weakness of their own time. Thus they judge absolute power as at once necessary and illegitimate [*illégitime*], and when they submit to its laws, they can only despise it and themselves.[45]

This passage referred to the degradation of the French under Napoleon. To understand its full force, it must be placed next to the second epigraph at the head of this paper. There Tocqueville had expressed one of his principal purposes in writing the *Democracy*—to attempt to show men living in a democratic age how to avoid degradation and tyranny. Tocqueville believed in 1835 that Bonapartism was the alternative to a constitutional democracy with a participating body of citizens. In this passage from his 1842 address, he repeated his original point, but made it clear that in his 1835 texts he had been referring to Napoleon. His views did not change in 1840. Bonapartism was not the only threat to an ordered liberty in a democratic state. But it remained high on his list of potential dangers.

IN TOCQUEVILLE's other political writings and speeches in the 1840s, whenever he had occasion to discuss Napoleon and Bonapartism, he continued to use the same frame of reference he had used in the *Democracy* and in his address to the French Academy. His own independent position in the chamber was based in part upon his repugnance with the principles of the left party. For this party operated upon what M. Jardin has described as a mythology combining "Jacobin principles and above all a nostalgia for the Empire."[46] Throughout his service in the chamber, Tocqueville continued to show his knowledge both of the details of Napoleonic legislation, and of the system that united it to the administrative structure that continued to be strengthened by the July Monarchy.

In 1846, Tocqueville had occasion to discuss at length a book on administrative law, a subject he regarded as crucial to understanding the spirit [*l'esprit*] of modern French law, government, and society. In Tocqueville's judgment, French administration and civil law were far more distinctive and had influenced political ideas, acts, mores [*moeurs*] much more than the constitution and institutions of the July Monarchy.[47]

Tocqueville once again applied to new circumstances Montesquieu's concept of the general spirit of political systems. Napoleon during the Empire had transformed the administrative system in order to dominate those he ruled more absolutely than any previous French regime:

> Napoleon only conserved or reestablished the system founded by the Constituent Assembly. Certain parts of that system he improved and completed, but what he changed most profoundly was its spirit. Wherever the Constituent Assembly had placed a council with executive powers, Napoleon substituted a single subordinate directly responsible to him. Wherever the Constituent Assembly had established popular elections, Napoleon substituted persons chosen by the sovereign.[48]

Returning to a theme developed in 1842, Tocqueville now provided a detailed account of how Bonaparte had transformed the Revolution into a despotism. Napoleon went beyond what had existed before him:

> To strengthen further this administration already emancipated from any control by citizens, Napoleon made even his most minor officials immune from legal action before any court of law. Although there had been attempts made to establish such a rule in absolute monarchies, no despot had ever dared to write it into a legal code; no country in the world had ever before admitted this as a legal principle. Thus without much modifying the mechanics of administration, without much changing its external appearance, Napoleon succeeded in appropriating to the needs of absolute power that vast machinery.[49]

Napoleon also saw how constructing parallel systems of offices and bodies could serve his purpose of monopolizing power and neutralizing opposition:

> Napoleon loved advice, provided only that he controlled completely those charged with giving it. . . . Thus he placed a municipal council besides the mayor; the general council of a department besides the prefect; the Conseil d'Etat besides the Emperor.[50]

Ultimately, Tocqueville argued, despite Napoleon's personal contributions to the transformation of the republic into a despotic empire, the bureaucratic state apparatus was not created by him. General causes were operative, of which he availed himself. It would be a mistake to think that a system that outlived regimes and revolutions could be explained by reference to individuals or assemblies. For general causes, a social revolution had created the conditions for the administrative system. Neither accidents, nor particular causes such as the will of an assembly or the genius of an individual could explain the creation and maintenance of such a durable structure:

> Surely our administrative system was not born by accident, was not created either by the arbitrary will of an assembly, or by the egoistic genius of a great man. No, it was the necessary result of that social revolution which operated in France at the end of the last century, and continues to operate in different phases throughout the world.[51]

Before leaving Tocqueville's treatment of Napoleon and Bonapartism in the 1840s, two questions must be considered: Was Tocqueville here subscribing to historical pessimism, a deterministic theory based on general causes? Did he believe that administrative centralization was inevitable in a democratic society? Had he stopped thinking and writing about the American alternative he had described and tacitly prescribed in 1835 and 1840? Actually the two questions are linked. Comparisons of the "two great free nations in the world today" were used by Tocqueville in the 1840s to demonstrate that there was nothing inevitable about the continental European trend toward administrative centralization.[52] In his 1846 report, Tocqueville used references to the United States and Great Britain to argue that alternatives existed to the French administrative system perfected by Napoleon:

> I have had occasion to discuss this subject many times with the best informed men of America and England. . . . Not one of them would wish to adopt our administrative system in its entirety, bearing as it does the imprint of Napoleon's powerful hand. Nor do they believe that in the long run such a system is compatible with liberty.[53]

In 1847 and 1848 Tocqueville repeated this conjunction, using Napoleon as a negative model and the United States as a positive one. In a report to the Academy of Moral and Political Sciences, Tocqueville treated a book by Cherbuliez with the provocative title, *Democracy in Switzerland*. Tocqueville left no doubt about his judgment of Napoleon's legislation after his invasion of Switzerland:

> Napoleon . . . granted equality, but not liberty. The political laws he imposed were so framed that political life was paralyzed. Power exercised in the name of the people, but put well out of its reach, was all placed in the hands of the executive authorities.[54]

Again American examples provided the positive standard. In this case they were contrasted with Switzerland. Tocqueville used the comparative method to prove that democracy and its principle of the people's sovereignty may be used to attain very different results:

> M. Cherbuliez thinks that the imperfect institutions of the Swiss cantons are the only ones democracy can prompt or even tolerate. My comparison will prove the contrary, and show, how starting

from the principle of the sovereignty of the people, elsewhere, with more experience, skill, and wisdom, it has been possible to obtain different results. I take as example the state of New York. . . .

In the state of New York, as in the Swiss cantons, sovereignty of the people is the recognized principle. . . . In general, in no case do the people retain in their own hands any part of the legislative, executive, or judicial power. . . .

The laws of New York State . . . are framed in a way to combat the natural defects of democracy. But the Swiss institutions . . . would seem to have been devised to make them worse. In New York they hold the people back but in Switzerland the only thought would seem to be how to make it irresistible.[55]

Other examples of Tocqueville's repetition in 1848 of points originally made in 1835 occur in the twelfth edition of the *Democracy*. In his preface, written after the overthrow of the July Monarchy and the establishment of the Second Republic in 1848, Tocqueville reasserted the values and the continuity of his thought. He showed no signs of retracting earlier errors, of correcting the analyses and recommendations of 1835 by reappraisals made in 1840. On the basis of his work fifteen years before, he claimed to have foreseen the Revolution of 1848. Indeed after it, the *Democracy* now had a topicality and point it had lacked in France when it was first published. Repeating the set of antitheses first stated in 1835 and recalled in his conclusion to the 1840 volumes, Tocqueville recalled his American model to French readers:

American institutions, which for France under monarchy were only subjects of curiosity, ought now to be studied by republican France. . . .

Let us not turn to America in order to copy slavishly the institutions it has provided for itself, but rather to learn which institutions best suit us. . . . Let us borrow principles rather than details. The laws of the French Republic can and ought to be different from those of the United States. But the principles on which the constitutions of the states rest—the principles of order, balance of powers, true liberty and a deep, sincere respect for law—are indispensable for all republics.[56]

In 1848, Tocqueville was reasserting his estimate of the United States as a potential model of liberal democracy for France and the rest of Europe. As political and social theorist, Tocqueville continued to utilize the same repertoire of concepts he had developed in both parts of the *Democracy*. His writings in the 1840s on Napoleon and Bonapartism demonstrate both the continuity and the brilliance of his applications of these concepts to new situations and problems in French politics.

Throughout the 1840s, Tocqueville continued to return to themes he had first emphasized in his 1835 volumes and with which those of 1840 were fully compatible. Thus the dramatic shifts in his political thought, which allegedly occurred between 1838 and 1840, left few if any traces on Tocqueville's work from 1840 to 1848. Tocqueville further developed his views of Napoleon and Bonapartism as permanent dangers to liberty and to the proper understanding of popular sovereignty; his philosophy of history and theory of historical explanation continued to play a larger part in his interpretation of events past and present than has been hitherto recognized, particularly by social scientists.

BETWEEN 1848 and 1850 Tocqueville rose higher in French politics than ever before. But even before Louis Napoleon's coup of 2 December 1851, Tocqueville knew that his political career had come to an end. He played out his part as a deputy, was arrested during the coup, and smuggled out a letter of protest to the *London Times*. Thereafter he refused to participate in what passed for political life in the Second Empire.

Tocqueville had already begun the search for a subject on the same level of importance as the *Democracy*. It has long been known that Tocqueville first conceived of his project as a study of the first Napoleon and his empire, and that Tocqueville's model was Montesquieu's *Considérations*. Stated in a letter from Tocqueville to Kergolay in 1850, this text has been available since its publication by Beaumont in 1861. Yet some of its key passages have not yet been analyzed. Taken together with other correspondence of Tocqueville, they indicate that it was his continued interest in Napoleon and Bonapartism that connected the *Democracy* and *The Old Regime and the Revolution*.

By his own account, Tocqueville originally conceived of writing a work on Napoleon and the Empire in 1841 or 1842. In short, it was approximately when he was preparing his reception address to the French Academy in 1842, or less than two years after the publication of the 1840 *Democracy*. Thus Tocqueville's concern with Napoleon and Bonapartism was among the most important links between the *Democracy* and *The Old Regime*. Indeed Tocqueville's own account does not refer to what has generally been regarded as that earlier work most closely related to *The Old Regime*, the essay written in 1836 at the request of John Stuart Mill and translated by him.[57]

Tocqueville wrote three letters describing his project. What he wrote Kergorlay from his convalescence at Sorrento contains the most complete account of it:

> I have long thought . . . of choosing from that long period which extends from 1789 to our own time, and which I continue to call the French Revolution, the ten years of the Empire: the birth, development, decline and fall [*décadence et chute*] of that fabulous enterprise. . . . Certainly it is among those acts of the French Revolution which permit judgment of the whole drama. . . . My doubts stem less from the choice of subject than from the problem of how

to treat it. My first thought was to rewrite, in my own fashion, the work written by M. Thiers. . . . But upon reflection, I hesitate. . . .

Another way of envisaging the subject has occurred to me: not a long work, but a short book; a volume perhaps. I would write, not a history of the Empire, but a work of reflection and judgment on that history. . . . Above all, my task would be to make comprehensible the principal causes that have produced the Empire and its consequences. . . . The inimitable model for this genre is Montesquieu's book on the greatness and decline of the Romans.[58]

In this letter, Tocqueville notes only that he had long thought of writing on Napoleon and the Empire. But in June 1852, while still at work on his original project, Tocqueville wrote that he had first conceived of it more than ten years ago, or approximately in 1841.[59] After the publication of *The Old Regime*, Tocqueville wrote Montalembert a long and careful letter to thank him for his praise of the work. Tocqueville noted that his project was first conceived more than fifteen years before 1856, or about 1841:

The book I just published and its continuation have been turning about in my mind for more than fifteen years; the project ripened and its form was determined during my major illness in 1850. Ever since I have been thinking about it continually.[60]

In the course of the 1850s, Tocqueville changed his conception of the book. I cannot detail that development here. But the evidence points to his intention to write a three-volume work. The closing book was to deal with Napoleon and the Empire within the context of the French Revolution. What would it have contained?

Any attempted reconstruction of that work would have to be inferred from Tocqueville's treatment of Napoleon and Bonapartism in the *Democracy*, that is during the decade of the 1830s; his further development in the 1840s, which has been

the subject of this paper; and finally, his notes, drafts, and correspondence during the decade beginning with 1850. Even the
best informed set of conjectures can provide only a shadowy
outline of what Tocqueville might have concluded, had he lived
to complete the work. While writing the first volume of *The
Old Regime*, he made extraordinary discoveries in his research;
he himself was surprised by the ultimate shape of his book.
Thus we cannot do more than surmise what Tocqueville would
have written had he been able to add years of research to three
decades of reflection on Napoleon and Bonapartism. Yet there
can be little doubt that with Tocqueville's death a very great
work was lost applying his distinctive theory of historical explanation to his judgment upon the fate of revolution and democracy in France. Surely that final volume of his trilogy
would have rivaled in interest and importance the first part too
often mistaken for the whole of Tocqueville's projected work,
The Old Regime and the Revolution.

Had Tocqueville completed his design, his book would have
treated subjects of extraordinary interest in terms of an analysis
previously developed by him in ways that have proved unu-
sually suggestive. Which aspects of the French Revolution, of
modern democratic societies and political systems, had facilitated the development of Bonapartism? Which theoretical arguments could be and have been used as justifications for them?

Like Montesquieu, Tocqueville held that institutions do not
determine everything, "that political societies are not what their
laws make them, but what sentiments, ideas, habits of the
heart, and the spirit of the men who form them, prepare them
to be."[61] In his draft chapters on the Directory as having prepared the way for Napoleon, Tocqueville was already applying,
in his own fashion, Montesquieu's distinction between *moeurs*
and *lois* to the French Revolution, to the formation of a new
political culture, and to the explanation of Napoleon and the
Empire.

In his work after 1850, the political point of Tocqueville's philosophy of history became clearer than ever before. The Bonapartist phenomenon, he argued, must be seen as less the achievement of an inimitable genius than the first instance of a knowing manipulation of democracy and democratic theory in order to subvert self-government. Tocqueville assigned to both Napoleons and to Bonapartism a degree of importance far exceeding what Marx and Engels reduced to a temporary and special case.

We have also lost Tocqueville's analysis of the interplay between an extraordinary individual and a set of opportunities created by the most complete and unprecedented revolution that had yet occurred. Could such a combination of exceptional leadership with revolutionary conditions occur again? To admit that Napoleon was a genius did not imply for Tocqueville that the prerequisite of Bonapartism is the presence of an individual with the extraordinary abilities of Napoleon. This was confirmed by the victory of Louis Napoleon, considered by almost no informed observer as possessing his uncle's abilities. Tocqueville had good reasons for not abandoning his early concern in the 1835 *Democracy* about Bonapartism as one possible outcome of certain structural and intellectual weaknesses of democracy in a society undergoing a series of revolutions.

Tocqueville as Historian: Philosophy and Methodology in the *Democracy*

JAMES T. SCHLEIFER

EVERAL misgivings face me when I consider Alexis de Tocqueville as a historian. The topic is neither the most glamorous in the *Democracy*, nor has it much immediate connection to the problems and puzzles facing modern democratic societies. Moreover, Tocqueville's historical philosophy and methodology have already been examined with great care and insight by several commentators. In addition to a general examination by Marvin Zetterbaum, we have more specific, but nonetheless rewarding studies by Albert Salomon, Edward Gargan, Melvin Richter, Roger Boesche, and François Furet.[1] And most books devoted to Tocqueville at least touch on some of the questions involved in considering the subject.[2] Nonetheless, the drafts, autograph manuscript, and other working papers of the *Democracy* contain several newly discovered fragments that, by adding illustrations, nuances, and some unexpected developments and twists to Tocqueville's ideas, will enrich our understanding of Tocqueville as historian. I believe that the topic merits further exploration.

Since I have begun with cautions, let me present two or three others. For this essay, my perspective is largely limited to the *Democracy*. A few cross-references to the *Souvenirs* or *The Old Regime* will be made, and I am assuming no profound disjuncture of philosophy or methodology among Tocqueville's books. But my discussion here is closely restricted to Tocqueville the historian, as seen in his greatest work, *Democracy in America*. Nor does this paper attempt to evaluate the accuracy of Tocqueville's interpretations of particular historical events or developments, such as the colonial foundings, the American Revolution, or for that matter the rise of classes in the Jacksonian era. My focus is rather upon Tocqueville's basic approach to history, specifically some major characteristics of his historical philosophy and methodology.

Finally, much of the new material to come is drawn from deleted passages and discarded versions of the *Democracy*; such sources raise a host of difficulties. Why did Tocqueville choose not to present a particular fragment? In some cases, we know from marginal comments or other clues that a piece was judged too controversial, or too contradictory, or too poorly stated, or too much beside the main point, or simply too long for an already lengthy book. But in other cases we can only guess at Tocqueville's reasons for the deletions. And how would Tocqueville have corrected a given piece? Resurrecting a discarded paragraph or an essay, unpolished and not intended for public view, presents undeniable dangers. The intrinsic interest in watching Tocqueville's mind at work will have to be my excuse.

Tocqueville's short chapter from the 1840 portion of the *Democracy*, "Some Characteristics of Historians in Democratic Times," may serve as a summary statement of much of his philosophy of history.[3] Two earlier versions of the chapter title reveal his intention more clearly: "How Equality of Conditions Influences Certain Historical Doctrines," and, even better, "The Influence of Equality of Conditions On the Way In Which History Is Envisioned and Written."[4]

He opened his discussion with the assertion that whereas historians in aristocratic times attribute almost all human developments to the action and influence of individuals, those in democratic times explain history by citing general causes. The former are seduced by the prominent actors on the stage; the latter, by the apparent insignificance and weakness of all the players in the human drama.

But in all ages, Tocqueville insisted, a variety of both general and particular causes are at work.[5] The difficulty is that in times of equality the particular or "secondary and fortuitous"[6] causes are less important and far more difficult to discern and explain than they are during periods of aristocracy, when special influences are more obvious and powerful. Many historians during democratic ages are therefore led by laziness and intellectual mediocrity to write glibly of great causes. Hence his first criticism of historians in times of equality: they pay too much attention to general causes and mistakenly ignore the influence of particular ones.[7]

Tocqueville then raised a second objection. Not only do democratic historians tend to exaggerate the influence of general causes, but they also too readily create systems, imposing an artificial "sequence and methodical order"[8] on human events.

From the historian as system-maker, Tocqueville moved to his third and most serious charge. Many of those who write history in democratic times are tempted to abandon the principle of human free will; out of general causes and systems they construct chains that bind nations "to an inflexible Providence or to some blind necessity," such as geographic position, origin, antecedents, or character.[9] To Tocqueville the moralist, such fatalism was unacceptable. The doctrine of necessity led to self-doubt and to public paralysis. Without choice, human beings lost any spur to action and any sense of responsibility for their own destiny. Deterministic beliefs endangered the moral objective that Tocqueville had always in mind: to foster human dignity and individual independence in the age of democracy.

What do we learn then about Tocqueville's philosophy of history from this small chapter? At least four major beliefs emerge: 1) an insistence on the variety of causes (and the complexity of causation); 2) a rejection of system-making; 3) a denunciation of determinism; and 4) a conviction that moral concerns must be fundamental to any historical approach.

But what he said in these few published pages is merely the calm surface of a turbulent pool. Some fascinating undercurrents of thought and argument lie hidden in the drafts and working manuscripts of the *Democracy*.

We know from our capsule chapter and from other parts of the text of the *Democracy* that Tocqueville distinguished roughly between general and secondary historical causes. Among the general causes, he counted: the intangibles of ideas, attitudes, values, character, and spirit (what Tocqueville called *moeurs* or mores); social conditions; legal and political institutions; and the circumstances of heritage (including origins or points of departure) and physical setting. Of these—again primarily for moral reasons[10]—he ranked first, moral and social influences; second, laws; and third, circumstances.[11]

What Tocqueville meant by secondary causes is more problematical. The *Democracy* shows more than a hint of confusion. How were particular or fortuitous or individual causes (or influences) related? Were these terms interchangeable? In a fragment written in the margin of an early version of his chapter on historians, Tocqueville remarked: "There are two things that must not be lost sight of: *individual influence* and *accidents*."[12]

He explained in a longer commentary:

There are two ideas in this chapter that one must be careful not to confuse. The destiny of a people may be modified or changed by the accidental influence of a powerful man, such as Napoleon, I suppose. Or even by an accident of chance such as a plague or the loss of a battle. One can refuse to believe in the influence of individuals and believe in that of accidents. During democratic centuries, the influence of *individuals* is infinitely less than during aristocratic centuries, but the influence of *accidents* is not diminished.

But the modern historical system consists in saying not only that individuals, but also that accidents can not modify [several illegible words; possibly "the destiny"] of nations. So, for example, the

glory of a particular battle would not be able to prevent the definitive collapse of a particular nation because a pre-existing chain of
long-standing causes destined that nation to inevitable destruction.

It is evident that all that I said in the preceding chapter applies
to *individuals* and not to *accidents*.[13]

Unlike individual actions, which varied in influence from aristocratic to democratic times, accident played a rather constant
part in history. Despite some remaining uneasiness that his
point was "exaggerated because when you go back to the origin of accidents you arrive almost always at individual action,"[14] Tocqueville acted on his distinction. In successive
drafts of his chapter on historians, he systematically deleted almost all references to accident and interlined the terms "special" or "individual" influences.[15] Tocqueville conceded that
the importance of individual influences would fade as equality advanced, but the role of chance, what he once called "this
hidden will of God,"[16] would remain unchanged. Those who
write history in democratic times neglect fortuitous or accidental causes at the peril of their theories and reputations. A rem-
nant (even a large one) of mystery, of the inexplicable, always
remained. Wrote Tocqueville: "In all human affairs an immense part is left to chance and to secondary causes which escape entirely from predictions and calculations."[17] "Chance is
always there, forming a shadowy corner in our picture of the
future."[18]

For Tocqueville, as we have seen, historical causes were mul-
tiple and complex. And the dense tangle of causes—including
chance—made single grand theories or neat historical systems
untenable. In a passage dated "March 8, 1836" he declared:

> Not a man in the world has ever found, and it is nearly certain that
> not one ever will find, the central point at which all the rays of gen-
> eral truth (which come together only in God) or even all the rays of
> particular truth meet. Men grasp fragments of truth, but never

truth itself. Having admitted this, it would follow that any man who presents a complete and absolute system is, by the very fact that his system is complete and absolute, almost certainly wrong or lying. And any man who wants to impose such a system on his fellows by force should be considered, *ipso facto* and without preliminary examination of his ideas, as a tyrant and enemy of the human species.[19]

These intense, even angry words give us a glimpse of how deeply Tocqueville believed in the uncertainty and incompleteness of human knowledge.

The difficulty was that men were always looking for simple answers, not only out of ignorance and laziness, but also out of a mistaken ideal of perfection. In a long, previously unpublished essay, Tocqueville elaborated.

General idea which I have wanted to emerge from this work: [that] simple ideas are not always the most beautiful nor those which lead to the best results. [several illegible lines]

Usually the simpler ideas are, and the more easily reduced to a single point, the more men judge them perfect, efficacious and beautiful. This human judgment comes partly from the pride of the human mind and partly from its weakness. Man wants to understand and produce, but complications tire him. And when he encounters the idea of some single cause working all by itself, he looks no further. He takes hold of it and contents himself there. He is always ready to sacrifice part of the result for the ease of the means.

However, if we cast our eyes on the works of the most perfect Being, of the Creator of man, of man's eternal model, God, we are surprised by the strange complications which present themselves and are obliged to grant perfection in the grandeur of the result and not in the simplicity of the means.

God links together a multitude of bones, muscles, nerves, each of which has a separate and distinct function. These first are themselves but the products of a multitude of primary causes. In the midst of such a complicated machine, He places an intelligence which is seated there, but is not actually a part. An invisible bond unites all of these things and makes them work together toward a unique end. This assemblage feels, thinks, acts; it's a man, sovereign of the world, second only to Him who created. The same diversity is found in all the works of the Creator.

God shows us [several illegible words] that great results can only be attained with the help of a great diversity of efforts, of a variety of ordinary things [reading of the last phrase uncertain]. If your machine can function as well with one gear as with two, make just one; but make ten if that serves the purpose you have in mind. If the machine so constructed produces what you want from it, it is not less beautiful than if it were simpler. The error of men comes from their believing that very great things can be produced by very simple means. If that were true, they would be right partially to identify the idea of beauty with the simplicity of means.

So God, if I can put it this way, establishes the idea of grandeur and perfection not in executing a great number of things with the help of a single means, but in making a multitude of different means contribute toward the perfect execution of a single thing.[20]

Here we see even more clearly why, despite his famous successes, Tocqueville eschewed the role of bold prophet.[21] Human understandings and pretensions paled next to the majesty of God's creation. Also, we should note that in this essay, Tocqueville's appeal to God, to Providence, is not the invocation of a "salutary myth."[22] As in so many other passages from his working papers, Tocqueville's talk of God has the rich tone of faith, not the hollow ring of utility.[23]

If simple explanations were out of reach, if the search for systems seemed misguided, human ingenuity would still find some way to easy answers. In the autograph manuscript of his book, Tocqueville presented an additional, but deleted, criticism of the kind of history written during times of equality. Too often the democratic historian is a slogan-maker "who prefers talking about the characteristics of race, the physical conformation of the country, or the genius of civilization and other great catchwords which I can not hear without involuntarily recalling the 'abhorrence of a vacuum' which was attributed to nature before the discovery of air pressure."[24] Historians in periods of democracy, Tocqueville observed, are wrong not only "in wholly denying the special influence of individuals,"[25] but also "in often being content with great slogans when great causes elude them."[26] "The human mind is always the same: slogans are invented when causes can not be found."[27]

As many commentators have remarked, the text of the *Democracy* demonstrates the breadth of Tocqueville's social and historical examination. The fragments from the working papers that we have just examined also speak to the point. His belief in the pluralism and complex interplay of causes led him to a remarkable effort to study democratic society in almost all its aspects. Tocqueville's sense of the wholeness of human existence made it possible for him, for example, to develop by 1840 a pioneering sociology of modern democratic culture. This habit of trying to see society in its entirety and to grasp the shifting relationships among the parts leads us to the question of Tocqueville's understanding of how change occurs.

Melvin Richter has alerted us to the notion of "functional equivalence."[28] Each nation shows a unique set of connections among varied causes and forces. In a given society any particular element—an institution, or habit, or belief, for example—might play a role totally different from its role in another society. From nation to nation, the same element can fulfill quite different functions. And more important, as the needs of a given society evolve, the function of a specific part of that society can change. To illustrate: if a people lose their strong religious heritage, they might still be led to think of something more than immediate selfish ends, if they were taught to broaden their perspective by the daily give-and-take of participation in local self-government.

Roger Boesche has recently proposed a brilliant analogy that

snaps this theory into view: the cultural mobile.[29] Together all
the pieces of a society make a balanced whole, each contribut-
ing in a precise way to avoiding disorder. To change one element requires compensating changes elsewhere in the mobile.
This not only gives us an image of "functional equivalence,"
but also graphically portrays Tocqueville's (and Montesquieu's)
understanding of the interplay of causes. Moreover, as Boesche
has shown, it explains why Tocqueville, despite his reluctance
to foretell the future, was so effective at prophesying. The
mobile allows the careful observer to see what changes might
occur in a given place to make up for a shift elsewhere in
the complex, but highly delicate, structure of society. With
Boesche's wonderful image we can grasp, perhaps better than
ever before, Tocqueville's vision of historical causation.[30]

THE PREMIER place that Tocqueville assigned to moral and
intellectual causes—to *moeurs*—made purely materialistic explanations of human affairs unacceptable to him. The repudiation of such theories emerges repeatedly from his working
papers. In an early and quite different version of his chapter on
the good morals of Americans,[31] Tocqueville discussed why
neither physical setting nor race alone could adequately explain
the morality of the New World republicans. To make geography a determining cause would be merely to repeat a favorite
error of earlier philosophers and historians, Tocqueville asserted. Moreover: "It is a materialistic doctrine against which
my conscience rebels and which facts daily belie."[32]

To make race the major determinant would mean succumbing to the fashion of the times. "Nowadays," he reflected in another fragment,

> people talk constantly of the influence exercised by race on the con-
> duct of men. . . . Race explains all in a word. It seems to me that I

can easily discover why we so often have recourse to this argument that our predecessors did not employ. It is incontestable that the race to which men belong exercises some power or other over their acts, but then again it is absolutely impossible to pinpoint what this power is. So we can at will either infinitely restrict its action or extend it to all things according to the needs of the discourse; valuable advantage in a time when we require reasoning with little cost, just as we want to grow rich without trouble.[33]

Elsewhere he resolved: "To say in the preface if not in the book. Idea of races. I do not believe that there are races destined to freedom and others to servitude; the ones to happiness and enlightenment, the others to misfortune and ignorance. These are cowardly doctrines. Doctrines however. Why? That results, during democratic times, from a natural vice of the human mind and heart which causes these people to tend toward materialism. This idea of the invisible influence of race is an essentially materialistic idea."[34]

"I see nothing in the physical condition of man," he concluded in still another discarded draft, "which disposes him to one kind of ideas rather than another, and nothing in historical facts leads me to believe that [a] particular intellectual disposition is inherent to one of the human races rather than to the others."[35]

Here too Tocqueville's major, and often unstated, objection to such materialistic doctrines is moral.[36] Humanity has little or no control over its physiography or biology. If the destinies of nations depended on what cannot be changed, the shape of the future would be essentially out of human hands. "The idée-mère of this book is directly the contrary, since I," Tocqueville affirmed, "start invincibly from this point: whatever the tendencies of the social condition, men can always modify them and avert the bad while adapting to the good."[37]

The allure of determinism, like that of materialism, seemed almost irresistible to Tocqueville's contemporaries. His original

manuscript discloses, for example, that his chapter on historians was in part a dissent from the historical philosophy of
François Mignet, who in his work on the French Revolution
excused the Terror as a *necessary* response to historical developments.[38] On the jacket-sheet of his chapter, Tocqueville
wrote: "The historians of antiquity did not treat history like
Mignet and company."[39] And in a draft, he commented: "Idea
of *necessity*, of fatalism. Explain how my system differs essentially from that of Mignet and company. Do a satirical portrait
of them without naming individuals. Show that even apart
from the pretention of a genius able to embrace the necessities
of the political world, there is great intellectual weakness and
great distaste for work. Explain how my system is perfectly
compatible with human liberty."[40]

Given the propensities of democratic times, Tocqueville
wondered

How can we escape from the doctrine of necessity? Superior men
who know its weaknesses willingly adopt it nonetheless, for, if its
usefulness to societies has not been proven, it can scarcely fail to
serve the greatness of those who currently lead societies. That at
least is certain.

Mediocre men avidly seize upon the doctrine of necessity because it can be expressed as a single, very simple idea; from it deductions are easy to make, and consequences can be seen at a
glance; it embraces enough to seem very inclusive; and everything is
tied together by a link visible enough to allow the whole to be
grasped in a moment. In this way very great results can be gained
with very little effort. A man is astonished suddenly to discover the
singular depth of his genius. [And] people believe that in a way they
hold the world in their hands. Any idea which flatters the pride of
superior men and the vanity of everyone else cannot fail to rule the
world.[41]

"At all costs," Tocqueville summarized, "get rid of the idea
of necessity which is the canker of the future."[42]

But the historical web of causes sometimes disheartened even Tocqueville and drove him close to determinism. "For who could indicate the narrow limits of what we call our free will? Man blindly obeys: the Being who has created him, seen only in His works, an all-powerful Being whose infinite grandeur escapes man's reason as well as his senses; first causes which he does not know; second causes which he can not change; [illegible word] his fellow-beings; sometimes chance; and often, finally, the fragile work of his own hands."[43]

Ultimately, however, such fatalistic notions were, once again, immoral. "I believe," Tocqueville declared in a draft, "that nations, like men, are free at nearly every moment of their existence to modify their fate."[44]

But did Tocqueville contradict himself? His fundamental concept of the march of democracy appears to be at odds with much of his stated historical philosophy. While denouncing Mignet, for instance, he admitted that he too had a system. Wasn't advancing equality, as portrayed by Tocqueville in his 1835 Introduction, an all-embracing general cause? Wasn't the "providential fact" of democracy a remarkably successful slogan or catchword? And most troublesome of all, what freedom of choice is left for humanity in the face of relentless leveling? Tocqueville recognized his own vulnerability, and in a fragment written after the appearance of the 1835 *Democracy,* he remarked with some astonishment: "People have not reproached me as I expected for my seeming to fall into the *mania* of the century. I reproach myself, however, because I do not want to fall into it. They absolve me, but I accuse myself."[45]

In the well-known concluding paragraph of his book, he tried definitively to make his position clear. Once again he asserted that his interpretation of history was perfectly compatible with human liberty.

I am aware that many of my contemporaries maintain that nations are never their own masters here below, and that they necessarily obey some insurmountable and unintelligent power, arising from anterior events, from their race, or from the soil and climate of their country. Such principles are false and cowardly; such principles can never produce aught but feeble men and pusillanimous nations. Providence has not created mankind entirely independent or entirely free. It is true that around every man a fatal circle is traced beyond which he cannot pass; but within the wide verge of that circle he is powerful and free; as it is with man, so with communities. The nations of our time cannot prevent the conditions of men from becoming equal, but it depends upon themselves whether the principle of equality is to lead them to servitude or freedom, to knowledge or barbarism, to prosperity or wretchedness."[46]

This famous image of the circle of possibilities—Tocqueville's effort at self-absolution—echoes an idea that he once heard from his lifelong friend, Louis de Kergolay. "Dare to state somewhere L.'s [Louis's] idea that an alternative must be found between absolute affirmation, certitude, and pyrrhonism, that only the system of probabilities is true and human, as long as probability spurs action as energetically as certitude does. All of this is poorly said, but the germ is there."[47]

So in the end, Tocqueville denied that the links between causes and consequences were fixed, and he emphatically rejected, as an affront to his conscience, any determinism, especially historical or physical determinism. He acknowledged that origins, race, climate, and physical setting, all had some influence, but he believed that that influence remained elusive, imprecise, unknowable. Circumstances of all kinds set limitations for humanity, but within the circle of possibilities, men were free and responsible for their choices and actions.

TOCQUEVILLE, in his published chapter on the characteristics of democratic historians, said explicitly very little about historical methodology. Although he criticized the tendency of democratic historians to ignore particular or individual influences, he applauded their search for profound, underlying causes. He also implied that methodology must adapt to the times, that a method suitable for the historian in periods of aristocracy might well be inappropriate for someone writing when equality reigned. A marginal fragment went even further: historians should adapt their approach to the era they are studying. Historians of democratic times are wrong "to follow the same method when they are recreating periods of aristocracy."[48]

Other significant elements of Tocqueville's methodology have been frequently examined, including his peculiar way of moving from observations to organizing principles (*idées-mères*) and then to a host of logical deductions, his search for origins or points of departure, his love of comparison, his intensive research about certain historical developments, his pose of "neutrality," and his use of new words.[49]

For us, in the age of quantification, however, perhaps the most striking characteristic of Tocqueville's methodology is his almost total avoidance of statistical evidence.[50] Once again, portions of his working papers reveal at least some of the reasons for his attitude. "I have not believed it necessary," he declared in a draft, "to burden my work with statistical details."[51] A marginal note at the end of his 1835 Introduction disclosed: "Why I have not included many numbers and statistics. Change so rapidly. Insignificant."[52]

In 1835, in the pages of the *Democracy,* he presented a comparison between the public expenses of France and the United States, [53] and an unpublished version of that discussion moves beyond such cryptic explanations. There he engaged the theoretical issue of what numbers can actually tell the researcher.

I know that minds are very busy comparing the expenses of the United States to ours. If it were not for the public disposition, I would not have prepared this chapter. For I am convinced that such a comparison is necessarily incomplete and therefore unproductive, and that even if it were complete, it would not reveal the truth. It can only be useful to those who look for figures to support their ideas and not to those who want truth to emerge from figures.

There are people who try to disparage those who are interested only in statistics. I, however, admire them, for I know that nothing in this world is more difficult than to reach a sure conclusion from statistics. It is the uncertainty of the science which discourages me more than its dryness. Statistics have a mathematical form and a certain air of scientific exactitude which attracts practical minds, but then statistics bring [people with such minds] to despair by constantly exciting them in the pursuit of a truth which is always escaping their grasp. . . .

[Even if you arrived at the total public expenses of each of two countries during a year and then compared them,] it would be necessary to redo it several more times; for in statistics the result of a year is only an indication, not a proof.

But suppose that someone had managed to obtain, for a ten year period, the total of public expenses for two countries. The most difficult task remains. We have the facts, but no ideas yet. The principal end of the operation is not to prove that one country pays more than another. For us, the figures are only a means by which we want to discover the reasons why one of the two nations pays more than the other. The reasons are many, however, and difficult to appreciate. They are not tangible to the senses. Only the mind's eye can discern them; only intelligence can grasp them. But the figures which establish fact do not indicate the reasons for a fact; they do not even hint at them.

I assume that the normal and habitual situation for a nation is to be constantly surrounded by enemies; so much so that one fortieth of its population must always be under arms and maintained at the expense of the taxpayers. I assume that the normal and usual situation for another is to inhabit a wilderness without neighbors. Reason, without figures, tells me that the expenses of the first nation must be greater than those of the second. Add that independently of this cause there is another equally powerful which arises from different laws. Again reason alone decides the question. Figures offer no help.

So statistical operations have served to establish a fact. But what is most difficult and most useful is to find the reason for this fact; and for this philosophical application, statistics abandon you to your own resources.[54]

This admittedly rough essay clarifies at least some of the reasons for Tocqueville's cautious approach to statistics. His skepticism came, in part, from his assumption that nonquantitative factors were more significant for explaining historical developments; in part, from his conviction—already familiar to us—that truth was ultimately indefinite and elusive; and in part, from his belief that the key functions of the social, political, or historical theorist were not fulfilled by statistical studies. These crucial tasks—interpreting, posing questions, probing for causes—demanded imagination and insight, the powers of the mind. For some thinkers, numbers might be a useful tool; for none could they substitute for thought. In short, his distrust of numbers arose from his larger conviction about the role and importance of ideas in shaping and understanding human affairs. For him, history was most essentially a philosophical, rather than a factual enterprise.

Also from the pages and working manuscript of the *Democracy* emerges a wonderful dialogue between Tocqueville and Montesquieu. As he composed, Tocqueville repeated, revised, and reversed the observations of his great predecessor. Tocqueville, for example, echoed Montesquieu's belief that political institutions are relatively, not absolutely good. He amended Montesquieu's understanding of republican virtue by demonstrating that enlightened self-interest might also lead to public-mindedness. And he rejected Montesquieu's assertion that the principle of despotism is fear; for Tocqueville it was religious fervor that most effectively supported despotic government.[55]

For Tocqueville's philosophy of history, Montesquieu was clearly the mentor. The two theorists recognized the plurality of causes and distinguished between general and secondary

ones. Each stressed, as the key to understanding, the fundamental moral dimensions of a society, its temperament, character, or spirit, what Montesquieu called the *esprit général* and
Tocqueville labeled *moeurs*. Each made much of the role of
ideas in history.[56] Both recognized and tried to investigate the
enormous range of human activities; and the two searched dili-
gently for the hidden connections among the bits and fragments
of society. Neither presumed to be a system-maker.[57]

But if Tocqueville essentially echoed Montesquieu in all of
these ways, he differed—or at least thought he differed—on
one significant matter. Tocqueville's specific repudiation of earlier philosophers and historians who had attributed too much
to climate and physical setting seems aimed at Montesquieu,
among others. Raymond Aron has pointed out, however, that
Montesquieu's reputation for physical determinism is unde-
served. He has reminded us that, if Montesquieu seems at times
in his *Spirit of the Laws* to present a deterministic interpretation of climate and physiography, elsewhere in the same
work he denies such determinism. Instead, Montesquieu, like
Tocqueville, describes possibilities or probabilities for societies.
A particular setting permits certain options, which human
beings then have the responsibility to narrow and to pursue. According to both Montesquieu and Tocqueville, physical circumstances are simply one part of the "wide verge of
the circle" drawn around human freedom. Neither—despite
Tocqueville's misapprehension—was willing to entertain fatalistic doctrines. So on causation, Tocqueville, although he was
less ambiguous about the influence of physiography, largely followed Montesquieu.[58]

On methodology, however, another interesting divergence
exists. In his work, Montesquieu cited classical examples frequently; he did not doubt that they offered valuable lessons for
the nations of his day. But Tocqueville, as he wrote the *Democracy*, struggled with a growing sense that the ancient republics
had little to teach modern democratic societies. His misgivings

even extended to the usefulness of comparisons with the republics of Renaissance Italy.[59]

Tocqueville explained some of the reasons for his doubts in the margin of his chapter on great revolutions.[60] After noting that the small democracies of the ancient world were perhaps naturally instable, he wrote: "Show in a note, in a few words, that these were not democracies. Men of leisure. Show how what was called a *democracy* in antiquity and in the Middle Ages is not really analogous with what we see today. At Florence: no middle class; capitalists; workers; no agricultural class; compacted and manufacturing population."[61] And in a discarded draft he declared: "In this matter [of social and political instability], I would like people to stop citing on every occasion the example of the democratic republics of Greece and Italy."[62]

At times his hesitations hardened into conviction. In the 1835 *Democracy*, after surveying the education, habits, and practical experience of citizens in the United States, he concluded: "When I compare the Greek and Roman republics with these American states; . . . when I remember all the attempts that are made to judge the modern republics by the aid of those of antiquity, and to infer what will happen in our time from what took place two thousand years ago, I am tempted to burn my books in order to apply none but novel ideas to so novel a condition of society."[63]

Despite such declarations, antiquity remained, of course, a significant source of examples for the published *Democracy*. Yet there is more to tell. The earlier drafts and the holograph manuscript contain considerably more references to classical (and Renaissance) history than appeared in Tocqueville's final text; many were deleted as the composition went forward. At times, as he revised, Tocqueville seemed about to shake off or slip away from the traditional expectation—so obvious in Montesquieu—that a serious work of political theory should cite classical examples. At times he seemed to have decided that the lessons of antiquity (or Renaissance Italy) were fundamentally inappropriate to the new age. So as he wrote, he pruned. But he could not bring himself to eliminate all classical citations; contrasts and comparisons drawn from antiquity were sometimes too tempting to resist. Ultimately, Tocqueville hesitated. Only the actions of his pen, repeatedly striking out mentions of Greece and Rome, hint at the growing distance between him and Montesquieu on this matter. Tocqueville's inclination to break free here from the tradition so well exemplified by Montesquieu is still another measure of the modern nature of his work and thought.[64]

A comparison of Tocqueville and the modern French *Annales* school of historians, descended from Lucien Fèbvre, Marc Bloch, and Fernand Braudel, presents another fascinating set of parallels and dichotomies.[65] Both the man and the school stress the multiplicity and complexity of historical causation and take a pluralistic approach to history. Among the levels and rankings of causes, both put first the ideas, attitudes, opinions, habits, and values that people use to order their lives; what Tocqueville called *moeurs*, the *Annalistes* label *mentalité*.[66] Both are interested in the totality of society and especially in the interconnections among society's various spheres. Such an acute awareness of the intricate web of history leads both Tocqueville and the *Annalistes* to admit a residue of the unknowable and inexplicable in human affairs. Both also recognize the complex interplay of human and nonhuman forces and settle for an explanation on what H. R. Trevor-Roper has called "social determinism with a difference."[67]

But contrasts there are; and at least four stand out. First, the *Annalistes* have developed a system of causes much more intricate than Tocqueville's plain, but not necessarily simple, distinction between primary and secondary causes. Fernand Braudel, for example, distinguishes the long, medium, and short-term waves of history, and focuses on the interplay of these three great levels of historical development.[68]

Secondly, the *Annales* school signals, for some, the end of the traditional concept of *histoire artisanale*.[69] The ideal of the individual historian laboring like a skilled craftsman over his work is rejected as outmoded. But Tocqueville clearly saw his work as art. His working papers show him painstakingly shaping ideas and phrasings. Paragraphs, sentences, even individual words were cast and recast for just the right nuance and cadence. The original manuscript of the *Democracy* also demonstrates that his chapter on history in democratic times was one of a package devoted to literature and was intimately connected as well to Tocqueville's chapter on general ideas.[70] Once again, we see that for Tocqueville, history was primarily philosophy and literature, the product of one writer's skill at a demanding craft.

Thirdly, the *Annaliste* usually attempts to include major quantitative elements in his analysis; measurement is crucial to his story. One of the founders, Marc Bloch, warned, it is true, against too much reliance on statistics. In words that echo Tocqueville's essay on the limits of what numbers can explain, Bloch wrote: "Human actions are essentially very delicate phenomena, many aspects of which elude mathematical measurement."[71] Yet such a caution has not diminished the rigorous commitment of the *Annales* school to statistics as a historical tool. Tocqueville's distaste for numbers and his suspicion of their mystique of certitude remain in sharp contrast.[72]

Finally, unlike the *Annalistes*, Tocqueville did not try to create a philosophy of history, nor did he develop a school. System-makers he distrusted. And although the influence of his ideas has not been insignificant, no clear group of *tocquevilliens* has ever emerged to propagate his approach to history, to spread his methodology or philosophy. Tocqueville has never been institutionalized in some *sixième*. His accomplishments —though impressive—remain nonetheless idiosyncratic.

Let me end my comparison with a speculation. Although the differences between Tocqueville and the *Annales* school come more easily to mind, the similarities are significant. How can we explain the parallels, rough though they may be? Is it because both the man and the school reflect the long and great French tradition of history, political theory, and sociology? Did that tradition, which of course includes the figure of Montesquieu, somehow suggest at least some of their presuppositions and color at least some of their interpretations? Heirs to the same national heritage, did they start out with some of the same fundamental assumptions about the complexity of human affairs, about the limitations and possibilities of human nature, and about the way in which the world works? Are there, in short, some elusive shared elements of approach, tone, and background? Whatever the explanations, between a leading theorist of the nineteenth century and the commanding historical school of the twentieth, there are intriguing and undeniable resonances with which we need to reckon.[73]

THE MATERIALS that we have just examined include several previously unpublished essays. One especially full and beautiful piece sets forth Tocqueville's argument about the superiority (almost divinely ordained) of complex rather than simple explanations. The others, more incomplete, present arguments about the dangers of closed systems, about physical causes, about accident and the doctrine of necessity, and about the limitations of numbers.

We have seen that the *Democracy* was composed by Tocqueville with great self-consciousness; so even brief draft fragments and cryptic marginal comments reveal something about his personal emotions, reactions, and intentions. As he wrote, his uncertainties (toward the appropriateness of classical models), his anger (toward those claiming absolute systems), his critical judgments (toward his contemporaries, such as François Mignet), and many other strong feelings and opinions spilled onto the page. Later, they were often deleted and perhaps forgotten. But in Tocqueville's working papers they have remained, ready for retrieval one hundred and fifty years later.

Perhaps most important, Tocqueville's manuscripts underscore the moral dimensions of his thought, particularly of his views about historical philosophy and methodology; as he worked on his book, he wrote candidly about his personal beliefs and his conscience. Whether he was considering chance, the web of causes, Louis de Kergolay's concept of probability, or statistical tools, he returned repeatedly to the elusiveness of truth and to the limitations of human knowledge. Yet curiously, this sense of human weakness did not deflect him from his larger purposes. He always began with the premise of human responsibility. Ultimately, Tocqueville believed in a moral universe where the Creator had granted humanity the power and the obligation to act.

PART III
Appraisals

Tocqueville's Ideal Types

ROBERT NISBET

D
emocracy in America was conceived by its author in an age rich in reification. Typologies, entelechies, ideal types, and abstractions of all kinds flourished during Tocqueville's life. New words appeared to give identity to purported historical forces and trends; old words were lifted from age-old specific uses to uses of a metaphysical character. The word "genius" had meant no more than a given talent earlier; now it became a romantic *Geist*. *Isms* were to be found in an abundance never even approximated in prior centuries in world history. To think deeply was to reify and to generalize—Blake's warning notwithstanding.

The waning of Christianity in the minds of intellectuals had much to do with this explosion of abstractions. The death of God was largely the experience of intellectuals, and as often as not it served as a mere pretext for unloading some gigantic, secular, City of God on the people. Comte, Hegel, and Marx were all masters of reification and of the secularizing of the sacred.

Not since St. Augustine's Rome had so many intellectuals been seized by intimations of "collapse," "breakdown," and "destruction." But it must always be remembered that the prophets had hope. As fast as they were declaring one world dying or dead, they were heralding a new one in which reason would triumph, usually cloaked in garments of science and ethics. What had once required the premise of God now required only the forces and dynamisms that could be shown to be instinctive in man and made manifest in history. Inevitably, in such a hothouse of secular prophecy, generalities and abstractions pullulated.

Tocqueville was aware of this. Characteristically, he saw the phenomenon as one rooted in democracy. "If aristocratic na-

tions do not make sufficient use of general ideas, and frequently
treat them with inconsiderate disdain, it is true on the other
hand that a democratic people is always ready to carry ideas
of this kind to excess and to espouse them with injudicious
warmth." He uses himself as an example of the toll taken in
writing by the indiscriminate use of general and abstract nouns:

"I have frequently used the word equality in an absolute
sense; nay, I have personified equality in several places; thus I
have said that equality does such and such things or refrains
from doing others. It may be affirmed that the writers of the
age of Louis XIV would not have spoken in this manner; they
would never have thought of using the word equality without
applying it to some particular thing; and they would rather
have renounced the term altogether than have consented to
make it a living personage."[1]

With all due respect to Tocqueville's personal candor in that
passage, it is doubtful that he was aware of the breadth and
depth of the use that he made of abstractions in his great study
of democracy. He thought of himself in general as being above
the epidemic use of entelechies and typologies in his age. He
considered himself democracy's rigorous historian, analyst,
even its scientist, with his conclusions grounded in empirical
observation. Did not his nine months in America prior to beginning the writing of *Democracy in America* qualify him as a
participant ethnographer of the new nation? Did he not avoid
the sterilizing effects of the habitual use of abstractions and
generalities by rooting his concern with political democracy in
the actual ways of living in a democracy, that is, American
democracy?

He seems to have thought so. More to the point perhaps are
the worldwide audiences reading his book who thought so and
who continue to think so. Rarely does a month pass in which
some fresh tribute to Tocqueville's classic work isn't made,
tributes in which he is lauded above all for his masterful understanding of the American character, for his penetration of the

integument of American society, down deeply and sensitively to the very "habits of the heart" of Americans, to the ways they lived and died, thought and acted, generation after generation. Such was the genius of Tocqueville in this respect, it is often said, that in his book he gave us more than a portrait of Americans as they were in 1830; his portrait covers at once Americans past, living, and yet to come. He took with him to America both microscope and telescope. "The greatest book on one nation ever written by the citizen of another" is an almost constant theme, especially in America, of appreciation of *Democracy in America*.

But in all truth, the book is not. There are indeed insights into the ways of Americans in this work, which have the ring of reality for the age in which Tocqueville thought and wrote. He was as sensitive a mind as ever left the shores of his country, but it's more than a little much to credit him with a work that, in point of truth, he didn't even attempt to write. Tocqueville said as much. "I confess that in America I saw more than America; I sought there the image of democracy itself, with its inclinations, its character, its prejudices, and its passions in order to learn what we have to fear or to hope from its progress."[2] That passage lies of course in the Introduction to *Democracy in America*. It is well known but not, apparently, known well or well enough. For Tocqueville meant exactly what he said. That is why he eventually wrote the greatest book ever written on the subject of democracy — considered *sub specie aeternitatis*, stripped of all its purely local and temporal attributes, and presented to the world as Aristotle, Machiavelli, and Hobbes had presented the political state.

Tocqueville could not have written such a book had his mind been engrossed in the Americans first and democracy second. As he tells us, he saw more than America; and in the process he saw less than America, the living America of 1830. Harriet Martineau's *Society in America*, published in 1837, is a better study of American life. Her assessment of women and

family life, to take but one example, is considerably more real-
istic than Tocqueville's. So is her general encompassment of
American political, social, and cultural life.

The best book on Americans ever written, certainly by an
outsider, is *The American Commonwealth*, by Lord Bryce, published in 1888. Institutions, authorities and freedoms, opinions,
values, the whole texture of American life come alive as the
true political ethnography Bryce sought to make it. No distant,
cosmic image, but America was the subject. Bryce loved
America (there is legitimate doubt that Tocqueville did) and he
spent in recurring periods many years in America, traveling its
length and breadth, ever fascinated by the diversity of its
people. To this day his book makes for valuable reading into
turn-of-the-century America and for fertile reflection on such
matters as equality, freedom, social structures, public opinion,
"why great men are not chosen president," "the fatalism of the
multitude," and so on. He caught America in its dynamic reality, its flux, disorder, and order alike. No visitor ever loved a
foreign country more.

We owe to George Pierson the illuminating phrase "Tocqueville's second journey to America." It tells us much about what
is good and less good in *Democracy in America*. Tocqueville
returned to France in 1832 and went to work immediately on
his promised monograph on prisons in America—the ostensible purpose of his departure nine months earlier from France.
The book presented him with no problems and it was published, to critical favor, in quick time. He then set to work on
Democracy in America, whose idea had almost obsessed him
during his visit. But he no sooner began the writing than he
was forced to stop. He knew far too little about American government, economy, or society to do such a book. He knew it.
Thus the "second journey" began: that of his own reading in
Paris libraries about America and Americans, and, more valua-
bly, reading and note-taking by two young Americans living in
Paris, whom he was able to engage both as research assistants

and as living repositories of Americana generally. Thus between 1832 when he returned to France, equipped with his journal of American experiences, and 1835 when the two volumes of *Democracy in America* came off the press (the two volumes form Part One of the whole work), a great deal of "visiting" of America had been done; but this time through a fair amount of reading on his own and a good deal more by his two invaluable American assistants. As we know from his letters, the writing of Part One, even with that assistance, caused him a great deal of writer's anguish—more than Part Two would cause him.

Part One is a great book, but not a very good one, assessed by standards we are entitled to apply by virtue of the title. There is an obvious secondhandedness. How could there not be, given the shortness of his stay and then his mode of composing it at home? As we know, there is a strongly Federalist cast to the book, the result in significant degree of his near vacuuming of Justice Story's *Commentaries*, after his creative agonies began. There are extraordinary omissions: among them the entire American educational system, including its notable colleges. He is thin and bare on the American states and their colonially rooted loyalties. Thus something very important about American loyalties and pluralist passions went begging.

He heard an American use the phrase "tyranny of the majority" while in conversation one day. The phrase began to haunt him; from a conversational commonplace it became a very metaphysical attribute of democracy. In his mind, before finishing Part One, it became a vast suffocating force, exceeding, he says, even the Spanish Inquisition in its power to stifle thought. No later visitor to America, not even Bryce, who searched for it, could find this tyranny of the majority; only the usual "tyrannies" of minorities.

Tocqueville dropped the phrase in Part Two, but the "public opinion" he writes of there has its roots very clearly in the earlier stereotype. He likened public opinion to a religion, with the majority the religion's "ministering prophet."[3] He muses in

Part Two over the boundless conformity that is exacted by
public opinion, the shrinking of the individual self in its awe of
public opinion, and the mediocrity that is the legacy of all writers and artists in American democracy. There isn't a hint
in Parts One or Two of those currents that were already at
work in the formation of such literary giants as Melville, Hawthorne, Whitman, Thoreau, and Emerson. In truth, much of
what Tocqueville wrote on culture in America is imaginative
nonsense.

LET US acknowledge immediately: Tocqueville is a genius, one
fully entitled to occupy space in the shelves next to Aristotle,
Machiavelli, and Montesquieu. His *Democracy in America*
remains even today the most suggestive and fertile work on
democracy and its general attributes yet written. But it does
not follow that a genius in abstract political philosophy must
thereby be an able ethnographer of a people, or a historian of
the first water, or even a scholar as that word is used carefully.
There is no evidence that he read widely and deeply in preparation for writing the *Democracy*. Certainly references to philosophers and chroniclers of notable democracies of the past and
present are few and far between in the book. Apart from the
spasm of reading that went perforce into the writing of Part
One of *Democracy* and into archival work for his later study of
the French Revolution, it doesn't appear that Tocqueville gave
much of himself to scholarship in the ordinary sense.

   A belief has grown up that Tocqueville was a lifelong student of Pascal, Montesquieu, and Rousseau. The only textual
basis for this triad in reference to Tocqueville that I have found
is in his *Correspondance*. There we find Kergolay, in a letter
written apparently in October 1834, advising Tocqueville to
read these three writers for their mastery of style. Two years
pass. Then in a letter to Kergolay dated 10 November 1836 we

find Tocqueville briefly assuring his friend that he does indeed pass time reading those three authors. We might have assumed as much, given the classic rank of all three in almost every educated Frenchman's reading. But it stretches the evidence considerably to argue any persisting, serious intellectual influence of their works on Tocqueville's mind. Particularly is this the case when it is suggested that Tocqueville derived major ideas in his classic from Rousseau. In truth, a very wide chasm separates the political values and perspectives of these two philosophers. The ideal society that Rousseau dreamed of in his *Social Contract* and his *Discourse on Political Economy*, a society saturated with the application of power to human nature as the means of ensuring that the individual "will be forced to be free," is very close to a Tocquevillian nightmare.

A mind that did influence Tocqueville deeply—who left in his notes eloquent testimony to this influence—was Edmund Burke's. He is critical of Burke for what he perceives as Burke's failure to see the roots of the revolution in the old regime; but this does not prevent Tocqueville from declaring Burke's *Reflections* "the work of a powerful mind, full of that practical wisdom which in a free nation some men acquire almost instinctively." The major themes in Tocqueville's study of the French Revolution are the major themes of Burke's *Reflections*, the chief difference being in format: in Burke, a fierce indictment; in Tocqueville, a measured treatise.

We learn from George Pierson, and also in greater detail from James Schleifer, that Tocqueville studiously avoided reading others' works on America once he began the writing of the *Democracy*. He wouldn't even read Harriet Martineau's excellent *Society in America*, published three years before Part Two of the *Democracy* was published. Perhaps he had heard of the "mental hygiene" practiced by his contemporary, Auguste Comte, then writing his classic *Positive Philosophy*, also in Paris. Comte, to keep his mind uncluttered and creative, foreswore all reading during the period of his writing.

Some have considered the *Democracy* a work in historical scholarship. And it is true, especially in the early chapters of Part One, that Tocqueville digs into some distinctly historical issues concerning America, its settling, growth, and its shaping by both geographic and commercial influences. Whatever Tocqueville's mind touched, in whatever degree of seriousness, something of acuteness almost certainly results. His treatment of the westward expansion of America is particularly arresting, and it is no exaggeration to say that he produced a theory of the effects of the frontier on the American mind that awakens thoughts of Frederick Jackson Turner and his famous frontier hypothesis.

But Tocqueville plainly regards history as an excursion; more pertinently perhaps, an auxiliary pursuit to be gotten over as soon as possible. It is fair to suppose that he regarded with some impatience the materials on American history, along with those on the constitutional substructure of American political society. Each was necessary but not crucial to Part One; this Tocqueville surely believed; and he was overwhelmingly right. What is ever true of Tocqueville is his compulsive use of intuition and logical deductions from the empirical; rarely the empirical for itself. George Pierson writes:

> Tocqueville was not, in practice or intention, a real historian. For an untrained amateur . . . he made exceptionally intelligent use of original documents and secondary works. But he was not interested in recording the past; and he so thoroughly slighted the backgrounds of his subject that he, in seeking explanations, came to mislead himself.[4]

The mind that lighted up the historical reality of the French Revolution as few others ever have come close to doing had very little of either interest or use to offer on the American Revolution.

If Tocqueville was not a scholar in the ordinary sense of the word—anymore than Plato was, along with a few other titans in the history of thought—and if he cannot accurately be called a historian as the result of his mode of the use of data in connection with conclusions, what may we call him? According to Pierson, he regarded himself as a scientist. This word, one of the multitude of coinages that occurred at the beginning of the nineteenth century, was fast on its way by 1830 to becoming not only an accepted but an honored word. The word was free of any associations with clericalism, and it bespoke an exactitude that was lacking in the older disciplines.

There were, however, two diametrically different meanings to the word "science." It could mean the kind of work that was done by physical scientists—such as chemists, geologists, and astronomers. Here the major step was one of acquiring ever-fresh data, as the individual scientist worked his way toward a result. Hard data from which inferences could be drawn were the dream of every scientist, then as now. The test of any hypothesis or principle in this kind of science was the congruence of principle and the data—or in applied science, in the success of the mechanical operation that was sought. In this sense of science, conclusions were verifiable—or, in Karl Popper's better concept, "falsifiable." In France the monumental study of the European working classes by Frederic Le Play was just getting under way, one calculatedly based upon the methods and techniques of the physical sciences. There were or would be others of comparable aim and success, by Vidal de la Blache, Demolins, Quetelet et al. who were the real forerunners of contemporary social scientists.

But a second conception of true science current in Tocqueville's day was considerably more seductive to those like Tocqueville who were blessed with intuitive and speculative minds. This conception of science goes directly back to Descartes and to his powerful exposition of it in his *Discourse on Method*. Descartes detested scholars; he mocked classical students who, he said, spent a lifetime finding out what every ignorant serving girl in ancient Rome knew; he thought the burning of libraries would be salutary to progress. What Descartes proposed—subversively, even terroristically, so far as scholarship is concerned—was straight intuition complemented by the geometric rigor of deductive logic. Begin with a clear idea or image, one that is "self-evident," and then by the same kind of derivation found in geometry, work toward a hierarchy of ever-wider and more inclusive "truths." At no point in this process was the mind to become sullied by facts or experience, for these are notoriously unreliable. They are the products, after all, of our gullible senses, not our rational minds. Using this logico-deductive method, and always working from an initial vivid idea or image, one would have a royal road to knowledge— absolute, not relative knowledge.

Even as Tocqueville got under way on his *Democracy in America*, Auguste Comte, also working in Paris, was writing his famous *Positive Philosophy* with its demonstration of the hierarchy of all the sciences and its grand conclusion that the time was right for the emergence of a new social science, to be called "sociology." Abstraction, generalization, endless logical ascents from small to large principles, so-called, and incessant speculation elevated into dogma are the hallmarks of Comte's lengthy work. That it and the lectures from which it derived were lauded by half of Europe's illuminati testifies to the appeal that Cartesianism continued to have, in moral philosophy and the social sciences at least. Cartesianism had been the very life of eighteenth-century revelations of "natural rights," the "natural order," "natural history," and a whole host of "self-evident" axioms from which the way could be opened to all manner of flights of the imagination. As the immense popularity of Comte's writings in the 1820s and 1830s made clear, Cartesianism was still very much alive and as seductive as ever in the nineteenth century.

Tocqueville may or may not have heard of his contemporary, Comte; there is no known contact between them;

Tocqueville's mind was a far more observant, resourceful, and imaginative instrument than Comte's; no one reads Comte today. Tocqueville lives on triumphantly. But this having been said, the truth remains: Tocqueville worked essentially by the same Cartesian method that Comte did—that of the initial clear, self-evident, hard idea or image of something, followed by imaginative but rigorously logical deductions of further truths, all abstract, but susceptible to occasional illustration by the data from one's reading or direct observation.

Interestingly, Tocqueville, at the very beginning of Part Two of his classic, declares Cartesianism to be the natural mode of thought in democracies. Democratic peoples, disinclined by nature to the sustained study of books, impatient of hurdles put in their way by asserted arbiters of learning, and eager to shake off any shackles of dependence upon an intellectual aristocracy, take naturally, Tocqueville informs us, to the philosophical method that had been so ardently recommended by Descartes. If Everyman was to be his own priest, his own governor and lawgiver in politics, and his own seer, then Everyman might just as well be his own philosopher-scientist. As Descartes remarks at the very beginning of his *Discourse*, no man has ever been heard to complain of insufficient common sense. It is, notes Descartes dryly, the most generously distributed of all nature's gifts.

Whether the American collective psychology or that of any other democratic people is *ipso facto* "Cartesian" is hardly a matter for serious discussion. The attribution is not one of Tocqueville's more brilliant strikes. What is more important, indeed very important, is his own possession of an enthusiastically Cartesian mind. Tocqueville is as much in the Cartesian swim as anyone before him, even the eighteenth-century *philosophes* with whom he did not generally agree or sympathize. In his Introduction, Tocqueville calls for a "new science of politics . . . for a new world." It was not, however, a new science that

Tocqueville himself proffered, but one as old as introspective reason, one made newly "modern" by Descartes two centuries earlier.

As Pierson points out, Tocqueville worked from four very simple ideas. The first is a belief, nay, a conviction of necessity and inevitability, a concept of predestination translated into the field of social evolution. The second, a world principle of history: specifically, a universal leveling of human differences, leaving them eventually in a vast homogeneity from which individuality and creativity are alike expunged. Third, a logical and historical conflict between aristocracy and democracy that has a dialectical quality to it; each abstraction is given the role of protagonist in western history. Fourth, the absolute superiority of moral forces over physical forces in human history.[5] That superiority does not anywhere in Tocqueville's work shine more effulgently than in his refutation of his friend Gobineau's racial theory of history.

It is impossible for the student of nineteenth-century thought to miss the affinity between Tocqueville and such system-builders of the age as Comte, Hegel, and Marx. It is by no means a complete affinity; there never is in such likenesses. But from Tocqueville's Introduction to Democracy in America all the way to the final pages of Part Two, there is an indelible impression left of the same kind of cosmic principles of change or development, of patterns of uniformity, and of inexorabilities and immanent ends that we are accustomed to seeing in the century's major philosophers of history. True, he strayed briefly into the concrete. He went to America to see what a democracy looked like. True, his mind was already made up with respect to the fundamentals of democracy and the leveling process in history. His mind was not often on America as rigorously as it was on Europe and especially on France. He missed vast amounts of telling material about Americans. But, unlike an Auguste Comte, he did stray forth with substantive as well as catalytic result from the solitary, introspective, and intellectually driven existence he cherished at home. Moreover, he made an almost equally rewarding visit to England during the gestation period of *Democracy in America*. It is possible that England furnished his mind with examples with respect to some of the attributes of aristocracy, just as America had with respect to democracy.

But all this duly and properly said, the important features of Tocqueville's mind were not experiential or experimental; they were Cartesian to the hilt. Pierson is again correct in his assertion that Tocqueville induced into his materials (American or English or French, we may add), the master ideas of which they were deemed to be expressions. "That done, he had the key. And rigorous, logical thought would *deduce* from the fundamental force that he had discovered all the consequences that it held for the given society."[6] From there on, Tocqueville would brood and brood, educing ever-new, ever-different consequences of the axiom-image of democracy he had begun with, which he slowly widened with the help of some observations to the point where free and full deductive imagination would carry him safely to all the rest, including the distant future.

I suggest that even those materials that Tocqueville leads us to believe he came upon for the first time in America—the separation of the judiciary from the executive and the legislative, the separation of religion and the state, decentralization, localism, and free voluntary associations—were already in his mind before he arrived there. Paris was a hotbed of ideologies, utopias, proposed revolutionary reforms, and of a dozen or more different prescriptions for a free democracy. Among these were the proposals of Lamennais, a romantic intellectual very much in the public eye.[7] He had begun as a devout, ultramontane Roman Catholic, was the author of the deeply traditionalist *Essay on Indifference* (Paris, 1817), and he had even been offered, it was said, a seat in the Sacred College; he had, however, worked his way to a social philosophy that was more and more antiecclesiastical as well as antistatist. (He would be excommunicated from the church in 1834, to the amazement of Catholic Europe.)

There is a great deal in Tocqueville's philosophy of politics that had been clearly thought out and published by Lamennais before Tocqueville ever went to America. By the late 1820s, Lamennais was widely known for his newspaper *L'Avenir*, published in Paris, the masthead containing Lamennais's central principles for political reform. These were: freedom of voluntary association; decentralization of governmental administration; invigoration of local government; separation of church and state; and full independence of the judiciary. Nor were these principles, at least in their entirety, solely those of Lamennais. The vivid memory of Jacobin centralization and nationalization had led more than a few intellectuals of the day to work with such principles in their projected reforms and revolutions. But Lamennais throughout his life, through the Revolution of 1848 in which he served as a member of the constitutional committee, held these principles in unique regard. So of course did Tocqueville.

The only reference to Lamennais I have encountered in Tocqueville is in the *Recollections*. There he refers to Lamennais as a fellow member of the constitutional committee of the Revolution of 1848, to Lamennais's continued espousal of localism and decentralization, and also, in a less charitable spirit to his "priestly shuffle," even after all these years.

In sum, Tocqueville would perhaps not have been as quick to feature decentralization, localism, and free association in the United States had he not been prepared by French, indeed European, controversies over these matters. It was not the American Revolution, but rather the French Revolution, that first dramatized these issues. From the beginning of the French Revolution, the Jacobins, drawing on the *philosophes*, Rousseau foremost, sought to centralize the government, to collectivize the nation, to foster a spirit of *patrie* among the French, and, in the process, to destroy or severely weaken all the associational loyalties such as the aristocracy, the church, and the guild, which by their existence militated against the combination of centralization and individualism the makers of the revolution so cherished.

These issues pressed on Tocqueville's mind throughout his life; beginning before he visited America and continuing through his *Reflections* and, notably, through *The Old Regime and the French Revolution*. The last, published in 1856, two decades after *Democracy in America* first came off the press, is justly famous among all students of the French Revolution to this day. It is a remarkable accomplishment. But, as Tocqueville himself declares at the very beginning of the book, "it is not my purpose here to write a history of the French Revolution." It is rather an effort to capture the nature of the revolution, in ideal-type after ideal-type, in portraits and landscapes of the revolutionary intellectuals, the monied class, the bureaucrats, and above all, *étatisme* and *individualisme*.

To return to *Democracy in America* and its true provenance: the pretense of wrestling with American events and issues is carried off well enough in Part One; but it becomes almost absurd in many sections of Part Two. In the rolling hills of Tocquevillian prose on democracy and its future, there are occasional references to Americans, but they are essentially unimportant and sometimes misleading, as in the section on American culture that begins Part Two and in such chapters as the ones on American women, the American worker, and "Why the Americans are So Restless in the Midst of Their Prosperity," the last having more of a Balzac-in-Paris flavor than anything American at that time. The genius of Part Two, and it is genius of highest order, lies in the abstract chapters where no country at all is mentioned, only the entity democracy *sub specie aeternitatis*, or else where the referent is denoted as France or Europe. Paul Janet, who admired Tocqueville, correctly wrote in 1840: "It is certain . . . that the problem that disturbed M. de Tocqueville and that brought him to the United States is the problem of European democracy. . . . Tocqueville describes America, but he thinks of Europe; hence those contradictory observations that cannot be applied at the same time to both."[8]

THE MOST useful way in which to think of *Democracy in America* is neither as history nor ethnography but as an ideal-type. Max Weber was far from being the only user of ideal-types in the nineteenth century. Among the principals, there are Marx, Maine, Tönnies, and, as noted, Tocqueville, also to be reckoned with.

An ideal-type is a theoretical construct that aims at both generality and concreteness. It is emphatically not an average. On the contrary it seeks out the distinctive, even at the risk of exaggerating or overlimning. Only those attributes are portrayed that will, when brought together effectively, give new meaning and shed light in a novel way on surrounding institutions and cultural patterns. Vividness, distinctness, and concreteness of image are the aims of the creator of an ideal-type.

Thus, Weber took such attributes as the following for his ideal-type of capitalism: First, the rational; that is, capitalism conceived as an economic system that had expunged as much of the merely traditional, nepotic, and feudal economy as possible. Second, production for an impersonal market through the use of an equally impersonal mass of workers. Third, production for profit, defined as the net left after all expenses, including the owner's, have been paid. Fourth, a bureaucracy in as full a sense as that found in the modern government, in each instance a replacement for the feudal and patrimonial. Fifth, a rational cost-accounting that theoretically prevents the intrusion of noneconomic factors.

An ideal-type, it must be stressed, is organized around a philosophy of history, or at the very least a distinctive patterning of events and personages in the past. According to Weber, capitalism is but one of many manifestations of the rational in the modern world—to be seen alongside rationalized armies, churches, schools, and foundations—all of them emergents historically from the traditional and/or the charismatic. A spirit of bureaucratization is inseparable from modernity. The old directness of cleric and communicant, of teacher and pupil, of commander and soldier, and of owner and worker is now gone, or else it is disappearing rapidly, to be replaced by more rationalized techniques and relationships—those from which the nonessential, the "nonrational," has been eliminated as far as possible.

With every ideal-type is linked—also as an ideal-type—its opposite. Weber saw much of western history as the evolution of a society that was solidly rooted in tradition to a society overwhelmingly characterized by rational or bureaucratic norms. He found in the Protestant ethic (more exactly the Puritan ethic) the principal, but not the sole, cause of the great transition from the patriarchal-traditional economy to the rationalist-capitalist one. Unlike Marx, who sought causes in the material, specifically the technological, realm, Weber found his dynamic in the nonmaterial, in the religious dimension of human experience.

When the typologies made famous by Sir Henry Maine, Karl Marx, Ferdinand Tönnies, and Emile Durkheim are examined, we find essentially the same use of ideal-types that I have just described in Weber. There is not space for any particularization of these types in this essay; it is probably unnecessary in any event. Maine's Status to Contract, Marx's Feudal to Bourgeois, Tönnies's *Gemeinschaft* to *Gesellschaft*, and Durkheim's Mechanical to Organic societies are well known. In each instance we have the kind of intellectual construct and also the implicit philosophy of history as well as social taxonomy that I have just described in Weber. What is involved in every one of these constructs is a kind of landscape painting in which some one feature is emphasized and highlighted. Finally, however deeply

researched ideal-types may be, and however elaborately gar-
nished with empirical instances and illustrations, they are yet
essentially intuitive, artistically generated types. First comes the
all-important vision, the image of whatever body of phenomena
is under consideration; next comes the whole rigorous series of
deductions from the image, with ever-new characteristics
educed from the image. And animating the ideal-type, or rather
the linked pair of types, a theory of history, one deterministi-
cally anchored in the ideal-types.

Aristocracy and democracy are ideal-types for Tocqueville in
just as full a measure as Status and Contract are for Maine and
Feudal and Bourgeois are for Marx. Into each of his two con-
stitutive categories, Tocqueville stuffed hundreds of specific
traits, ranging from the microlevel to the macro level in size
and importance, from the psychological to the social, the political to the economic. Tocqueville holds his two great ideal-
types, Aristocracy and Democracy, in a kind of dynamic tension, a dialectical opposition, quite as Marx and Weber do
with their paired opposites. As James Schleifer has written:
"Tocqueville liked to think in contraries . . . his mental inclinations simply caused him to see concepts as *pairs in tension.*"[9]

The aim of course is to show how these paired opposites and
their dialectical conflicts are the engines carrying western society to its ultimate destination. For Marx, this destination is socialism; for Weber, a world of monolithic rationalization; for
Tönnies, an eventual "pseudo-*Gemeinschaft*" to hide the pains
of *Gesellschaft*. For Tocqueville, the destination is a vast,
unwrinkled plain of homogeneity, equality, and mediocrity. It
leaves him in melancholy. True, he ascribes to God a possible
power for seeing human justice and happiness in this future leveling; but it is not a power that Tocqueville credits himself
with; nor even a desire for such a power, given the inevitable
fruits of its triumph in the world. Tocqueville's landscape of
the future is of a whole world eventually made empty of the
traits of aristocracy—differences, individual achievements,

honor, hierarchy, heroism, and so forth—but, by virtue of the driving engines of *démocratie*, equal, homogeneous, popular, pantheistic, and doubtless contented. The future that Tocqueville paints is not very different from that presented by Tönnies and Weber, each of whom was plainly troubled by visions respectively of *Gesellschaft* and rationalization. In all three visions, Tocqueville's perhaps foremost, there is a nagging worry about the position of individuality, about authentic community, and, not least, about individual liberty.

To return to Tocqueville's specific uses of his ideal-type, there is a veritable museum of them in Part Two of *Democracy in America*. As both Pierson and Schleifer emphasize in their studies of Tocqueville, there is no longer even the pretense of drawing from monographs, reports, and other empirical studies in the making of Part Two. From Tocqueville's intuitive conviction at the start of a deep spirit of Cartesianism that inheres in the democratic mind all the way to his final, somewhat mournful ruminations on the future of democracy, pluralism, and liberty, we have a very feast of ever-fresh and new ideal-types, all squeezed, as it were, from the master type, democracy.

Tocqueville's dynamic motor for his philosophy of history is equality—conceived as a historical process rather than as a simple condition. "In running over the pages of our history," he writes in the Introduction, "we shall scarcely find a single great event of the last seven hundred years that has not promoted equality of condition." Those stirring words come early in Tocqueville's Introduction. Marx said as much about the role of class conflict, Tönnies about secularization and individualization, Weber about the principle of rationalization. But for Tocqueville, the great transformation, the change from aristocracy to democracy, has been accomplished by the profound and ineradicable hunger for equality in the minds of men. Every revolution in history, Tocqueville repeatedly declares, has been caused not by the passion for freedom but rather by the desire for equality. The historical process is made self-aggrandizing by the fact that no degree of equality ever reached in practice is deemed sufficient. Each substantive advance toward equality is accompanied by a veritable explosion of expectations for an even higher level of equality. There is a kind of dialectical process involved, as of course there is in the Marxian theory of history.

It is striking how alike Tocqueville and Marx are in their bare dynamics of history and its somewhat teleological momentum toward a foreseeable future: in Marx, socialism and communism; in Tocqueville, equality and homogeneity. For Marx, the canvas of the historical pageant is economic; for Tocqueville, it is political; for Marx, the efficient cause is class conflict; for Tocqueville, it is an iron process of leveling. Both Marx and Tocqueville saw modern history, however, as the triumph of forces that were first present embryonically in the body of what Marx called the feudal and Tocqueville the aristocratic, and then these forces were released with gathering force and momentum in capitalism and democracy, respectively. Tocqueville's philosophy of history is fully as deterministic and purposive as Marx's. Finally, each worked from a vividly conceived ideal-type, capitalism and democracy, and from this capacious and endlessly fertile construct, each derived, deduced, a long series of smaller ideal-types. The history of the Western interest in each of these two remarkable minds has been one of a constantly changing focus on what is deemed essential. The varied interpretations of Marxism over the past century-and-a-half have been fully equalled in number and variety by the changing interpretations, or emphases, in the appreciation of Tocqueville. Both Marx and Tocqueville are treasure troves of ideal-types, large and small, one and all the products of intuition and the logicodeductive imagination.

The power of an ideal-type is immense. It is like the power of a great book or poem or painting or song. Once put in thralldom to an ideal-type—Tocqueville's, Marx's, Freud's, whoever's—we are likely to see the external world in a permanently different way. Many find it easier and more natural to blur or distort the external world, to crusade passionately for this or that rendering, than to give up an iota of a cherished ideal-type.

Of Prophets and Prophecy

DANIEL T. RODGERS

Democracy in America began as a piece of reportage, metamorphosed into a work in political philosophy, and became, at last, a book of prophecy. That is not the straightforward progression it may at first blush appear. The making of high theory out of reportage goes on every day, but prophecy is a rarer and more interesting phenomenon. Still more so is the canonization of prophets, the picking out of a handful of writers as gifted not merely with wisdom, or truth, or influence, but with prevision: the ability, not given to most mortals, to see in the tea leaves of their time a startlingly accurate picture of the future.

That status has been Tocqueville's for well over a generation now. We have read Democracy in America in many ways since the beginnings of the modern Tocqueville revival in the 1940s, but in none more eagerly than the prophetic mode. We have cultivated the pleasures and pains of recognizing our twentieth-century selves, and the burdens of our modernity, in the America he described. We have granted that extraordinarily talented young Frenchman the prize of a tea-leaf reader extraordinaire. But in this quarrying of Democracy in America for its prevision of our contemporary dilemmas, we have rarely noticed how much that reading of Democracy in America diminished the book or stirred the tea leaves of history into confusion. What manner of prophet was Tocqueville? And what manner of readers have we ourselves been to insist so hard on the theme of prevision? To begin to read Democracy in America afresh demands some harder thought about prophecy.

T O C Q U E V I L L E did not not begin his reputation as a seer of the future, but rather as an observer and historian. The first American reviewers of *Democracy in America*, all but over-whelmed by the novelty of being taken so extraordinarily seri-ously, even admiringly, by a European writer, bestowed their praise on the book's descriptive sections, not on the orphic pas-sages that would so rivet the attention of later readers. By the 1880s, James Bryce was interested enough in the prophetic side of *Democracy in America* to compile a checklist of Tocque-ville's successful and unsuccessful predictions.[1] But Bryce was not profoundly impressed with Tocqueville's batting average, and in this he was not alone.

It was the Tocqueville revival of the 1940s and 1950s that stamped *Democracy in America* with the reputation of previ-sion, and it did so quickly, powerfully, and enduringly. In the postwar readers' guides to *Democracy in America*, the pro-phetic theme was everywhere. Here was a work of "prophetic insight," Phillips Bradley wrote in the Alfred A. Knopf edition of 1945 with which the resurgent postwar interest in Tocque-ville began, so fertile "in confirmed perceptions that even a gleaning of the whole yields an abundant harvest of caution and counsel for our time." *Democracy in America* was "a tract for our times," Richard Heffner bolstered the point in his introduction to the Mentor edition of 1956, the cheap, mass-produced edition that stocked the bus stations and the neighborhood bookstores: the work of a "master prophet." Robert Nisbet, who has perhaps done more than any other modern social philosopher to boost Tocqueville's reputation as a thinker of the first rank, wrote in 1966 that sociological the-ory was best seen as a great magnetic field suspended between the nineteenth century's two master prophets, Tocqueville and Marx—of whom the victor, the more disturbingly accurate predictor, Nisbet claimed, was Tocqueville. Even now, in the best of all modern introductions to *Democracy in America*, Thomas Bender prepares student readers for the "premonitions

of our modern condition" that they will find uncannily pre-
figured in Tocqueville's pages. He has been a prophet of our
modernity for over a generation now, and a powerful one.[2]

There was a side to Tocqueville, of course, which invited, indeed all but panted after that response. The second volume of
Democracy in America was written in the orphic style of a man
increasingly obsessed to read the future, to guess the shape of
the "half buried" world rising under his feet. But there are
many ways to admire Tocqueville's achievement other than as
a tea-leaf reader for another century's discontents. Shaggily uneven, fraught with internal contradictions of mood and idea,
Democracy in America was the work of a man doing what
most of us are too timid to do—thinking deeply and furiously
hard about his own, politically charged times. There is still no
better way to read the book than that. Alternatively one may
read it, jammed as it is with aphorisms and generalities, as the
work of a provocateur and moralist, a work still capable of
jolting us out of our easy mental tracks. One may read it, if one
likes, as a classic in political theory. But we have not, I think,
been content to rest our affections or our quarrels with *Democracy in America* on these grounds. For forty years now we have
scoured the book for what it got right about modernity; we
have pushed it on students as a book in which they can see the
controlling features of their own America, revealed under the
skin of Andrew Jackson's time. We have filled in the space between our America and Tocqueville's with the peculiar gasp of
admiration we grant the prognosticator who somehow gets the
future right.

But such a reading is not without its costs. One of the most
important consequences of that focus has been to concentrate
our reading of *Democracy in America* with intense narrowness
on a handful of its particularly startling passages. I do not
mean simply the trumping of such lucky guesses as Tocqueville's offhand prediction of a future great power rivalry between the United States and Russia. I mean, rather, that our

preoccupation with the prophetic quality of *Democracy in America* has induced us over and again to condense the book into those small number of phrases that seem best to prefigure the urgencies of our present moment.

Those urgencies have taken two strikingly different forms since the beginning of the postwar Tocqueville revival. For Tocqueville's readers in the 1940s and 1950s, the heart of *Democracy in America* was the first volume's section on majority tyranny. To those chapters the editors guided their readers with a heavy, anxious hand. There, Phillips Bradley wrote in 1945, was to be found "the real *raison d'être* for the writing of the *Democracy*."[3] There, Richard Heffner concurred, Tocqueville's message for our times was concentrated. Through the course of the 1950s' agonized debate over mass culture and conformity, Tocqueville's name became virtually synonymous with the phrase "tyranny of the majority." David Riesman—although he was careful to note that the conformistic American Tocqueville had seen, holding his opinions in reserve lest he lose caste and business among his neighbors, was a figure radically different from the quicksilver manipulator of roles and interpersonal signals who seemed to Riesman to dominate the postwar American middle class—nonetheless ransacked *Democracy in America* for *The Lonely Crowd*'s epigrams.[4] Others were not so careful. In the tendencies of Jacksonian America, it was said, Tocqueville had had the gift to see the postwar man in the gray flannel suit: an emergent world of Levittowns, McCarthyism, and conformity, hidden in the potentials of early nineteenth-century democracy. This was, if my memory has not tricked me, the way Tocqueville was taught in the college curriculum when he came into vogue in American history and civilization courses. He was the seer of a public life grown moblike, over-charged with energy, rolling over the fragile, precious reserves of distinction and individuality.

When toward the end of the 1960s, that world of mass markets and cold war terrors dissolved into a startling new

cacophony of politics and lifestyles, one might have expected a
certain cautious reassessment of Tocqueville's prophetic abilities. Instead the bottom line of Tocqueville's prophecy was
overhauled to suit the altered circumstances. *Democracy in
America*'s first volume, controlled as it is by the specter of
majority tyranny, student readers in the 1980s are now advised, will probably not compel their attention. It is the
long-neglected second volume of 1840 where we now suddenly
find Tocqueville's eye to have been keenest. Our prophetic
Tocqueville of the 1980s is the seer not of mass society's heavy,
conformistic pressures but of enervation and withdrawal, of a
public life in decay. The key to *Democracy in America* is now
the spirit that Tocqueville called "individualism": the scurrying
of men and women into the private, petty affairs of family and
self, leaving the public sphere to the centralizers, the quiet
horsemen of paternalism and bureaucratic power, who move
in where public commitments fail. Here, in this bleak portrait
of trivial affairs and private preoccupations are the sections of
Democracy in America to which contemporary readers of the
1980s will now find themselves uncannily near, Thomas Bender
writes. From roughly opposite poles of the political spectrum,
Richard Sennett and Robert Nisbet have quarried the same
lines of volume 2 for that common theme.[5]

The point is not simply that Tocqueville changed his mind
—though, like most agile thinkers, he did. There was a side to
Tocqueville reminiscent of Henry Adams: playing with alternative scenarios of disaster, unable to decide whether the world
rising about him would end in fire or ice, in mob rule or en-
tropic decay. The more important point, however, is that
when Tocqueville's predictions of 1835 grew tattered, we
traded volume 1 in for volume 2, the specter of conformity for
the specter of enervation and withdrawal, without doubting
either prophetic reading of the book. We have hungered to see
ourselves in his pages—not Jackson or Louis Philippe—but
modernity.

IN THIS eagerness we have rarely paused to ask what sort of prophet Tocqueville really was. For prophets come in three quite distinct molds, and they read the tea leaves of their moment in distinctly different ways. The oldest prophets did not so much predict as know. They were messengers of fate, mouthpieces of the Lord, to whom the strange dreams and burning bushes spoke with a clarity barred to others. In modern times, prophets of this sort have been eased out by those who only guess. The guessers themselves, however, fall into two fundamentally different camps: those who work by extrapolation, and those who work by something closer to intuition. The mark of the extrapolators is the density of their concern with present-day facts and their obsession with explanatory laws. Extrapolators tend to care deeply about the mechanics of change; they are drawn to the rhetoric of science; they think their way into the future, as it were, on straight lines and causal threads. One thinks in this regard of H. G. Wells, of Herman Kahn, and above all of the later Marx, deep in the fact-crammed bowels of the British Museum.[6]

The intuitional readers of the future tend to work in quite different ways. They think their way into the future, not along causal threads, but by the gift of seeing under the mundane surface of everyday life the half-concealed patterns of a world in birth. Their imaginations do not run toward explanatory laws but toward horizontal relationships, not toward facts but toward typologies and ideal types. *How* one gets from the world falling into ruins to the world about to be born is not their central question. Their preoccupation is to read the shape of the future, the chick in the thinned and cracking eggshell. They work not by extrapolation but by hunch and metaphor. One thinks of Comte, of Carlyle, of Weber. And of Tocqueville.

For to reread *Democracy in America* and its accompanying notebooks looking for the telltale signs of our modernity in the womb of Tocqueville's America is to realize with a start how bold a hunchmaker, how reckless a leaper between observations Tocqueville was. Take his fearful prediction of the impending tyranny of the majority. He made up most of it, it is clear, out of the frightened talk of the ex-Federalists and proto-Whigs, reeling from Jackson's victory, with whom he had conversed so much in America. He arrived in the United States just in time to see the final break-up of the deference politics of the eighteenth century: when Jackson's heavy-handed use of the power of patronage was still new and (to Jackson's opponents) deeply frightening, when the machinery of mass party mobilization was just beginning to be hammered into place, when on the radical flanks of Jackson's party men were talking of popular, majoritarian sovereignty with an expansiveness that shivered the nerves of those still committed to the complex constitutional balances of an older, far less direct democracy. Tocqueville hardly spoke to a partisan of the new democratic order. "I have almost got proof that all the enlightened classes in America are opposed to General Jackson," he confided early to his notebook.[7] It was the American defenders of the *ancien régime* with whom he sensed a kindredness of spirit. They bent their young listener's ear with their dire, Madisonian fears of majoritarian democracy. Into the first volume of *Democracy in America* these fears poured, vivid and little changed.

To these conventional anti-Jackson prejudices, Tocqueville himself added a deeper and more novel worry: that what the political mob could not accomplish, the tyranny of public opinion might complete. Here his most vivid American informant was a Baltimore doctor, a bit of a freethinker it would appear, who told Tocqueville that in America the slightest hint of irregular religious opinions would instantly strip a professional man like himself of his clients. "Public opinion does with us what the Inquisition could never do," Dr. Stewart told Tocqueville in a phrase that worked its way virtually unaltered into Tocqueville's *Democracy*. In Baltimore, Tocqueville heard his first vivid description of a democratic, press-smashing mob. In Ohio, he had fallen in with a young reactionary lawyer, who confessed that he would never publicly admit to the antidemocratic opinions he was willing privately to confide to his French acquaintance.[8]

What drew the meager anecdotes into a pattern, however, was Tocqueville's own private surprise at the absence of so much of the cultural landscape familiar to him in Paris. The absence of an openly reactionary aristocracy, which made no secret of its loathing of the mob, and of a literary underground, seething with anticlerical sentiment and satire of bourgeois morality: this remained an enduring conundrum to him. Out of that surprise, together with an aristocrat's shock at the apparent sameness of conversations among the common and middling folk, flowed his famous conclusion that in no country he knew was there "less independence of mind and true freedom of discussion than in America."[9]

But it should not reflect particularly adversely on Tocqueville that that famous hunch was concocted largely out of preoccupations private to the peculiar sliver of Americans he talked to, and to Tocqueville himself. Jared Sparks, the Boston historian who had first offered Tocqueville the "tyranny by the majority" phrase, concluded upon reading *Democracy in America* that Tocqueville had "entirely mistaken" the point. The editors of the *Democratic Review,* pointing to the Democratic Party's uphill battle against a vigorously anti-Jackson press, complained they had no idea what Tocqueville was talking about in adverting to the majority's monopoly over public opinion.[10] In 1830s England, Tocqueville's passages on the tyranny of the majority passed quickly into the shibboleths of those terrified that Chartism might break apart the cautious democratic reforms of 1832. In the United States, on the other hand, reviewers of all political stripes protested that Tocqueville had read far too much into the passing phenomenon of Jackson's early popularity.[11] Theirs was not simply the defen-

siveness of a generation hypersensitive to foreign criticism.
Sixty years later, Daniel Coit Gilman noted that Tocqueville's
"tyranny of the majority" chapters were impossible to connect
to the America he knew—either to Gilman's America of the
1890s, split into a myriad of ethnic subcultures and still rever-
berating with Populist discontent, or the America in birth at the
moment of Tocqueville's visit, just beginning to feel the explo-
sive dissenting energies of abolitionism.[12]

Preoccupied by the spectacle of so politically timid an aristocracy, by the puzzle of a country without a genuinely reactionary party or a proper Bohemia, Tocqueville, in short, had
not seen anything like the man in the gray flannel suit at all.
His hunch that majoritarian democracy might make things
hard for those who failed to think in step had precious little to
do with Reisman's world of gladhanders and sales personnel, of
mass fads, mass media, and pressing corporate loyalties. It was
hardly Tocqueville's fault that even the language for this sort of
polity escaped him, that he had to make do with Madisonian
talk of better constitutional checks and balances.

As for the now-celebrated chapters on privatization, here it
is quite clear that Tocqueville did not have democratic America
in mind at all. There was much he could have seen to support
the point, we now think, in Jacksonian America. The cultural
revolution launched in the early years of the nineteenth century
by middle-class Americans with new ideals of social discipline,
temperance, and family order on their minds held within it tendencies both toward moral imperialism and toward quiet domestic retreat.[13] A particularly farsighted observer might have
seen as much beneath the frenetic associational, do-gooding
spirit with which Tocqueville was so impressed. But, in truth,
Tocqueville does not seem to have seen it at all. It was not until
he had returned to France—to narrow, provincial Normandy,
to which he had transferred his writing project in 1838—that
the term "individualism" (or as we would now call it, privatization) took shape in his vocabulary. To the theme of public

enervation, America always seemed to him the great exception. He readily granted that the language of American politics was poor in words for public life. The term "virtue," in its classic, republican sense, meant, he thought, nothing to the Americans. But in talk of "self-interest rightly understood," they had a way of talking about the common good serviceable enough to sustain a terrific, meddling, public-spirited energy.

It was barely democratized France that he had in mind when he wrote of men consumed in the "trivial, lonely, futile" activities of the self.[14] It was England he had in mind when he wrote of democracy's gravitational attraction toward centralized authority, in an oddly distorted and, as it turned out, an incorrect reading of the new Poor Law of 1834.[15] America in 1831–32 had seemed him full of startlingly centrifugal tendencies. Here "there is no, or at least there doesn't appear to be any government at all," he wrote his father soon after he reached New York. "All that is good in centralization seems to be as unknown as what is bad."[16] But by the time he wrote his arresting passages on bureaucratic power, Jackson's America had all but passed from his mind. It was Napoleon who haunted Tocqueville by the late 1830s: the specter of yet another round of Bonapartism, ushered in this time not by revolution but by the listless indifference of a bourgeoisie for whom liberty and honor had lost every shred of public meaning. In the short run, this was an acute prediction, weighted with tremendous import in Tocqueville's France. As a prevision of Reaganomics, jacuzzis, and yuppiedom, however, is it is hard to see that it was anywhere close to the mark.

It was, in short, out of thin stuff that Tocqueville made the predictive hunches for which we have so eagerly celebrated him. We allow as much in intuitional prophets. We do not ask diviners why their guesses work. If Tocqueville was acute enough to sense some of the shape of modern times, does it matter where he found it? He haunts us—even when we catch a glimpse of his rickety prognosticating machinery at work—

with the timeless charges of an acute political moralist. Does it matter that the structures of his and our America are alike only on the wings of a loose and vague metaphor he called democracy?

THE RUB comes in Tocqueville's refusal to play the role of a merely intuitional prophet. The part he yearned for, clearly, was closer to that of the later Marx. He would not merely describe the world he sensed rushing into being. He would explain it, harness his phenomena to a causal engine. That engine, of course, was equality. It was the "nodal point" of his observations, he wrote at the outset of volume 1, the central historical fact from which all the others derived.[17] In America, equality had paved the way for democratic majoritarianism. Equality of condition fueled the tremendous associational energies of the Americans; it clamped on their minds the shackles of their neighbors' opinions. In Europe, by the same token, it was love of equality, he was convinced, on which the new model Bonapartes would ride. An homogenized citizenry absorbed in the gains of the self was no fodder for revolution, he thought. Where equality ruled, the demagogue "exhausts himself trying to animate [the] indifferent and preoccupied crowd."[18] But toward stealthily centralized bureaucracy, democracies went as silent sheep, without bleat or murmur.

Each of these points was but a variation on a common theme. The creed of equality—though at first blush it might seem to diffuse that spirit of independence in which liberty flourished—was as likely to lead, Tocqueville always suspected, through a secret back door, to novel and yet still stronger forms of tyranny. This has long been taken as the gist of the analytical Tocqueville: the historical law ratified by his uncannily predictive guesses. Between equality and the furious centralizing energies of modern nation-states, Robert Nisbet

writes in a gloss on Tocqueville, there is "a fateful affinity."
Hannah Arendt condensed the Tocqueville-derived point more
simply: equality is a "danger to freedom."[19] And yet for
Tocqueville this too was hardly a law, but hunch and metaphor.

Through what secret byways were democracies lured toward
that hindering, restraining, enervating, stifling, stultifying bureaucratic despotism Tocqueville so vividly feared by 1840? His
line of reasoning proceeded on two levels. The first—his insistence that in aristocratic families the claims of history pulled
men out of their petty concerns and endowed them with a vig-
orous sense of public responsibility—strikes us now as a somewhat embarrassing piece of special pleading for Frenchmen of
Tocqueville's own kind. Since Tocqueville's day, the lures of
privatization have run at least as hard through the salons of the
aristocracy as through the countinghouses of the bourgeoisie
or the workshops of the masses. Tocqueville's second line of argument was the more powerful: that in a polity controlled by
love of equality and resentment of aristocratic distinctions, the
"ever-fiercer fire of endless hatred felt by democracies against
the slightest privileges" beats against every privileged person
except the state itself.[20] In the state, and only there, were democracies willing to bestow authority: wholesale and without
reservation.

This was a powerfully haunting and yet—it seems to me—
quite erroneous prediction: a hunch that hindsight hardly sus-
tains. Centralized, liberty-extinguishing states we have had in
abundance, but very few of them have sprung, as Tocqueville
imagined they would, from equality. The first of the great modern, bureaucratically centralized states, with a hand deep in the
everyday affairs of its citizens, as Tocqueville himself knew
well, was prerevolutionary France, riven with inequalities. The
second—Weber's own iron cage—was Wilhelmine Germany,
where war discipline and Junkerism, not egalitarian democracy,
held the reins. At a time when the United States, so steeped

in egalitarian talk that its immigrants boasted of eating white bread and meat like aristocrats, was struggling to establish the rudiments of a civil service, the war-nurtured states of turn-of-the-century Europe had already laid in place the apparatus of centralized state power Tocqueville so deeply feared. Even now, where the civilian employees of the United States Defense Department are eightfold as numerous as the employees of the Department of Health and Social Services, it is clear that war is the far better promoter of centralized, massively bureaucratized power than the flickering spirit of equality. There are Bonapartes abroad in the world, but, as always, they ride in, not on cries of equality, but of order and martial discipline.

It is true that where equality is so long resisted that it arrives only through the guns of revolution, the result has repeatedly been to funnel massive amounts of power into the central, revolution-consolidating apparatus of the state. But it was not this sort of revolution that Tocqueville had in mind in the haunting final passages of *Democracy in America*. These "great revolutions," springing out of deeply entrenched systems of caste and privilege, he thought (erroneously, as it turned out) would become more rare. The sort of despotism egalitarian societies had to fear was very different: a continual, barely noticed accretion of state authority, fueled by the accumulated resentments of its (almost) equal citizens, until they turned at last to sheep in the care of their absolute and despotic protectors. Midway through the age of Thatcher and Reagan, that hunch hardly seems a compelling item of prophecy. Tocqueville failed to foresee that democratic citizens might be at least as prickly about their rights as aristocratic ones. He failed to foresee that in democracies, the populace might take out the accumulated resentments of private life not on the privileges of private wealth but on the state itself, marching under the banner of tax revolts and anti-bureaucratic resentment. Our current political condition— marked not so much by political enervation as by a powerful

rage to dismantle what shreds of public life we still possess—
Tocqueville failed to foresee altogether.

Not only has history failed to attend overly well to Tocqueville's ventures in prophecy, but his hunches, fears, and premonitions fell themselves a good ways short of explanatory,
predictive law. Tocqueville never thought, while in America, to
take even the roughest factual measure of the equality that so
absorbed him. He stirred together tendencies he felt in Jackson's America, elitist and commercial Britain, and centralized
France into an ideal type that by the late 1830s floated increasingly free of any specific political referent. Under his keywords,
as George Wilson Pierson wrote long ago, he tended to assimilate virtually every visible phenomenon of the world he sensed
in birth.[21] His causal engine, equality, in short, was hardly a
causal engine at all, but a big, accordion-like metaphor.

TO GET closer to the discontents of the twentieth century
would have required a different language, one less beholden to
classical politics, than the language Tocqueville possessed. The
conformistic 1950s, beset by the terrors of exposure to a suddenly diminished and dangerously armed world, enraptured by
agencies of persuasion the likes of which no one in the 1830s
had the least presentiment, was a radically different society
than Tocqueville foresaw. Our current scuttlings toward private pleasures likewise have their roots deep in phenomena of
which Tocqueville had no inkling: the economics of a closed
and pinching world system, the cyclical energies and exhaus-
tions of modern politics, and the power of differential market
advertising. John Stuart Mill came closer to the lineaments of
our modernity in his objection that the great bulk of Tocqueville's phenomena were characteristic not of democratic societies but of "commercial" ones.[22] Tocqueville groped for that

sort of language in *Democracy in America;* in his chapter on the dangers of a manufacturing aristocracy, he came closest to it. It was not entirely his fault that in the France of the 1830s and out of the circle of which he came he did not possess the words for it.

Does it diminish Tocqueville to acknowledge his deep flaws as a prophet? He was a diviner, a huncher, an extraordinarily acute observer of much that fell under his ken. If his picture of Jacksonian America was flawed, no other European saw it better. The timelessness of *Democracy in America* comes not from its prevision of the future of democracy, or from its occasional lucky guesses, but from its untarnished moral seriousness. As long as politics endure, there will be a need for Tocqueville's warnings against the mob, the *Gleichschaltung* of the mind, the bloated structures of state power, the erosion of public life and public commitments. Where the pleasures of private life triumph, the horsemen do not always ride in, but life surely decays. In that moral alone, in the example of a man thinking hard and engagedly about public life, there is more than enough in *Democracy in America* to sustain another century-and-half's reading.

But the world Tocqueville sensed in birth is not the modernity that besets us. In his farthest flights of prophecy, Tocqueville did not see the forces that have wrenched our world so far from his. He got a great deal wrong—not the least about the tendencies of equality. To think he had his eye on us has been for too long our private, oddly egocentric folly. It is time to stop reading *Democracy in America* as a book of prophecy; if we are to see the beasts in the eggshell of our times, we must do that, in different terms, ourselves.

Many Democracies:
On Tocqueville and
Jacksonian America

SEAN WILENTZ

HAT DOES *Democracy in America* have to tell us about American politics and society in the 1830s? The question may seem obvious, even impertinent. Since the Tocqueville revival of the late 1930s and 1940s, countless scholars have turned to *Democracy* as the single most insightful commentary on the Jacksonian era. Seemingly, there is nothing about Jacksonian politics, social relations, and culture about which Tocqueville was not an authoritative critic.[1] Nevertheless, it is time to reexamine *Democracy*'s historical significance. Over the last fifteen years, revisionist work on various subjects, much of it by social historians, has made it difficult to sustain many of Tocqueville's impressions of this country. A few historians have directly rebutted Tocqueville; many more have challenged what John Higham once called "the Tocquevillean idea that all Americans are basically alike."[2] Although attempts at synthesizing these findings into an intelligible whole have only just begun, we certainly have a far more comprehensive understanding of Jacksonian America than either Tocqueville or his later admirers down through the 1960s could have had. This understanding allows us to undertake a fresh and more critical appreciation of Tocqueville's masterpiece.

TO CITE recent scholarship—and *Democracy*'s many critics— is not to say that Tocqueville lacks for contemporary American disciples. A wide range of historians, political theorists, and sociologists still regard *Democracy* as a trustworthy entry-way into the hearts and minds of Jacksonian Americans, with lasting relevance for our own time. Robert Bellah and his colleagues' study of the corrosive sociology of American individualism, *Habits of the Heart*, exemplifies *Democracy*'s abiding influence: A reviewer, summing up the book's frame of reference, aptly commented: "Once again the starting point is Tocqueville."[3] From very different perspectives, Richard Sennett, Thomas Bender, and John Diggins have all rooted historical analyses of current cultural and political problems in Tocqueville's description of the 1830s.[4] Andrew Jackson's most thorough modern biographer, Robert V. Remini, has concluded that "Tocqueville remains the surest and best key to unlocking the mysteries of Jacksonian America."[5] And various journalists, moonlighting academics, and other pundits have been unstinting in their praise of Tocqueville as the man who discovered the lineaments of modernity in Jackson's rural republic.[6]

Much of this writing glosses over *Democracy*'s bad hunches, misinformed reporting, and ideological biases—shortcomings in *Democracy* that those who specialize in studying Tocqueville are now quick to point out.[7] There appear to be several reasons for this glossing over. Christopher Lasch has detected a political subtext in some neo-Tocquevillean writing, a tendency "to exalt bourgeois liberalism as the only civilized form of political life."[8] On a different tack, Daniel Rodgers points out elsewhere in this volume that many of Tocqueville's disciples have been too eager to read *Democracy* (or some portion of it) as prophecy, taking Tocqueville's own claims to prevision too seriously—and thereby misreading the present into the past that Tocqueville described. Just as troubling is the persistent slighting of so much important recent work about the past, work that should encourage a more distanced handling of *Democracy*.

Take, for example, what historians are now saying about one of Tocqueville's central themes, equality of condition in Jacksonian America. Tocqueville claimed that equality was the fundamental fact of a democratic order. By this he did not mean that an absolute material equality existed in the United States: Most of what he wrote about American conditions concerned not absolutes, but a relative equality, in contrast with the Old World. However, in asserting that American class differences existed within an egalitarian framework, Tocqueville made a variety of claims—about the rapid circulation of wealth, the plebeian origins of American fortunes, and the fluid structure of American opportunity—that now seem to have been dubious. Plainly, Tocqueville overestimated the proportion of the country's free population that was middle class— or, as he put it, "comfortably off"—while he slighted the opulence of the wealthy and the poverty of the poor.[9] Even more important, *Democracy*'s treatment of democracy and equality seems at odds with another recent discovery—that over the same period during which American politics grew more democratic formally, inequalities of wealth and power declined hardly at all; if anything these inequalities became more severe.[10]

Likewise, recent historians have moved well beyond Tocqueville's treatment of another of his key topics, religion. Tocqueville was remarkably sensitive to the importance of religion to American political culture. His basic insight about how religion promoted social order in a democracy—"Despotism may be able to do without faith," he wrote, "but liberty cannot"— was profound.[11] More than ever, historians have come to agree with Tocqueville about the centrality of religion to American social life and social change in the 1830s and after. But as current work also suggests, Tocqueville never fully came to terms with the specifically evangelical Protestant character of the Second Great Awakening. Nor does *Democracy* elaborate the social processes (and conflicts) that helped produce the great religious revivals of the Jacksonian era. As Paul E. Johnson has written, Tocqueville treated religion as a form of personal rectitude and social control but he effectively ignored the question of who, in American society, was controlling whom.[12] It was precisely from the connections between transcendent religious experiences and shifting power relations—between employers and wage-earners, middle-class patriarchs and middle-class women, masters and slaves—that the religious passions of Jacksonian America gained so much of their force. In the northern states, evangelicalism became, among other things, a vehicle for promoting new forms of work discipline, public morality, and feminized family government.[13] In the south, masters adapted evangelical notions of stewardship to their emerging defense of slavery as a positive good, while slaves interpreted Christianity very differently, as a parable of endurance and deliverance.[14] Throughout the country, the sociology of American religion was more complex and conflict-ridden than Tocqueville had appreciated.

Democracy was far more acute about another American institution, slavery. A great deal of current scholarship echoes Tocqueville's judgment that slavery fundamentally shaped the mores and social conditions of Jacksonian America in ways that distinguished the free states from the slave states. But Tocqueville also misjudged vital aspects of southern life, notably the cultural perseverence of the slave communities. In *Democracy* we read that "[t]he Negro has no family; for him a woman is no more than the passing companion of his pleasures, and from their birth his sons are his equals." Historians, to the contrary, have identified kin networks and family ties, along with slave religion, as some of the most powerful bonds among the antebellum slaves—extraordinary sources of dignity and mutuality, which helped fend off the worst social and psychological hardships of bondage.[15] Tocqueville, it seems, too quickly deduced cultural disorder from the very real horrors of enslavement; his writings thus bypassed important features of both American slavery and an emerging Afro-American culture.

On women, family life, and gender, *Democracy* certainly raised themes of interest to recent historians. Although they were freed from the restraints of aristocratic authorities, Tocqueville observed, American women had lost their independence in the bonds of marriage—and had done so voluntarily.[16] Once confined to their dependent state, as wives and mothers, American women undertook their true vocation, to elevate the nation's moral tone by scrupulously attending to their private duties, following the canons of what historians now call "the cult of domesticity."[17] No less a promulgator of this cult than Catharine Beecher recognized in *Democracy* a near-perfect delineation of the advanced state of American women.[18] Yet Beecher (and Tocqueville) notwithstanding, *Democracy* contained at best a partial account of American womanhood. Quite apart from the female slaves, many women— women in small farming households, the women of the laboring poor— had neither the means nor the desire to live their lives in accord with emerging Victorian middle-class standards. At various flashpoints—notably between urban reformers and poor women—these differences exploded, as the champions of domesticity sought to remake "unruly" females and families in their own image, and the "unruly" resisted.[19]

More generally, Tocqueville appears to have slighted ideological differences and conflicts among free Americans, in and out of party politics. Not that he omitted discussion of these conflicts: "What strikes one most on arrival in the United States," he wrote, "is the kind of tumultuous agitation in which one finds political society."[20] In the end, though, Tocqueville was far more impressed by Americans' shared values, based on their common republicanism, individualism, and respect for the Constitution—"a tacit agreement and a sort of *consensus universalis*," which he thought precluded deep and lasting ideological divisions.[21] Today, historians are more wary. Closer examination of Americans' shared political vocabulary has revealed different versions of what these words meant; these clashing interpretations surfaced in bitter conflicts between Whigs and Democrats, labor unions and employers' associations, squatters and land speculators, abolitionists and slaveholders, and various other groups. In the 1980s, Americans can listen to Ronald Reagan and Coretta Scott King speak eloquently about the affirmation of equality and social justice without assuming that they mean anything like the same thing. So in the 1830s, behind Tocqueville's "tacit agreement," lurked far more powerful conflicts than *Democracy* captured—conflicts that would bring about (among other things) the bloodiest civil upheaval in the history of the nineteenth-century western world, an upheaval Tocqueville anticipated but thought the republic would avoid.[22]

All of this revisionism is, understandably, upsetting to those who wish to regard Tocqueville as some sort of Olympian authority, the surest and best key to Jacksonian America. Occasionally, *Democracy*'s admirers have struck back at the supposedly low-minded revisionists: One historian has seen fit to label another historian's challenge to *Democracy* as "a feeble effort to bury the noble Tocqueville in Brooklyn under a pile of tax receipts."[23] Put this way, the important historical issues become personalized and therefore trivialized, as if the point is to "prove" or "disprove" Tocqueville, or vote *Democracy* up or down. Nothing that historians discover about Jacksonian America can rob *Democracy* of its unique value as an ambitious attempt by an extremely perceptive man, thinking with all his might, to understand democracy (and America) in the broadest possible terms. Certainly no one can hold Tocqueville responsible for not knowing things that it has taken scholars a century-and-a-half to learn. *Democracy* may be regarded as a classic not because it is "right" or "accurate"—Tocqueville, himself, a compulsive self-doubter and reviser would almost

certainly have conceded as much—but because of the breadth
of its author's moral and political concerns and the cogency
of his questions. Revisionist efforts will have been wasted if
they lead historians merely to denigrate Tocqueville, or to neglect him, as historians before the 1930s tended to do.[24] But
Tocqueville's admirers serve neither the man nor his work if
they try to elevate them above subsequent research, or try to
isolate Tocqueville's ideas from what we have learned (and
continue to learn) about their contexts. Instead, given all we
now know about Jacksonian America, it is time to reread *Democracy in America* alongside current reinterpretations not as
prophecy, nor as some timeless diagnosis of modernity, but as a
historical artifact.

Approached in this critical historical spirit, *Democracy in
America* loses some of its glamor, but retains considerable stature. *Democracy*'s great strength—indeed, its genius—was that
it marked a breakthrough in conservative thinking about property and mass democracy, a breakthrough that Tocqueville
intuited, then elucidated earlier and far more fully than his
American friends and informants. The book's shortcomings,
meanwhile, are instructive, because they point out the danger
of projecting a single ideal of democracy as the essence of Jacksonian politics—and, for that matter, of our own politics.
Tocqueville articulated a new conception of democracy in the
1830s, one that would become increasingly important (indeed,
dominant) in the United States over the decades that followed.
What he failed to comprehend was that this democracy was but
one of several American democracies that had emerged out of
the social tumults of his time.[25]

TO UNDERSTAND the dimensions of Tocqueville's achievement, it is important to recognize that he visited, and then
studied, an America in flux. Even if we concede that every

historical moment is, in some sense, a moment of transition, there are ample grounds for describing the half-decade from 1828 to 1833—and even more specifically the period immediately surrounding Tocqueville's brief stay in 1831—as a turning point in American history. The sheer pace and drama of events, crowding in upon each other, reinforce that impression: The election of Andrew Jackson, the Virginia suffrage and slavery debates, the great Finneyite revivals in Rochester, the emergence of immediatist abolitionism, Nat Turner's rebellion, the bank war and then the nullification crisis, the rise of radical labor movements and trade unionism in the northeast, the drive for graduation and freeholds in the west, the gestation of this country's first mass democratic party system. In a matter of weeks (and sometimes days) Americans witnessed the fall of entire chunks of the gentry's old regime and the opening up of issues of section, class, and race that would dominate the nation's politics for decades to come.

Aléxis de Tocqueville disembarked in New York City and stepped into the middle of this political maelstrom—unprepared. He and his friend de Beaumont had come to look at penitentiaries and to ponder the New World's lessons for the Old; crossing the ocean with his head full of Montesquieu and Guizot, he had expected to find a classical republic in the United States, where independent citizens exercised selfless civic virtue on behalf of the commonwealth. Such, after all, was what eighteenth-century political writers had said a republic was supposed to be; such was the kind of republic Americans boasted they had created.[26] It took Tocqueville less than a month, spent talking mainly with some of the leading men of New York City, for him to change his mind. It was not virtue that made the Americans a people; Tocqueville saw little enough of virtue. Individual *intérêt* was the secret of American politics.[27] For the rest of his visit, and then over the next nine years, Tocqueville puzzled over his discovery. Again and again, he asked himself the same question: How did the Americans,

lacking virtue and the traditional forms of aristocratic authority, manage to maintain stability and order? From these ruminations—and with his attentions often fixed more on his native
land than on the United States—he constructed his grand
themes, always claiming that in America he saw not simply
America but an image of democracy itself.

It is hardly surprising that Tocqueville, immersed in so many
different events, understood them in terms of a contrast between democratic America and aristocratic Europe: Such were
the terms of intellectual inquiry he and his generation of educated Frenchmen had absorbed, above all from *De l'Esprit
des Lois*. Nor is it surprising that, in explaining that contrast,
Tocqueville fastened on the problems of virtue and self-interest, stability and order: Such were the preoccupations of
enlightened aristocrats in France (and Britain) in the 1830s,
alarmed by the specter of popular revolt and democratic reform. Tocqueville made no pretense about where his sympa-
thies lay: Although inclined toward democratic institutions, he
was an instinctual aristocrat who despised what he called "the
mass." "I have a passionate love for liberty, law and respect
for rights— but not for democracy," he wrote at one point.
"There is the ultimate truth of my heart."[28]

Not quite so obvious is that Tocqueville's preoccupations
haunted his American friends and informants as well—a point
recent historical research has emphasized.[29] To be sure, upper-
crust Americans, far more than even enlightened Old World
aristocrats, had made their peace with republican principles; indeed, they were often insistent republicans, champions of the
American Constitution. But no less than the young Tocqueville,
the mainly ex-Federalist, soon-to-be Whigs from whom he
learned so much were frightened by the seemingly irresistible
democratic tide—a tide they feared would destroy the orderly
American polity inaugurated in 1787 and bring to power either
a lawless mob or an American Napoleon. Their world—a
world of political deference, virtuous obligation, and elaborate

checks and balances on the popular will—had been swept
aside by the election of Andrew Jackson and the ascendancy of
Martin Van Buren. The Jacksonians' consolidation of power
only confirmed that, henceforth, party loyalty, the shameless
pursuit of self-interest, and demagogic flattery of the electorate
would be the cardinal American political virtues; some even
saw Jackson as the much-feared military dictator. And on the
horizon loomed even more dangerous mobocrats, men like the
artisan radical, Thomas Skidmore, and women like the feminist
agitator, Frances Wright, who supposedly would dissolve the
moral bonds of civilization and destroy whatever checks on
popular rule remained.

This was a conservative, self-serving, at times cranky view of
American political culture in the 1830s, and it quickly became
Tocqueville's. He expressed his fears (and his informants' fears)
amply in the first volume of *Democracy in America* in his de-
pictions of an irrational American people, goaded by semilit-
erate party hacks, destroying great institutions like the Second
Bank of the United States for little more reason than to see if
the institutions would fall. Beyond that, Tocqueville discovered
an even deeper problem, a singular timidity on the part of worthy gentlemen—the kinds of men who might be expected to
understand and exercise civic virtue—in the face of majoritarian rule. In public, Tocqueville's wealthier friends actually
lauded the democracy they so distrusted, "careful to avoid
showing that [they were] hurt" by the state of things.[30] To do
otherwise, Tocqueville reported, was to court utter marginality,
or (even worse) physical attack.

It took no special gifts to collect these views and assemble
them into a book. Had Tocqueville done only that, his writings
would be nowhere near as interesting as they are. Had he gone
on, as American conservatives like Rufus Choate did, to pre-
scribe ways to institutionalize classical virtue in the United
States, he might be as well-known today as Rufus Choate.[31]
Instead, Tocqueville scrutinized the peculiar American demo-

crat more closely than his American friends had yet done—and he found that despite the potential tyranny of a democratic majority, there really wasn't so much to worry about after all. Perhaps, Tocqueville suggested, Madison and his successors had misjudged the American majority (and therefore misjudged democracy). Perhaps, in a democracy, popular self-interest could be turned into a kind of virtuousness, less exalted than the classical variety, but enough to shape an orderly, moral, public-spirited citizenry.

As John Diggins has pointed out, Tocqueville managed to transcend his fears and those of his American friends only by breaking with the prevailing modes of political inquiry. Instead of approaching democracy and democratic manners through a study of American laws and institutions, he tried to study democratic manners directly, to see how they affected politics. He did this not by taking any extensive surveys of American social structure—he hardly had the time or information for that—but by juxtaposing what he saw in America (ever-symptomatic of democracy) with what he knew best, post–1830 France. He came to understand America, and democracy, in terms of a series of absences: The absence of a peasantry, the absence of a proletariat, the absence of an idle aristocracy. In America, all citizens worked and none lacked property or the means to obtain it; the pursuit of equality and material desires was universal. Out of that pursuit sprang a pride in work and achievement—as duties to the community as well as the means to self-gratification—which encouraged the public spirit, led to the creation of voluntary associations, and secured political stability.[32]

Contained in this analysis, quite apart from its shrewd discussion of the Jacksonian middle-class mentality, was a revolution in conservative thought about property and politics—a revolution that, in America, had begun in Jefferson's day, but was not yet completed when Tocqueville visited the United States.[33] From the framers onward, Americans preoccupied

with order and stability had assumed that there was an inevitable conflict between the wealthy few and the poor (or prop-
ertyless) many. Unless the many were held in check, they would
use their majority power to despoil the few. Atop these gloomy
assumptions, American conservatives, with one eye fixed on
Europe, built their case for mixed government, the breaking up
of popular sovereignty, and the elevation of virtuous men of
property to political leadership. "We have no experience that
teaches us that any other rights are safe where property is not
safe," the young Federalist Daniel Webster warned during the
Massachusetts constitutional convention of 1820.[34] Unfortu-
nately, that convention, and subsequent developments elsewhere, portended the ascension of the self-interested many and
an all-out assault on virtuous politics and property rights. All
was lost unless some scheme could be devised that would sub-
merge men's individual desires in what conservatives believed
to be the rightful, orderly objects of government—but no such
scheme seemed in the offing. "Montesquieu has somewhere a
reflection to this purpose," an ironic, embittered Rufus King
wrote to an associate in 1822, "but gives no hint in respect to
the formation of so extraordinary a plan."[35]

Less than a decade later—and nearly half-a-century after the
ratification of the Constitution—Tocqueville could see things
differently. Not that the danger of majority tyranny had completely passed away: Tocqueville still found it in the American
state legislatures as well as in the reign of public opinion. But
contrary to the fears of founding fathers like Madison and
John Adams (and of pessimistic Federalists like Webster and
King), America had not become more and more like Europe,
with its sharp distinctions between the few and the many. Democratic America had given rise to an exceptionally large middle
class—an amorphous group of entrepreneurs, businessmen,
shopkeepers, and commercial farmers, far larger than any comparable group in Europe. Tocqueville easily—all too easily
—equated this class with the many. In America, Tocqueville

observed, "everyone, having some possession to defend, recognizes the right to property in principle."[36] In this sense,
America was a classless society, despite its manifest inequalities
of wealth: The many, who either owned property or could reasonably expect to do so, would never strip the wealthy few of
those property rights that they themselves held so dear. The
framers' glorified notion of mixed government, which Tocqueville took to be a "chimera" anyway, was of little relevance in
such a democratic republic; were it ever actually established, a
truly mixed government—checking the power of the many
with the privileges of the few—would only plunge the republic
into revolution or anarchy.[37] Rather, in the politics of classless
America—democracy in its most advanced state—the few
could embrace both democracy and the people.

Tocqueville, in short, after nine months of travel and nine
years of study, saw what it was taking his American friends a
generation to see: In America, mass democracy did not necessarily endanger property; equality could mean the right to pursue both democracy and property. Once they did discover this
truth for themselves, American conservatives proclaimed it to
the rafters—and completed the Jacksonian revolution by helping to create in the Whig party a political counterweight to the
Jacksonians and the radicals. There was not, Daniel Webster
(now a Whig) announced in 1838, any "clear and well defined
line, between capital and labor" in the United States, as there
was in Europe.[38] America, Calvin Colton told the electorate
six years later, was "a country of *self-made* men," where all
were bound together in their individual pursuits by mutual
dependence and an overarching harmony of interests.[39] The
prattling of Democrats and other alehouse agitators about the
few and the many, others asserted, were but attempts to foist
Old World doctrines on an exceptional, democratic people.[40]
Behind the petty squabbles of the day-to-day, the superficial violence of politics and the marketplace, was a greater democratic consensus promoting universal prosperity and upward

mobility, which all right-thinking respectable Americans, rich and poor alike, understood and tried to exemplify.[41]

Here was a vision of politics that, unlike the eighteenth-century Whigs's view, could reconcile pessimistic American conservatives to mass democracy. Just as important, it could become a popular political philosophy in a country gripped by rapid commercial expansion and social transformation. Native-born craft workers, small shopkeepers, petty-capitalist farmers, and Southern planters all found ample reasons to rally behind the Whig democracy; by the late 1840s, many leading Democrats, as well as Whigs, had begun subscribing to its essentials.[42] Nowhere, however, did any American expound that vision and its logic more copiously or brilliantly than Aléxis de Tocqueville. And no writer more fully explored this vision's possible implications for every aspect of American life, public and private.

READ THIS WAY, *Democracy* ends up saying a great deal about the 1830s, with significance far beyond the history of Jacksonian America. The book helps lay bare not simply an intepretation of American democracy, but a process whereby a particular set of assumptions about democracy emerged— assumptions congenial to those who had distrusted popular sovereignty, assumptions that were to become prevalent in much of the world over the nineteenth and twentieth centuries. In this respect, *Democracy in America* is of singular importance to historians curious about the larger meaning of democratization in the United States and elsewhere. In the jargon of one important stream of current scholarship, Tocqueville captured, if not something so grand as "modernity," then a signal moment in the modernization of politics—the decline of deference and the emergence of political individualism. Or, if you prefer, Tocqueville helps us understand how certain hegemonic notions about democracy, property, and equality took shape in America in the second quarter of the nineteenth century.

Yet to notice these broader meanings is also to confront the limits of Tocqueville's analysis. If *Democracy*'s sweeping antithesis opened up aspects of democracy that Americans were only beginning to understand in the 1830s, so too (as recent work suggests) Tocqueville reduced too much about Jacksonian America to a single conception of democracy. The turning point that gave rise to the Jacksonian political revolution—and the shift in conversative thinking that *Democracy* so nicely illustrates—also saw in this country the emergence of other, very different kinds of democracy.

Here lie *Democracy*'s instructive shortcomings. Jacksonian America may not have been Europe, but it did have an increasingly reactionary and powerful landed elite, the elements of a republican working class, and a troubled yeomanry. Tocqueville observed the elite—the southern slaveholders—firsthand, and he wrote about them eloquently. The emerging working class and the yeomanry he barely saw or understood. All played important roles in the political crises of the 1830s and raised problems that were far graver and more complicated than Tocqueville imagined.

Few passages in *Democracy* are as arresting as Tocqueville's contrast between the north and the south:

> [The Northerner] with a greater degree of activity, common sense, information, and greater aptitude, has the characteristic good and evil qualities of the middle classes. [The Southerner] has the tastes, the prejudices, the weaknesses, and the magnanimity of all aristocracies.[43]

Slavery, as Tocqueville argued, was creating two civilizations within the United States, with different conceptions of labor, money, and leisure. If we now think that Tocqueville overlooked important things about the slave south, his intuitive grasp of the cultural divide between free labor and slavery remains extraordinary.

Where Tocqueville's analysis of democracy fell short was in its failure to probe the deeper paradoxes of slavery and freedom. Like other antislavery writers, Tocqueville found the peculiar institution an oppressive anomaly in democratic America, the cruelist kind of inequality: "Amid the democratic liberty and enlightenment of our age," he believed, slavery could not survive.[44] Yet he never adequately explained why it was that southerners, including slaveholders like Thomas Jefferson, had been among the leading advocates of democratic principles and natural rights from the mid-eighteenth century on. He did not grasp how slavery could have underwritten the expansion of democracy for southern whites in the 1820s and 1830s. Nor did he explore the paradox further to wonder why, at the very moment when he visited America, white southerners—planters and yeomen—began insisting with increasing urgency that their personal independence and democratic liberties would be threatened by any effort to interfere with the slaveholders' property. That an "aristocratic" elite and "democratic" populace could defend the enslavement of blacks—and, beginning in the 1830s, the denial of free speech to whites—on democratic grounds and in states which boasted some of the most democratic constitutions in the world was a terrible fact of Jacksonian democracy that Tocqueville never fully sorted out.[45] Failing in that, he underestimated how the growing cultural divisions between north and south fed a political crisis that cut through shared interests ideals—and stunted "middle-class" democracy in the south. Alongside the American democracy Tocqueville described, there was another very different theory and practice of democracy—the slaveholder's democracy.

Tocqueville likewise showed only passing interest in the meanings that the slaves and American free blacks might have attached to democracy. Better than other visitors, he did resist the blandishments of plantation paternalists about slavery's benefits to the slaves. He expected that if the masters did not grant emancipation, the slaves would take it for themselves, by any means necessary. He also understood how racism intensified the sufferings of free blacks, in both the north and south. Yet Tocqueville showed little curiosity about the possible implications of the eighteenth-century democratic revolutions for the enslaved men and women and the free blacks of the United States. A Frenchman might have been expected to have been more interested: Just as Toussaint L'Ouverture and the black Jacobins of Saint–Domingue had viewed the French Revolution as the signal for their own uprising, so slaves and free blacks in various parts of the United States absorbed the democratic message of the American Revolution as an unfulfilled promise. But while Tocqueville sensed the slaves' and the free blacks' restiveness, he did not ponder how they might have had their own definitions of democracy—and how, in time, these might have influenced their own struggles for emancipation and equality.[46]

Tocqueville had even more trouble with the free labor north and the political implications of its economic development. He easily grasped the rapidity of that development—occasioned by the rise of banks, internal improvements, and early corporations—and how it distinguished the north from the south.[47] He glimpsed the poverty that accompanied the transportation revolution, and noted in passing that the larger American cities had acquired "a rabble more dangerous even than that of European towns" (which he expected would eventually require the raising of a national standing army).[48] But when Tocqueville saw these crowds, he saw a traditional *canaille*. He could not see—as far less brilliant visitors like Thomas Hamilton could —that for these people, and for a growing number of other Americans all across the north, the line of demarcation between capital and labor was growing sharper and more permanent.[49]

Tocqueville's great friend and admirer, John Stuart Mill, helped account for *Democracy*'s oversights in these matters.

While he praised *Democracy* lavishly, Mill also pointed out
that much of what Tocqueville saw—and especially what he
didn't like—was hardly peculiar to American democracy, or
the result of democracy at all. In a sense, even though Tocqueville had taken a step beyond classical political theory, he
remained too much the classicist, preoccupied with a limited
set of questions about politics and society. Or, as Mill put it,
Tocqueville "bound up in one abstract idea the whole tendencies of modern commercial society and [gave] them one name
—Democracy." In fact, Mill argued, many of the defects that
Tocqueville found special to the American democratic mind
were "the ordinary ones of a commercial class."[50]

Tocqueville was too ambitious and careful an observer
to miss completely what Mill was talking about. Buried in
Tocqueville's unpublished papers at Yale Univesity is a note
referring to "the great difficulty in untangling what there is
[about America] which is democratic, commercial, English, and
puritan." ("To be discussed in introduction," Tocqueville
added hopefully.)[51] He never really did untangle it all; still, toward the close of the first volume of *Democracy* and in the second volume, he looked for a language with which to describe
the specifically "commercial" problems of the 1830s. At a few
points he found it, especially in his trenchant, all-too-brief
chapter on how an aristocracy might be created by manufac-
tures.[52] But Tocqueville was too much a man of his class, his
country, and his political education to make more of this language—or to make a single concrete reference to the labor
movements and class conflicts of the Jacksonian north. He
could not appreciate that the ideals of the working men's parties, the city central unions, the land reformers, and the radical
wing of the Democratic party carried very different meanings
than those of other groups of Americans. He could not comprehend that for these people, the cry for equality sprang not from
irrational impulses or self-interest alone, but out of very real
fears that exploitative businessmen and manufacturers were im-

posing new forms of power and dependency on the productive classes, destroying the democratic republic in the name of democracy and equal rights.[53] Beside the democracy Tocqueville did see, and the southern democracies he only began to understand, there was yet another democracy, a democracy of the wage-earning classes that came to life in the 1830s and would come into its own in later decades.

Finally, Tocqueville had practically nothing to say about the American yeomanry and its view of democracy. The oversight is understandable; in contrast to the French peasantry, America's freeholding rural small producers must have all seemed pretty much alike. But there were important divisions in the American countryside, between cash-crop producing commercial farmers and the relatively isolated, self-sufficient communities of yeomen. The former—particularly in the grain and dairy regions of the northwest—fit fairly easily within Tocqueville's conception of the individualist American democrat. The latter, however, pursued their self-interests according to intricate, customary rules of inheritance, household production, and barter exchange, in a balance of personal independence and local communalism quite unlike anything Tocqueville described. The transportation revolution and the commercialization of agriculture dealt severe blows to the northern yeomanry in the first half of the nineteenth century, but yeoman communities did persist in more remote areas with poorer soils; in the south, meanwhile, the majority of the white population consisted of yeomen and their families. In all areas, the yeomen equated democracy with the right to obtain and work their land—and to maintain their communal solidarities—without interference by absentee speculators, commercial developers, and meddlesome politicians. The yeomen mounted all sorts of local political efforts to defend themselves in the 1830s and 1840s, from squatters' clubs to antibank movements; these would culminate, fifty years later, in the rural insurgencies associated with Populism.[54]

ULTIMATELY, the collisions among these different forms of American democracy would destroy the agrarian republic Tocqueville knew, not by the quiet action of society upon itself, but with considerable brutality and human suffering. By the 1880s, as James Bryce among others noted, the cumulative effects of civil war, emancipation, urbanization, immigration, and industrial capitalist growth had created entirely new structures of power, individualism, and commitment.[55] We are reminded of the transience of Tocqueville's time and place, of how the polity and social formations he analyzed carried the seeds of their own destruction.

But to leave it at that would be to miss all that lives in *Democracy*. For Tocqueville, it was only natural to see the great sameness of the Americans. Lacking the bold contrasts of Europe (by which he meant France)—Europe with its legitimist aristocrats and revolutionary workers—American political culture acquired a certain narrowness that seemed to ensure stability and public spirit despite the solitude of middle-class life. In this contrast, he saw the reasons why nineteenth-century conservatives could, at last, make their peace with democracy— first in America, eventually elsewhere. Yet where Tocqueville saw many things in Jacksonian America and called them one thing, there were in fact many democracies. Behind what he called the Americans' universal consensus there were fundamental differences about the first principles of democracy itself, born of the social changes that accompanied the democratic revolution. Over the decades that followed, these differences (and nothing so simple as *intérêt*) proved to be the central fact of American politics.

Of course, the specific vision of democracy that Tocqueville set down lived on long after the Jacksonian era. Although written in the 1830s, *Democracy in America* did at the very least anticipate what was to become the intertwining of capitalism and democracy, and suggest why so many Americans might come to understand democracy only in these terms. In recent years, there has been an extraordinary resurgence of this way of thinking, both at the centers of power and (to judge from the media) in the country at large. This leads to a final, more present-minded reflection.

Taking the long view, historians might well consider that while Tocqueville slighted the diversity of democracy in the 1830s, and while he failed to comprehend the social and political revolutions to come, the champions of middle-class democracy did ultimately triumph, smashing the slaveholders in the 1860s, marginalizing the more radical elements of working-class and rural unrest in the 1880s and 1890s, binding most Americans to what we now call capitalist democracy. Perhaps, after reexamining Tocqueville's historical significance, some of his old reputation as a prophet emerges intact. Perhaps, with a touch of perversity, one might even claim that *Democracy* presents a more accurate rendering of our own time than it does of Andrew Jackson's.

And yet one also wonders how much such a view misses about our own time and place. To look at contemporary America—with its warfare-welfare state, its extraordinary concentrations of private power, its place in world affairs—and then compare it to the age of Jackson is to be immediately reminded of how different we are from the America Tocqueville described. More important, it is also to be struck by the enormous disparities and contradictions between our social and political institutions and the hopeful vision of the middle-class American democracy that began to emerge in the 1830s. At other times in our past—the 1890s, the 1920s, the 1950s—that vision has appeared to be an all-encompassing, self-evident reality, only to be challenged by new and very different visions of democracy inspired by the gap between promise and actuality. We might expect that, as we wrestle with our own contradictions, new and different forms of democracy—possibly liberating, possibly not—have already begun taking shape without our fully realizing it. The portents are not especially good, now that public officials try to justify lying to the American people (and Congress) as essential to the national security and the future of democracy itself. But in addressing these matters, Tocqueville can only teach us so much. These are matters we must master on our own.

Bryce's America and Tocqueville's

ABRAHAM S. EISENSTADT

URSUING the subject with his characteristic energy, the wiry, red-bearded Scottish professor knew exactly what question he wished to lay before the students of his graduate seminar. The date was November 1883. The locale was the Johns Hopkins University of Baltimore, which had opened its doors only seven years before in the grand year of the Revolution's centenary, as the first American center of learning to devote itself exclusively to postgraduate studies. The seminar's subject was Tocqueville's *Democracy in America*. The forty-five-year-old professor was James Bryce. The problem he posed to his seminarians had special meaning for him: What did they find questionable in Tocqueville's *Democracy*? And, because the notable Frenchman's work had so much been an exercise in anticipating the future, how far had his predictions in fact been sustained by later events? Tocqueville had long served Europe's statesmen and intellectuals as a *vade mecum* to the terrain of democracy across the Atlantic. But he loomed inescapably before the learned, probing, unremitting Scottish professor who had already embarked upon his next scholarly enterprise. It was to be a comprehensive analysis of the American polity.[1]

Bryce had lectured at the Johns Hopkins two years before in 1881, in the final phase of his second visit to the United States, a railroad journey of several months and many thousands of miles throughout continental America. Now completing his third trip, he felt himself increasingly at ease in the American ambience. He had early gained entry into an ever-widening orbit of men whose company he would find most convivial: the learned men of the eastern cities, and particularly those of New England. His own credentials, of course, made the entry an

229

easy matter. He was a member of Parliament, a rising figure in
the Liberal party, and an increasingly close associate of the party's great leader, William Ewart Gladstone. He had occupied
the Regius Chair of Civil Law at Oxford since 1870. His prize-
winning history of *The Holy Roman Empire*, which appeared
in 1864, had long commanded the respect of scholars. When he
arrived at Harvard on his very first trip to the United States in
1870, he at once met many of the most prominent members of
America's intellectual fraternity: Henry Wadsworth Longfellow, Oliver Wendell Holmes, Jr., James Russell Lowell, Arthur G. Sedgwick, Horace Gray, Ralph Waldo Emerson, and
Charles William Eliot. Outside the immediate Cambridge orbit,
Bryce met Theodore Dwight, Simeon Baldwin, E. L. Godkin,
Henry Adams, and George Bancroft.[2]

The seminar served Bryce as a reflective pause on his determined journey in shaping his book on America. With the defeat of the Irish Home Rule bill in April 1886 and the fall of
Gladstone's ministry, in which he had served, Bryce could invest all of his efforts in completing his book. En route, he wrote
a long essay for what was then the most important voice of the
new social science in America, *The Johns Hopkins University
Studies in Historical and Political Science*. Appearing in September 1887, the essay carried the arresting title of *The Predictions of Hamilton and de Tocqueville*. Using *The Federalist* and
Democracy in America as the sources for his analysis, Bryce
said his purpose was to find out how far the authors of these
two notable works had been correct in anticipating what had
actually happened in the American republic. While everywhere
respecting the acuity of both men, Bryce showed how significantly they had gone astray in their predictions. Although
Bryce included Hamilton in his analysis, there could be little
doubt that Tocqueville engaged his principal concern. In the essay, Bryce summed up the charges that he and his seminarians
had leveled against Tocqueville four years before.[3]

Why should the historian and the political scientist carefully probe the predictions of such prominent authorities as Hamilton and Tocqueville? To do so, said Bryce, would throw a revealing light on the times in which these men had lived. More than that: by understanding how wrongly such profound political theorists had anticipated the future, we could learn "to temper our self-confidence in judging the phenomena of today." That was really the point Bryce wished to make. His essay conformed to his usual mode of writing: it offered a series of lists. Bryce began with a survey of the American polity in 1787. Depending very largely on *The Federalist,* he cited the predictions of both the opponents and advocates of the new American Constitution. He proceeded to specify the respects in which American life had changed from 1789 to the early 1830s, when Tocqueville had visited the United States. He then listed the salient points of Tocqueville's *Democracy* and, in particular, the prophecies that the notable French writer had ventured to make about the course of the American republic. He concluded with a list of those of Tocqueville's observations that, as Bryce put it, "have ceased to be true" and those of his predictions that were later proven false.[4]

One section of the essay dominated the whole of it. Entitled rather blandly "Tocqueville and His book," it offered the crux of what Bryce found questionable about *Democracy in America.* The Scotsman focused on three major points. First: Tocqueville's portrait of American life was in many respects wrong, because his method of analyzing it was wrong. Second: because his knowledge of English life and institutions was at best limited, Tocqueville had misunderstood the workings of the American polity. What he took to be expressions of America's democracy were in fact expressions of America's Englishness. Finally: Tocqueville's field of vision was so largely, indeed almost exclusively, French that it could not but distort what he saw.[5] We shall be exploring each of these items of Bryce's critique of Tocqueville's *Democracy.* Here were the central grounds on which Bryce confronted his predecessor, both to justify and to validate the important work he was now rushing to complete.

It was a remarkable confrontation: James Bryce versus Alexis de Tocqueville. So much about them seems to have been similar. Was it mere chance that the most profound and rewarding appraisals of American institutions were done by foreigners? Standing outside the pale of the republic's politics and society, they could better grasp its overall design, more objectively comprehend its nature. Aliens in America, they were also aliens in their own countries. Little need be added to what is already known about Tocqueville as an intelligence wandering endlessly between the two worlds he spent his life trying to describe and reconcile: the democratic world, struggling to achieve its ultimate triumph, and the aristocratic world, struggling to stave off that triumph and to retain its own ascendancy. Bryce had gained access to the highest reaches of English political and intellectual society, but the ever-lingering traces of his Scottish speech would be only one reminder that his acculturation was only a cloak over his essence: his Celtic birth and early education, his Presbyterian faith, his middle-class origins, his continuously close ties to his Scottish parents, his endless yearning for the glens and mountains of his native land, and the perennial travels he went on to satisfy that yearning.[6]

They went to America for answers, both for themselves and for their societies. Tocqueville's portrait of two ideals in conflict and of America as the embodiment of democracy was more than the product of his rich intelligence: it was an exercise in autobiography, no less a commentary on himself than on his age. His journey to America was at first a flight. But he understood very early that in explaining the great importance of America to France's rulers, he would be underwriting his own importance in the French world of letters, if not necessarily in Orleanist ruling circles.[7]

Bryce did not go to America to escape. He went not because

England repelled but because America beckoned. He belonged to a generation of the newer intelligentsia, many of whom had gathered at Oxford, who chafed under the existing order of politics and ideas. For Bryce, America was a kindred society. It offered an imposing model of the disestablished polity that he and his fellow radical Liberals would have to ponder in remaking their own. Bryce joined a larger company of English men of letters who were voyaging to the republic across the Atlantic, including individuals such as Arthur Hugh Clough, Leslie Stephen, Goldwin Smith, Matthew Arnold, Herbert Spencer, and, in particular, Albert Venn Dicey, with whom Bryce made his first journey. There was so much about America that attracted Bryce on each of the three journeys he took before writing his *American Commonwealth* that as his letters to his family disclose he regularly considered settling permanently in the United States.[8]

No less than for Tocqueville, Bryce's journey to America was an adventure in self-definition. And for him too it was a journey of ambition. A man nearing fifty, he had in many ways made his mark in English public life. But the station that Tocqueville had gained by virtue of his name and connections, even before the *Democracy* appeared, Bryce had gained by virtue of his persistent and arduous work as a historian, barrister, professor, politician, and writer. In a way that he surely could not have seen too clearly, his book on America would translate him to the highest reaches of his society. But to say that Bryce went to America on a personal adventure would be to miss the point that he was very much a public person and that he was adventuring as a prominent member of the Liberal party and as a distinguished spokesman of the British intelligentsia. No less than Tocqueville, he went to America looking for answers for his country and its problems. More than ever, as Bryce was well aware, the example of America was entering into the bitter controversies that were then raging in Britain over the course the kingdom should take.

All through the nineteenth century, during England's great age of reform, America stood as a model of democracy in operation, to be cited either to condone the virtues of popular government or to condemn its grievous failures. A kindred nation, one that had sprung from the loins of her English motherland, America had a special meaning in the older country's century-long debate over reconstructing her political institutions. That meaning became intense in England's periods of social crisis, and particularly so in the troubled decade of the 1880s. Major changes in the structure of the British polity were succeeding each other with great rapidity. Conflict and confusion immediately preceded the enactment of the Franchise and Redistribution Bills of 1884 and 1885; uncertainty about what they signified for British politics and indeed for the British constitution immediately followed. Bryce voiced his own concern and anxiety in a letter to an American friend:

> The suddenness of our political change here from storm to calm is without precedent but still more wonderful in the acceptance by both parties of this readjustment of seats which imports nothing less than a revolution. Such a topsyturvy among members of Parliament has never been seen before. And just when the impulse to change will be greatest, with a House full of new members, largely Radicals, Mr. Gladstone's influence, the most conservative in the country, will be withdrawn.[9]

That her politics were being further democratized made all the more urgent Britain's quest for instruction from America. Apprehensive about the impact of Britain's new democracy, her governing classes were asking themselves a whole series of questions to which American experience seemed particularly relevant. How far, they wondered, would Britain's broad electorate be able to vote informedly on the issues of the day? What could democratic America teach us about that? Britain's party leaders would surely have to fashion new social policies to respond to the calls of the newly enfranchised classes. To what extent, they asked, could the American example instruct us here? Could Britain, conforming more to her traditions than to her franchise, continue to be a polity of defined social divisions: of classes and masses? What could we learn from America on this question? The advance of political democracy made the House of Lords seem more than ever a vestige of earlier centuries and earlier Englands. Could the American Senate inform us about a more feasible role for a second chamber in the nation's government? Britain's constitution, hitherto so widely respected throughout the Western world, was now being exposed by new popular campaigns to increasingly frequent shocks of radical change. Could we not borrow from America those political institutions that appear to have given her government conservatism and stability? Roiling in her troubles with Ireland, Britain was looking for some device that would afford a solution to her perennial Irish problem. How far could American federalism offer us a serviceable model? Because the balance of continental power shifted dramatically in the 1860s, with immense consequences for world affairs, Britain could no longer hope to continue her hegemony in international politics. How far, and in what way, would we have to reckon with the almost sudden emergence of American power?[10]

Bryce's attempt to answer these questions defined in significant measure the nature and dimensions of his book. True enough, his broad purpose was to inform England and Europe about America. He intended, he wrote Thomas Wentworth Higginson, "to enlighten Englishmen about the institutions of the United States." To another friend in the republic, he explained "how little most Europeans know of many things familiar to every American and how often it is necessary, in order to prevent misconceptions, to re-state a fact or reiterate a view by fresh illustrations." As he contemplated his *Commonwealth*, he said, all of its 116 chapters were "parts of a whole, all connected in my own mind and intended to make the national aspects of American life more intelligible to Europeans."[11] If he had originally thought of a relatively shorter book of information about U.S. institutions, here was reason enough for the book to have grown voluminous: enlightenment, restatement, fresh illustrations, and instruction, in Bryce's careful and comprehensive presentation, filled up pages. As England's myriad problems kept intruding upon the mind of the very prominent Liberal M.P. during the turbulent mid-1880s as he was writing about America, inevitably his book expanded to the measure of the ever-intruding problems.

His book was in effect designed as more than a general compendium of information about America. As he indicated in his opening chapter, he had a more immediate, practical purpose. Over nearly two decades of a deepening knowledge of life in the republic, he had become ever more aware how little England's rulers knew about the details and workings of American politics. In lieu of hard-fisted facts, the men who ran England perceived the transatlantic republic through a mist of misunderstanding, myths, and ignorance. Into their misty view of America entered the axioms they had clung to about democratic or popular government.[12] Bryce's *American Commonwealth* consciously aimed to do two things: First, to give the men who ran Britain a massive introduction to the particulars of American politics in each of its central features: its national government; its state and local governments; its party government; and the role and sway of public opinion. Second, to ascertain for the guidance of England's ruling classes how far American institutions could be used in England. His answer, in sum, was not far at all. This was, as Bryce wanted to make clear, the most important lesson that one could learn from a highly informed and careful study of the democracy across the seas. The task that Bryce undertook was prodigious. He had to free America from the paradigm of democracy, and he had to free England from the paradigm of America. And in doing both he had to free American democracy from the grasp of Alexis de Tocqueville. Here then lay the importance of Tocqueville for Bryce.

How indeed could one contemplate America without also contemplating Tocqueville? The young French aristocrat had internationalized the discourse on democracy and the resonance of America. He had written for France, but he was particularly revelant to England. If this had been true in the 1830s and 1840s in the years of Wellington and Grey, it was even more true in the 1870s and 1880s in the years of Disraeli and Gladstone. England's new democracy seemed every bit as threatening as parliamentary reform had in the 1830s and as Chartism had in the 1840s. That it was now a time of creeping Chartism and that the franchise reforms of 1867 and 1884 had come in virtually under Tory sanction made the dangers of democracy no less insidious to the men who had gladly subscribed to the Victorian compromise. Democracy's new vitality aroused again Tocqueville's message, both about its dangers and about America as a view of its future. Because the premises of English society were once again being challenged, it was time for a Bryce. And because the American model was being appealed to, it was again time for Tocqueville. Bryce did not write the *Commonwealth* merely to question the *Democracy*. His motives were practical and immediate. But having decided that a democratizing England urgently needed a manual of instruction about America, Bryce could nowhere avoid the man who had written Europe's American primer.[13]

There was much that was similar about the two men and their works. Their own lives had pushed, indeed almost swept them to the American shore. The agitated times they lived in did more than try their souls: they galvanized their intelligence. Their books were essays in comparative analysis. They were manuals of instruction for the ruling classes of their respective countries. And in this sense, however widely their authors ranged, however deeply they probed the workings of the human polity, both books were tracts for their times.

But however comparable, Bryce's *Commonwealth* and Tocqueville's *Democracy* were very different works. That they spoke for different times, different polities, different problems immediately suggests the ways they differed. Tocqueville was trying to understand the new age of democratic revolutions, the civil war in each continental polity between the forces of aristocracy and democracy. Bryce wrote in a world where aristocracy had long since come to terms with democracy, and where democratization was no longer a revolution but a process. Seeing democracy in its widest dimensions, Tocqueville had written a study of society and politics, one that is correctly classified as "political sociology." Bryce's purview was more limited. Because it was part of his purpose to disconnect politics from society, his book centered very largely on America's political institutions. But Tocqueville's *Democracy* was at every point the explicit pursuit of a single idea: how liberty could be preserved in a regime of democracy, with particular reference to the American experience. His book detailed his personal adventure in exploring this idea. At times his *Democracy* reads like the ordered steps of proving a geometric theorem. Bryce wrote his *American Commonwealth* as a massive compendium of information. Its three volumes ran over fifteen hundred pages, packed tightly with almost countless details. Turning from one aspect of his exposition to another, Bryce gave his readers long lists of details about the institutions and workings of American politics. To his mind, his facts were precisely his theme.

Bryce's *Commonwealth* was far from being a uniformly negative commentary on Tocqueville's *Democracy*. Everywhere respecting the venerable Frenchman's perception and authority, Bryce wished however to challenge Tocqueville on the major themes that figured centrally in his own extensive study of the

United States. In seeking to analyze these themes, I shall address the following questions. What, according to Bryce, were the three highly controvertible premises of Tocqueville's study of American democracy? How did Bryce seek to refute each of these premises? Because Bryce wished no less than Tocqueville to seek instruction in the American polity, what lessons did he believe that one could validly find there? What conditions in the English social politics of the 1880s explain Bryce's challenges of Tocqueville's premises, as well as the lessons Bryce found for England in America? In the answer to these questions we shall come up with a further sense of the dimensions of each work and of the special meaning and importance of Bryce's great work on *The American Commonwealth*.

TO CALL *Democracy in America* into question, Bryce knew exactly where he had to begin: with Tocqueville's method. Several of the points that Tocqueville made about American democracy, said Bryce, "were true of America, but not of democracy in general, while others were true of democracy in general, but, not true of America." What was wrong with Tocqueville were the premises of his inquiry.[14]

In his essay on "Hamilton and Tocqueville," Bryce laid out his charge against those premises. The great French author had, in sum, studied America deductively. His view of the transatlantic republic had been filtered through certain axioms that he had held a priori. Indeed, asked Bryce, had he not granted as much in that famous sentence of his introduction. "I admit that I saw in America more than America; it was the shape of democracy itself which I sought." Seeing the democratic revolution as by far the most salient aspect of his own age, he was looking for the essence of democracy. It seemed to him that that essence could be found most clearly in the United States. Like Plato, he wished to distill the ideal of a polity, discarding from the ideal what he considered to be fortuitous. Thus, it was not democracy in America that he presented, "but his own theoretic view of democracy illustrated from America." Many of his chapters begin with a few large principles about democracy, which lead him to certain conclusions; in the process, he cites a few examples from the American experience that sustain these conclusions. The problem with Tocqueville's *Democracy* was that it was an exercise in deductive logic. He proceeded from preconceptions and prepossessions. He defined America in terms of his intuitions, selecting only those aspects of life in the United States that would "point and enforce propositions he has already reached." Indeed, said Bryce, Tocqueville pushed his premises too far. His book on America was in this sense a venture in scholasticism. However astute a man he was, however brilliant his *aperçus,* he had in many respects written a book of impressions and speculations. *Democracy in America* was "really a work of art quite as much as of science."[15]

In 1887, Bryce's critique of Tocqueville's *Democracy* lay almost covert within the scholarly confines of his article in the Johns Hopkins *Studies.* A year later he broadcast that critique to a large world of readers on both sides of the Atlantic in the opening pages of *The American Commonwealth.* He immediately noted that the only author with whom his own work invited comparison was Alexis de Tocqueville, whose masterpiece had appeared half-a-century before. And announcing that he had conceived his subject differently, Bryce no less immediately reiterated his questions about Tocqueville's conception. To the French political philosophers, America had stood out primarily as a democracy, indeed "the ideal democracy." Tocqueville's chef-d'oeuvre was therefore not actually a descriptive account of American life but "a treatise . . . upon democracy, a treatise whose conclusions are illustrated from America, but are founded, not so much on an analysis of American phenomena, as on general and somewhat speculative views of democracy which circumstances of France had suggested." As for himself, said Bryce, he had "striven to avoid the temptations of the deductive method." His own extended journeys to America had convinced him of the dangers of ready inferences. The observations he had formulated on his first trip he largely scrapped on his second; and these in turn he significantly modified on his third. He was very wary of ready-made theories. "I have striven . . . to present simply the facts of the case, arranging and connecting them as best I can, but letting them speak for themselves rather than pressing upon the reader my own conclusions."[16]

One had to begin at the beginning. Did it not becloud whatever understanding one might glean from America to label her a democracy? Nomenclature obscured understanding. What's in a name? For Tocqueville, thought Bryce, everything. In the New World, the French aristocrat had by his own avowal been looking more for a political type than an actual country. How could one perceive the true nature of American democracy if one emphasized far more that it was a democracy than that it was America? True enough, Tocqueville had been careful to try to separate the essence of American democracy from those accidental elements that had entered into the American environment. But his Platonism had let him to ascribe too little in America to anything but democracy.

This is why Bryce preferred to call America a commonwealth rather than a particular type of a polity. He did not decide on a title for his book until the very last weeks before its publication; he resisted the suggestion that he name it "the American republic." The word commonwealth was more comprehensive: it denoted a genus rather than a species, and it addressed the purport of a polity rather than its form. The idea of a commonwealth, in Bryce's perspective, suggested the continuing discourse about *civitas* that had engaged the great ancient and medieval minds and that had taken on a special meaning in the revolutionary England of the seventeenth century: in the England, that is, of Hooker, Hobbes, Harrington, and Locke. A commonwealth, to Bryce, denoted a polity whose society and goals were clearly commendable. In designating America a democracy, Tocqueville had, as Bryce saw it, transmuted form into essence. It could not have been more clear from Bryce's opening statement about the purpose and substance of his work that calling America a democracy would precisely vitiate his purpose and substantively misrepresent what he thought America really was. Tocqueville had been wrong to reduce all of American life to a political genre. "Democratic government seems to me, with all deference to his high authority," said Bryce, making his ritualistic bow to Tocqueville, "a cause not so potent in the moral and social sphere as he deemed it: and my object has been . . . to paint the institutions and people as they are."[17] In Tocqueville's age, democratic government was rare, and America clearly represented its most important expression. In Bryce's age, democracy was a spreading phenomenon, and America merely one instance of popular government. To understand the real meaning of America for Britain, which was Bryce's prime concern, he had to make clear her identity as America, rather than as a type of democracy.

We could not learn what the transatlantic republic had to teach, said Bryce, if instead of seeing America we saw democracy. From naming it a democracy, we proceeded to invest it with all the attributes that have been ascribed to a democratic polity. The danger lay in our falling into a nominative trap. We then argued from the paradigm of democracy rather than from its actuality. The great writers of political science had long since set up this paradigm, warning us about the dangers of democracy. Philosophers "from Plato downward to Mr. Robert Lowe, and popular writers repeating and caricaturing the dicta of philosophers, have attributed to democratic governments" a whole set of serious flaws (3:305). What were these flaws? Bryce listed them in one of the most important chapters of his book, one that he very pointedly entitled "The Supposed Faults of Democracy." The flaws included weakness and incapacity to act promptly, fickleness and instability, contempt for authority, a passion for destroying old institutions, and the influence of demagogues. He examined each of these in turn, showing that in fact none of them was true of the actual workings of American government (3:chap. 94).

Two of the dangers generally ascribed to democracy drew Bryce's special attention: the desire of a democratic people to bring everyone down to the same level, and the tendency of the majority to exert its tyranny over the minority. The charge that the citizens of a democracy wish to level down, said Bryce,

> derives a claim to respectful consideration from the authority of De Tocqueville, who thought it a necessary attribute of democracy, and professed to have discovered symptoms of it in the United States. It alarmed J. S. Mill, and has been frequently dwelt on by his disciples, and by many who have adopted no other part of his teachings, as an evil equally inevitable and fatal in democratic countries. (3:315)

Even granting that there may have been some basis for expressing this fear over half-a-century ago, the charge, said Bryce, could not be sustained by the facts of American life in the 1880s. Neither indeed could the charge that the American majority exercised a "wanton and improper use of strength" over those with whom it differed. The real problem with American democracy was not that the majority was tyrannical but that its individual citizens had a fatalistic sense about their will or disposition to differ with the expressed desire of the majority. Again, Tocqueville did not accurately understand the actuality of American democracy. "One is inclined to suspect," said Bryce, "that . . . struck by the enormous power of public opinion, [he] may have attributed too much of the submissiveness which he observed to the active coercion of the majority, and too little to that tendency of the minority to acquiescence."[18]

Whatever the deficiencies of the American polity, they were, in sum, not those that traditional philosophy had placed at the door of democracy. The fact was that traditional philosophy was alive and well in Bryce's England. Every time extending the franchise came under discussion, as it did all through the nineteenth century, the classic arguments about the dangers of democracy were rehearsed. England's statesmen knew much Latin and more Greek. And they also knew Tocqueville, whose book served as an object lesson not in the advantages of democracy but in its dangers. Who could forget the passion with which Sir Robert Peel, arguing against extending the franchise in Britain, had fairly universalized Tocqueville's warnings against "the tyranny of the majority"? In Bryce's day, particularly in the debates of the 1860s and 1880s over extending the suffrage, the perils of popular government were again sounded. There was a vast legion of Victorian critics of democracy, among the most prominent of whom stood W.E.H. Lecky and Sir Henry Maine.[19]

If Bryce's masterpiece had any single purpose, it was to wrench the United States out of the paradigm of democracy. Indeed, he wished to crack the paradigm itself. Where Tocqueville saw regularities, he saw exceptions. Where Tocqueville found a model, he found divergences. What defined a polity for Bryce was precisely its particularities. And in this way, a polity was far more than the sum of those particularities. Its essence lay in its uniqueness and its differences. In suggesting this, Bryce came up with what was in effect a counterparadigm and his own idea about what political science could properly try to do. His counterparadigm, which was of course his creation of a new model, depended very largely on what he considered lay at the heart of the newer political science of his own age: what he called "the laws of political biology." The inspiration for these laws he found in many sources, but above all in the teachings of Charles Darwin, which had an enormous influence on Bryce's ideas.[20]

If Bryce's laws of political biology were sanctioned by Darwin, their purpose was to dissuade the leaders of British politics from appealing to the forms and practices of popular government in the United States. From different groups in Britain were coming clamorous cries for emulating the American example: for converting the House of Lords into an American senate, for paying the members of the House of Commons, for scrapping the monarchy and setting up a republic, for making further constitutional changes extremely difficult, for vesting the judiciary with powers to safeguard the constitution, for setting up a quasi-federal arrangement of jurisdiction and power, for completely separating the established churches from the state.

To all these groups Bryce issued a stern caveat, one that he sounded in the opening paragraphs of *The American Commonwealth* and voiced again and again through its 116 chapters and more than sixteen hundred pages:

> Direct inferences from the success or failure of a particular constitutional arrangement or political usage in another country are rarely sound, because the conditions differ in so many respects that there can be no certainty that what flourishes or languishes under other skies and in another soul will likewise flourish or languish in our own. Many an American institution would bear a different fruit if transplanted to England. . . . Now and then we may directly claim transatlantic experience as accrediting or discrediting some specific constitutional device or the policy of some enactment. But even in these cases he who desires to rely on the results shown in America must satisfy himself that there is such a parity of conditions and surroundings in respect of the particular matter as justifies him in reasoning directly from ascertained results there to probable results in his own country. (1:11–12)

So if America was full of instruction for Europe, it had to be taken with the greatest care. This is what Bryce meant by "the laws of political biology." Transplant at your own risk. The warning phrase was *ceteris paribus*. But other things were very rarely, if ever, equal.[21]

Conceived in a Darwinian environment, Bryce's laws of political biology were not merely post-Tocquevillean, they were anti-Tocquevillean. It was basic to these laws that human life and institutions had evolved from homogeneity to heterogeneity. To see them correctly, one had to be right about one's premises of inquiry. One had to avoid the many traps of easy or convenient argument. Those who made facile comparisons between English and American institutions should be alive to the dangers of historical analogies. So too should those who made their case by a priori reasoning. Questionable analogies and specious reasoning were hardly the basis for understanding, let alone remaking, a polity's institutions (1:11; 3:487).

Bryce's case against Tocqueville grew out of his case against so many of his own contemporaries. It was perforce substantive and adjective, and practiced barrister that he was, Bryce had long known that the one was a dimension of the other. That he was also a highly trained historian and political scientist made him keenly alive to problems of method and the use of evidence. Certain error lay ahead for those who neglect "that critical examination of the premises from which every process of reasoning ought to start" (3:487). Bryce's study of America arose out of needs that were immediate, practical, and in a word that he so much liked to use, "edificatory." To dissuade his contemporaries from their ready recourse to the American model, he had to center on Tocqueville. He had to throw into question the argument from paradigms, the use of a democratic typology, the recourse to a priori reasoning, indeed the predictions grounded on what he considered to be so insecure a method of reasoning. That was the first of his basic charges against Tocqueville's *Democracy* and the one with which he surely had to begin. In an obvious sense, it was probably the most important.

MORE THAN Tocqueville's method lay open to question, said Bryce. The second major charge he leveled against the notable Frenchman was that he did not know England well enough to understand how English were the Americans. Granted that, although he was a foreigner, Tocqueville had a most creditable command of English history and even of English society. Yet for all that, he had failed to perceive "the substantial identity of the American people with the English." And, for all the years he spent studying democracy in America, what escaped him was perhaps the most revealing insight of all: "the truth that the American people is the English people."[22]

Bryce spelled out the details of his charge. Tocqueville was not really familiar with the workings of English politics and laws. How therefore could he appreciate that what he took to be American legal inventions were in fact applications of basic premises of English law? This, for example, was true of the coexistence of similar laws operating at different levels of jurisdiction and of the role of American judges in establishing the constitutionality of the statutes of the federal or state governments. But what had escaped Tocqueville was something far more serious. He had, Bryce readily granted, a close acquaintanceship with England's aristocracy and with her men of letters. But what he really did not know was "the ideas and habits of the English middle class," which in fact ran very close to those of the Americans. In sum, said Bryce "much that is merely English appears to Tocqueville to be American or Democratic."[23]

These were the points Bryce made in his 1887 essay on Tocqueville. They figured much less prominently in *The American Commonwealth*, which appeared the following year. He took them as givens. It was precisely his point not to write a book of theses and axioms about the United States as he felt

Tocqueville had done. But one can discover readily enough the elements of Bryce's argument, which he adroitly introduced at certain important points of his analysis of the American polity. The American polity was basically English in its laws and in the values of its people, and whoever interpreted American life without this understanding could only end up with misunderstanding and misinterpretation.

To grasp the real character of American law, Bryce insisted, one had to go back to its origins. Here is why, although disavowing any desire to write about the American past, he began his great work with two chapters that presented the historical context of America's legal and constitutional system. The men who drew up the constitution of 1787 did not experiment in new ways and with new doctrines. They followed the patterns of their state and colonial governments. But those in turn led them to "the British Constitution [which] became a model for the new national government. They held England to be the freest and best-governed country in the world" (1:42). What else had bound the colonies together but the English matrix and English common law? Between them there was no other political connection than the fact that they belonged to "the great free British realm . . . so that the inhabitants of each enjoyed in every one of the others the rights and privileges of British subjects" (1:22–23). They went to Montesquieu as the oracle of their political philosophy, accepting fully his idea that the English constitution was a model of liberty and balanced government (1:36). One can trace many features of American constitutional practice back to its English sources, said Bryce, and regularly find that Americans had adopted for themselves the "priceless heritage of the English Common Law, which the colonies carried with them across the sea, and which they have preserved and developed in a manner worthy of its own free spirit and lofty traditions" (1:345).

How far was it true, as Tocqueville would have had us believe, that the Americans were inventors and innovators, that they had devised a new set of institutions for their new world? Certainly not so far as their constitutions and laws were concerned, answered Bryce. They were "at bottom a conservative people, in virtue both of the deep instincts of their race and of that practical shrewdness which recognizes the value of permanence and solidity in institutions." To rightly understand their laws, one had to begin by understanding that the spirit of the men who drafted the constitution of 1787 was "an English spirit . . . which desired to walk in the old paths of precedent, which thought of government as means of maintaining order and securing to every one his rights, rather than as a great ideal power, capable of guiding and developing a nation's life." In effect, Bryce was saying, the principle of American liberty was a direct English inheritance, one that rested remotely if at all on the New England township, which Tocqueville had made virtually the centerpiece of his construct of American freedom. Bryce added one important corollary to his axiom about the conservatism of the Americans: it was a product of long schooling. The men of 1787 "had the experience of the English constitution." And, therefore, whatever degree of success the generations that followed them achieved in operating the American Constitution "must be in a large measure ascribed to the political genius, ripened by long experience, of the Anglo-American race by whom it has been worked."[24]

What made the Americans English was more than their laws, Bryce explained. It was their common ethnicity. This is the sense in which he used the word "race," one that regularly occurs in nineteenth-century English writing. What were the features of this shared ethnicity of the Americans and the English? Their conservatism, said Bryce, expressed their basic instincts. "A love for what is old and established is in their English blood." Their political institutions, very largely of English origins, gave them "the pride of forming part of the English race and the great free British realm." Sentimental forces bound the Americans to each other and to the English. They loved local independence and self-government and they shared no less "the sense of community in blood, in language, in habits and ideas." What, after all, were the constituent elements of which the American nation was formed? With some exceptions, they spoke the same language. They belonged to the same race. They professed the Protestant religion. They ran their politics and property under the same English common law. They had the experience of the English constitution. Their centuries-old practice in these laws gave them a trained shrewdness in the workings of legal institutions. How else, apart from this English legacy and ethnicity, could one explain the remarkable ability of the Americans to overcome the difficulties their constitution often threw before them? This is what Bryce concluded: "The devices which we often admire in the [American] Constitution might prove unworkable among a people less patriotic and self-reliant, less law-loving and law-abiding, than the English of America."[25]

That last phrase bears repeating: "the English of America." One can hardly sense how Bryce perceived the role of English ethnicity in American life unless one also considers what he thought of the non-English. He did not often speak of them, but when he did, his words turned from paean to lament. The most memorable of his chapters considered "why the best men did not go into politics (2:chap. 58)." Clearly, the best men were his American friends, who were very largely of English descent and who had supplied him, on his successive trips to the United States, with most of the information that filled the pages of his book. They constituted in sum the eastern establishment: its college and university presidents, its notable clergymen, its financial leaders, its reputable politicians, its journalists, editors, and novelists, and those who formed the upper echelons of its society. To be English, for Bryce, was no guarantee of respectability. Yet it was nothing fortuitous that his respectable Americans were largely those with an English genealogy, and that those who lacked a proper respectability tended also to lack the proper genealogy.

In Bryce's family tree, not all non-English were questionable, but those who were questionable were almost all non-English. Two groups in particular impressed him as ill-suited for democratic politics, and they could be found by and large in America's cities. These were, first, the teeming hordes of immigrants and, second, those great clusters of the lower classes whom Bryce called (using an English term) "the residuum." Predominant in both groups were the Irish and the Germans. If the residuum was uncertainly qualified for the workings of popular government in America, the immigrants were certainly unqualified. In his own age, when the shortcomings of America's party system and of her urban politics were scandalizing informed public opinion on both sides of the Atlantic, Bryce felt it imperative to find the roots of the failure in what he considered, in effect, to be a failed ethnicity (3:71–73).

But his concern went far beyond that. He was again reproving Tocqueville, and doing so by means of a strategem that impresses one as nothing less than highly adroit, if not indeed brilliant. It will be recalled that Tocqueville, in one of the most important chapters of the *Democracy*, had argued that three factors explained the continuing success of American liberal democracy. These were America's laws, America's mores, and certain accidental or providential causes. The adroitness of Bryce's stratagem was that he worked within the framework of Tocqueville's formula. He translated each of Tocqueville's terms from American into English. At the very beginning of *The American Commonwealth*, on that important page in which he laid out his differences with Tocqueville, Bryce insisted that the unique character of America could be ascribed not so much to its democratic government as to its Englishness. Or, as he put it: "to the history and traditions of the race, to [the race's] fundamental ideas, to its material environment"

(1:5). Elsewhere in *The American Commonwealth*, in discussing the federal system, Bryce again borrowed Tocqueville's formulas but reached his own conclusions. America's laws could not fully explain the success of federalism in the United States. It succeeded because of the nation's mores. After all, asked Bryce, in sensible Latin: *Quid leges sine moribus?* What are laws without mores? "They are," said Bryce, "moral and material influences stronger than any political devices (1:474)." And what had ensured the success of these devices other than precisely the moral qualities and mental habits of "the English of America?" Wherever Tocqueville found American innovations, Bryce found borrowings from the English.

Tocqueville had made American laws and mores the building materials of his grand construct of democratic society. By anglicizing both the laws and the mores, Bryce once again challenged the construct. Said Bryce: "Democratic government seems to me, with all deference to his high authority, a cause" not so potent in the moral and social sphere as he deemed it (1:5). Of course, that was not quite what Tocqueville had said. He did not see government as cause, and morals and society as consequence, but rather all three as part of a larger integer. Still, the sum of it was that where Tocqueville saw a fundamentally new society for the new age, Bryce saw an essentially English society transplanted and adapted. By changing its terms, Bryce subverted Tocqueville's formula.

Why was Bryce so intent on anglicizing the Americans and, in effect, on questioning Tocqueville's ideas about democracy? There were many reasons why, and they arose largely from the fact that Bryce was speaking for a later age and for another society. Two of these reasons warrant our attention at this point. Bryce wished to allay English fears. And he wished to support the growing Pan-Anglian movement.

The fears of certain elements of England's governing classes and intelligentsia stirred excitedly in the early 1880s during the debate over extending the franchise. The reform bills of 1884 and 1885 greatly advanced the movement toward democracy that had begun in 1832, each decade witnessing an increasing infusion of popular government into the English constitution. The spectre of democracy was surely haunting conservative minds; and to the degree that it could be incarnated, it lived in American government. Tocqueville had been democracy's admonishing prophet, if hardly its warm advocate. But what were his admonitions became their anxieties. Bryce's intent was to calm these anxieties with facts, history, reason and, in sum, reassurance. In frenetically seizing upon Tocqueville's model of American democracy, he suggested, the conservatives had failed to distinguish between what was American and what was democratic. The image of democracy they had invoked was a product of their invention, one that existed "only in the fancy of alarmist philosophers." But, as Bryce had carefully argued once before in urging the passage of the reform bill of 1867, the opponents of democracy had erroneously read the history of polities that they subsumed under that label in order to condemn the form altogether. They were no more correct in perceiving American democracy in the 1880s than they had been two decades before.[26]

In part, Tocqueville was responsible for the conservatives' alarm, because he had presented the American's essential traits (which, to say the least, opponents of democracy nowhere found alluring) as those of *homo democraticus*. But how, asked Bryce, would troubled English minds respond if they could more correctly understand *homo americanus* in the perspective of his origins and culture for what he really was: a variant form of *homo anglicanus*? Abandoning Tocquevillean abstractions would lead them to grasp the significance for the English polity of the fact that Americans were, in fact, of "English blood" and that they carried the basic sentiments of "their race." What it signified, said Bryce, was that the men of the republic loved their legacy and tradition, that "they did not seek change for the sake of change," that they were "conservative in their fundamental beliefs, in the structure of their governments, in their social and domestic usages." Beware simple historical analogies and simple political typologies, Bryce advised those of his countrymen who quivered before the franchise reforms of the mid-1880s. And what he spelled out explicitly conveyed an obvious implication. If *homo americanus* could hardly be classified as a Tocquevillean democrat, how much less so could *homo anglicanus*. Walter Bagehot's explanation of why the English constitution had continued to function smoothly in increasingly democratic times appeared yet to be valid: "England was a deferential country," and the electors, "influenced by rank and wealth," still responded to the direction of their "betters." This was surely so, said Bryce, with respect to the most important single force shaping the conduct of popular government: public opinion. In England, the opinions of the classes continued to guide those of the masses. Here was England's further guarantee against the recent electoral reforms: "though the Constitution has become democratic, the habits of the nation are still aristocratic."[27]

One can see, then, the importance for Bryce of underscoring the Englishness of the American democrat. By trying to rescue America from typology, Bryce was trying to rescue England from anxiety. Because their apprehension was misfounded, the conservatives who helped rule England had nothing to fear but fear itself. In the workings of the transatlantic republic, ethnicity counted no less than democracy. By insisting on the Englishness of the Americans, Bryce hoped to show that the new English world was safe not only for democracy but also from it.

In Tocqueville's configuration, America's laws and mores formed the essence of her democracy. But what if those laws and mores inhered not so much in America's democracy as in her Englishness? The question was particularly important for those who were invoking Tocqueville during the 1880s in England's roiling debates over popular government. Indeed, if

Tocqueville had failed to see that what he called the democratic mores of America were in fact the middle-class values of the English, then were there not serious questions not only about his paradigm of democracy but even more significantly about its relevance to England? Bryce's practical intent was this: by making America more of an England, he made her less of a democracy, and surely less of an object lesson on how to address the problems of popular government. Conversely, he made England more of an America: more of a polity, that is, where enduring laws and popular mores would permit the society to move steadily and conservatively during its trials.

In stressing America's Englishness, Bryce did more than question Tocqueville's model of democracy and sustain the way the English polity was working. He also voiced the ideals of the Pan-Anglian movement. Pan-Anglianism articulated the growing sense on both sides of the Atlantic, in the latter decades of the nineteenth century, that England and America were members of a larger community of ideas and institutions: political, ethnic, and cultural. They were, indeed, kindred nations. The Pan-Anglians were a small but vocal and powerful fraternity of key individuals in both nations: primarily their intelligentsia, but also their polititians, jurists, financiers, and clergymen. They commanded central positions in their respective nation's colleges and universities and its newspapers and journals of politics and literature. In Britain, they gravitated to Liberalism, a fact that prompted R. W. Gilder, the editor of the *Century Magazine*, to hail the Liberal triumph of 1906 as the advent to power of the "friends of America." In America, their politics tended to be Liberal Republican, Mugwump, or Progressive. The friends of Britain in America were very largely the friends of James Bryce: the men and women with whom he continuously corresponded, whom he regularly visited on his trips to the United States, and who supplied him with the intelligences that framed his *Commonwealth*. Their message, however variously stated, had one major theme: that, whatever issues had divided the two nations during the first century of America's independence, the time had now come for rapprochement and interdependence. Pan-Anglianism welled out of the deeper currents of social politics in each of the kindred nations and out of the international conflicts each was confronting. At the time of the Spanish-American War, George Haven Putnam, a prominent American publisher, wrote Bryce that "whether the relations with England take the shape of an understanding, or possibly at some later date of an alliance, it seems certain that the antagonism surviving the War of 1812, and the frictions of 1861–1862, have been outgrown, finally and forever." During the recurrent international crises of the ensuing years, Theodore Roosevelt avowed that, "as regards the British Empire and the United States, I am a dreamer of dreams." He hoped for "some kind of intimate association" among the English-speaking peoples.[28]

No one expressed the Pan-Anglian idea more clearly than Bryce. Addressing an American friend as he was putting the finishing touches to his great work, in effect disclosing the sentiment that had inspired it, Bryce wrote:

> Great Britain and the United States are natural allies; that is to say, each is held to the other by the natural ties of a common blood and speech, a common literature, a common love of freedom, as well as of common material interests, ties far stronger than those which draw either country to any foreign power. It is therefore of the utmost consequence to the welfare and prosperity of both, and important to the world also, which is interested in their peace and in the strength of the moral influence which they exert, that there should prevail a complete good feeling and cordiality between them.[29]

Bryce's intent as a Pan-Anglian was precisely to reverse the animus between England and America that had so impressed Tocqueville in the 1830s and to enhance the binational sentiment of rapprochement that was expanding in the 1880s. He wished to repatriate America. He wished to bring her back into the fold of the English-speaking peoples. His purpose was nowhere parochial. He did not wish to expand England's domain. His Pan-Anglian vision embraced an ethnic community in which both great nations figured as equals. By virtue of their advanced ideals and institutions, he hoped they would also figure as leaders of the transatlantic world around them.

IF TOCQUEVILLE knew England too little, said Bryce, he knew France too much. That was not quite the way Bryce put it, in directing the third of his major charges against the author of the *Democracy*. Tocqueville saw things American in French terms, Bryce stated. Thus, for example, he was surprised at the way Americans used associations as an integral part of their political activity. He was no less surprised at the practice of American legislatures of attempting different experiments in legislation. The practice ran against the workings of French law, which bore the heavy stamp of immutability put upon it by the Napoleonic code. However much he understood that he could hardly "assume the ways and ideas of his own country to be the rule," he was inclined to do so. Even in Tocqueville, said Bryce in a remarkable metaphor, "the tendency lurks." Preoccupied as he was with his own country, he took to be irregular or particularly distinctive those American features that stood in contrast to "the circumstances of France." He regarded as abnormal those things which were "merely un-French." For Tocqueville, France was the immediate "background of every picture whose foreground was the New World."[30]

The reason this was so, Bryce explained, could be found in the essential nature and aim of the *Democracy*. The great work on America was "not so much a political study as a work of edification." Tocqueville himself had declared as much in his famous introduction: "I wished to find lessons in America by

which our own country might profit." He had written a book
of warnings and exhortations. America had much to teach, and
France had much to learn. As Bryce paraphrased Tocqueville's
message, it was that France needed "to adjust her political institutions to her social condition, and above all to improve the
tone of her politics, to create a moral and religious basis for her
national life, to erect a new fabric of social doctrine, in the
place of that which, already crumbling, the Revolution had
overthrown."[31]

Both terms of Bryce's charge against Tocqueville's work
were of course related. The young aristocrat had gone to America to seek instruction for his homeland and what could he
carry in his luggage but French premises and French purposes?
Indeed, Tocqueville virtually conceded the validity of Bryce's
charge not merely by that opening avowal in the *Democracy*
that he was looking for instruction in America but also by the
confession that he made to his friend Count Louis de Kergolay: "Though I seldom mentioned France, I did not write a
page without thinking of her."[32] In the light of this, Bryce's
point must be granted. If the *Democracy's* frame of reference
was French, and its purpose moral and didacatic, then its accuracy as a portrait of American institutions and ideas could be
said to have had certain limitations.

But what is striking about Bryce's critique of the *Democracy*—indictment would probably be too strong a word—is
that is could be leveled against *The American Commonwealth*
as well. Bryce had conscientiously tried to avoid the errors that,
he believed, seriously marred Tocqueville's work. Their two introductions are a study in contrasts. Tocqueville declared that
he was looking for instruction. Bryce, on the other hand, said he
wished to resist lessons in general and Tocqueville's in particular. He preferred, so he said, to let the facts speak for themselves. And one imagined, looking at the sixteen-hundred
tightly packed pages, that this prodigious encyclopedia of facts
would surely, if not quite speak for themselves, then at least

permit the reader to arrive at an informed judgment. That Bryce believed he had fairly successfully stepped aside for the facts was evident from a letter he wrote his mother a few months after the *Commonwealth* appeared. Many hailed him for his impartiality and for his avoiding to indicate his own feelings on basic questions. "In fact," said Bryce, "this detachment never cost me any trouble or even thought at all: it came of itself without any exertion." For himself, he had doubted "any merit for the book beyond that of a careful collection of relevant facts." But whatever his stated intention, and whatever sense he had of having been impartial, the truth was that Bryce everywhere intruded upon his facts.[33]

It is not too difficult to see how Bryce too came to write a book of instruction and perforce of the personal premises that framed the instruction. For himself, no less than for Tocqueville, the question was how to reform his polity in an age of social turbulence. For both, democracy was the only possible guarantee against continuing domestic upheaval and, indeed, revolution. America stood just as prominently as the principal model of democracy in Bryce's age as she had in Tocqueville's. Bryce put this very well in one of the concluding chapters of his book: "The question which in one form or another every European politician has during the last half-century been asking about the United States is the broad question, How does democracy answer?" (3:304) To this, Bryce gave a highly qualified response. Democracy in America had succeeded despite itself, he said, indeed in the face of everything that one would consider to be the democratic essence.

That essence consisted of a feasible tie between the rationale of democracy and the means for fulfilling it. As a form of polity, for Bryce as well as for Tocqueville, democracy was government by the people and for the people. Both agreed that running the polity for the widespread advantage of all classes of society was decidedly preferable to running it for the greater advantage of a single class. But how should this be done? In

Bryce's age, there were two principal ways of doing it: England's cabinet government and America's presidential or congressional government. There was little question, as he saw it, about which was the more desirable. "The English system is the model for nearly all of Europe," said Bryce. The reason was that "cabinet government fuses the legislative and the executive functions of government" (1:369–370). This fusion effectuated government and rationalized democracy. For him, government by the people was far from being persuasive unless it could also act as government for the people; unless, that is, it could practicably translate into social programs the regularly registered preferences of the electorate. This English government did, and American government did not do.

American political institutions were seriously flawed. Most problematic was the uncoupling of two basic functions of government: the executive and the legislative, that is, formulating and administering policy and passing the laws that embody that policy. In this respect, the Americans failed to solve the greatest problem facing free peoples: "how to enable the citizens at large to conduct or control the executive business of the state." Far from working in concert, as did the major branches of English government, those in America were almost perennially in conflict. The divorce of power from policy making was as true of the government of the states as it was of the nation. The idea of federalism articulated the principle of diffusing power even further. And whereas, in England, parties were primarily advocates of significantly different social programs and therefore agents of unified action, in America they served no such purpose. They were private organizations, primarily concerned with getting the spoils of office. Unaffiliated to party programs, undirected by party leaders, law-making in the United States lacked consistency, just as national policies lacked continuity. Nor did it help to vitalize American democracy that the republic's "best men," as Bryce called them, did not go into politics. Men of great talent, who in England naturally gravitated to the House of Commons, sought other outlets for their abilities in the United States.[34] What was the result of all this? Bryce gives us this summary:

> There is in the American government, considered as a whole, a want of unity. Its branches are unconnected; their efforts are not directed to one aim, do not produce one harmonious result. . . . There is a loss of force by friction . . . such powers as exist act with little concert and resign themselves to a conscious impotence. (1:391)

If he found their democracy to be very questionable, Bryce understood that the Americans had fashioned it to their own measurements. They builded as well as they knew. The men of 1787, the conventioneers as he called them, confected a special brand of government, one that expressed their deepest convictions. They distrusted power and the agencies of power. They followed Montesquieu's reading of the English constitution, believing that liberty can thrive only where despotic power cannot. They took a strongly Puritanical view of human nature, basing their government "on the theology of Calvin and the philosophy of Hobbes." The government they fashioned, said Bryce, was "the least democratic of democracies." With these premises as their guide, they devised a wide variety of ways and means to contain the excesses of power. A century after these devices had been welded into the structure of American government, we can see, said Bryce, how artificial and questionable they are. We can surely see how they contradict, indeed violate, the rationale and workings of modern democracy (1:407–408).

Bryce's *American Commonwealth* is a detailed analysis of American political institutions. It is no less a detailed list of their shortcomings. Bryce takes his readers from one aspect of American government to the next on a carefully guided tour in infeasibility. Congress, for example, legislates ineffectively. In terms of the criteria by which one may judge the quality of law-making, says Bryce, one would have to conclude that Congress makes laws poorly. The handling of one of the most important items of American affairs—national finance—was, in a word, "unfortunate." Without a close link between the executive and the legislature and without an effective way of questioning the permanent officials who knew most about the nation's income and expenditures, American financial policy was at bottom inadequately conceived and ineffectively managed.[35]

Looking at the system in the large, Bryce found the whole construct of American government basically marred. Equal in power, the two houses of Congress were in perennial conflict. The presidency was a questionably conceived office, all the more so because the president and Congress were so poorly linked. What was true of the American Congress was true of the American presidency: because their roles were poorly conceived, their functioning was largely impaired. This impairment was in essence duplicated in the governments of the states, which rested on similar premises. And the whole nation's capacity to pursue an organized social policy was further encumbered by the American federal system, which again splintered and disintegrated power. Indeed, one had only to compare the political institutions of the United States and Europe to see how much the American system lacked the unity, efficiency, and vigor that government needed to be able to realize the purposes of democracy (1:71–72, 89–93).

But if their political institutions were questionable, the Americans were not. Here was Bryce's canny adroitness, his fine-handed legal dexterity. His argument was simple enough: Americans had transcended the flaws of their constitutions. They were able to live with their faulty system and to make it work. "The defects of the tools are the glory of the workman," Bryce repeated in variant phrasings in *The American Commonwealth*. Their startling achievement in the Civil War showed beyond dispute, he said, that "such a people can work any

Constitution" (1:394). Why was this so? The most important reasons inhered in the mores and characteristics of the Americans. They embodied "moral and material influences stronger than any political devices" (1:395). They were a people of hope, with an unbounded faith in the democratic system. They had a practical capacity for politics, "a clearness of vision for self-control never equalled by any other nation" (1:474). They felt, moreover, an enormous reverence for this Constitution, one that arose out of their deep conservatism.

Here Bryce came full circle. What was the source of this deep-seated conservatism? It was, as we have already noted, English. The Americans carried it in their "English blood," "the deep instincts of their race," those law-loving and law-abiding qualities of "the English of America" (3:62, 63; 1:474). Bryce had wrapped it all up rather neatly. What seriously impeded the republic's political institutions was American. What made them work, despite the impediments, was English. His formula fitted in perfectly with the premises and purpose of his chef-d'oeuvre.

Bryce's *American Commonwealth* was no less circumscribed by England than Tocqueville's *Democracy* was by France. At every point of the *Commonwealth* he referred to relevant English practices. Every major aspect of American politics invited a description of analogous English institutions. *The American Commonwealth* was nothing so much as a study in comparative politics. If it was a protracted journey through the notable defects of the political institutions of the United States, *The American Commonwealth* was no less a sustained affirmation of those of England. Bryce did not often permit himself such outright or sweeping statements as the one that "the working of the representative system in America seems somewhat inferior" to the British system (1:403). But a belief in the overall superiority of English political institutions lay deep in the premises that informed his book.

These premises articulated English political ideology and

English experience. Bryce's central chapters, those in which he reflected on the overall workings of American government and in which he compared the American and European systems, were in effect an Englishman's strong censure of the American way of running politics. To the degree that European politics was successful, it was because it was modeled on England; to the degree that American politics failed, it was because it was not. It was eminently sensible to him that England's natural "aristocracy"—the best men of her stratified society—should run English politics.[36] For that reason he cavilled at the American practice of electing congressmen only from their local districts or states. He never questioned the validity of the complete fusion of powers in cabinet government or worried about the virtually unlimited sovereignty of Parliament.

To say that he saw America through English eyes does not fully define the nature of his vision. He spoke as a Gladstonian Liberal. He believed in the efficacy of Parliament, the virtue of democracy, the merit of a qualified elite, and the validity of Liberal reform. He looked at the political world the Gladstonians had created, and he found it good. There was yet another dimension to his judgment of America. Born a Scotsman, acculturated as an Englishman, he was also a quasi Mugwump: that special genre of late nineteenth-century American reformers with whom he had a close connection. On his several visits to the United States, he formed close and enduring relationships with scores of the foremost members of the American intellectual and professional establishment. Indeed, it was their knowledge and attitudes, which he carefully collected in literally hundreds of interviews and through extensive correspondence, which served Bryce as his primary source of information about American life. In his own estimate, five-sixths of his volumes came from conversations with Americans in London and the United States. His friends were the genteel reformers of the gilded age, men who freely shared with him their deep misgivings about the functioning of American government.[37] But whereas they centered on the moral failures of the men who were running American politics, he broadened his critique to the failures of the institutions themselves. Underneath the critique ran the oft-repeated leit-motif that America's politics did not engage her best men. If in fact he judged America by this dual standard—as a Gladstonian and as a type of Mugwump—his primary ground of judgment was as a member of the English establishment. And in the creed of his own persuasion, he believed in government *of* the people, *for* the shared interest of the major classes, and *by* the best men of the polity.

How far was *The American Commonwealth* a work of edification? The problem with the *Democracy*, Bryce had said, was that Tocqueville wrote it with the clear intent of warning and instructing his countrymen. That he had perceived and judged America in French terms was closely related to Tocqueville's insistence on telling France's leaders what had to be done to avert danger. The errors he committed are those, said Bryce, "which every one who approaches a similar task has to guard against."[38] In a way, it might be said that Bryce sought very carefully to avoid duplicating Tocqueville's error. He did not succeed. Informed by English premises, his book aimed at preaching to the English. He undertook to guide them in the conduct of public affairs. He wished to tell them both what they could learn from America and how that learning could help them conduct English policy. Because the lesson he drew from America was so different from Tocqueville's, his readers could mistakenly suppose that there was no lesson at all. But to do so would be its own mistake. Bryce's *Commonwealth* was a book of its times and for its times. It summed up England's problems and offered counsel on how to address them.

The 1880s were a particularly troubled decade in England. The mid-Victorian social order—"the age of equipoise" of the 1850s and 1860s—had become increasingly unstable. The classes that had earlier accepted it were now at odds with each other, if not quite at war. Pressing questions arising from domestic and international crises besetting the English state now dominated political discourse. And for each of the questions, America seemed to offer a relevant answer. Should not the electorate have the right to run politics and to get its fair share of social benefits? Did not the example of the United States clearly support this right? But should there not be a limit to the ease with which English laws, indeed its constitution, could be changed? Again, did not American practice argue the virtue of setting such a limit? And what about the American Senate? Here was the very model of a second house that was truly representative and, if not popularly elected, then surely of a democratic nature, none of which could be said about the House of Lords. So far as Irish Home Rule was concerned, did not federalism, which permitted the constituent parts of the American union to go their several ways, offer a guiding principle? Above all, was it not clear that America was, as Andrew Carnegie was at that very time proclaiming, a democracy triumphant over England in every conceivable way, and a model worthy of emulation?

Here then was the turbulent context of Bryce's work. These then were the discontented groups he was addressing. Here too were the upbraiding questions about the mother of parliaments and of parliamentary democracy that he was trying to answer. Wherever one turns in all the long pages of *The American Commonwealth* on that extended journey through the whole range of American political institutions, Bryce is always carefully instructing his readers not to be misled by superficial similarities. Everywhere therefore he is giving detailed explanations about the workings of each major American organ of national and state government, no less than of the American party system and of the role of public opinion in the United States. No, the House of Representatives was not like the House of Commons. No, the Senate was not like the House of Lords. No, the American presidential system was not at all like England's cabinet system. No, the American states were not similar to the

English counties nor American local government to local government in England.[39] Indeed, *The American Commonwealth*
was an exercise in nay-saying or, to put it more accurately, a
study of incomparability. It was imperative that those who
were running English affairs understand the true nature of the
American polity. If they did not, Bryce felt certain they would
run a dangerous risk. Here then was the real purpose of Bryce's
book: to serve as a guide to the perplexed, a statesman's manual, a *vade mecum* to that journey through the United States
that England's ruling classes, in the new age of American economic and industrial superiority, now *had* to take, clutching a
compendious Baedeker in hand. He could not piece the Victorian compromise together again, but he could show how it
should not be done.

Indeed, this was precisely the point of Bryce's book of instruction: to teach what not to do and why not to do it. What
could we learn from America? In essence, that one polity could
not simply duplicate the institutions of another. Bryce had begun his book on America with that precept. In his introductory
chapter, he granted that American institutions were "no doubt
full of instruction for Europe, full of encouragement, full of
warning" (1:12). But instruction, he insisted, did not mean emulation; and the warning, he urged, was that emulation was
fraught with the danger of making simple analogies between
Europe and America. Some twelve hundred pages later, in his
final chapter on American political institutions, he repeated the
admonition he had begun with. Asking "How far could American experience be used by Europeans?" Bryce answered, "Not
far at all." However instructive democratic government might
be for Europeans, "it supplies few conclusions directly bearing
on the present politics of any European country, because both
the strong and weak points of the American people are not exactly repeated anywhere in the Old World." That England is
now a democracy is no reason at all for imitating certain key
features of American democratic government. America has

solved her own problems in her own way. But, he insisted, "no
one who knows America will expect the problems she has
solved . . . to reappear in Europe in the same forms." And then
came Bryce's urgent concluding sentence: "Nothing can be
more instructive than American experience if it be discreetly
used, nothing will be more misleading to one who tries to apply
it without allowing for the differences of economic and social
environment."[40]

Was *The American Commonwealth* a book of edification?
Most definitely it was. To his own generation he was proclaiming the laws of political biology, the most immediate of
which was that institutions could not be transplanted (1:12).
His great work on America was dedicated to the proposition
that England should not imprudently imitate her. Anxiety
over England's future under the regime of her new democracy
should not drive her to impulsive transatlantic borrowings. One
should not mistake the form of a constitution for its essence.
Had not Bryce amply shown that, despite its cumbersome and
often contradictory agencies, the American polity worked because of the temperament of the Americans, which was conservative precisely because it was English? Adding some American
devices to the English constitution was surely no answer. That
Bryce's urgent homily to Britain's leaders was negative did not
make it any the less urgent or homiletic. There was a very immediate and practical lesson that could be learned from America. In teaching the lesson, he had consistently indicated the
inefficacy and questionability of America's political institutions.
And no less consistently and persuasively had he argued the virtue and special appeal of those of England. Now *there* was a
tremendous lesson all of its own.

BRYCE'S critique of Tocqueville informed his own book on
America, defining its substance no less than its importance.

This nowhere means that *The American Commonwealth* was merely an extended reply to the *Democracy*: Bryce had too many other views of the republic to correct and too many other causes to serve. Indeed, his judgment of the *Democracy* is far more important for what it discloses about Bryce and his time than for what it says about Tocqueville. It enunciated two basic points about the *American Commonwealth* and its author. Bryce's model of social science prescribed his method. His Anglo-American outlook prescribed his substance. Each was of course a function of the other. Together, as we have already seen, they gave Bryce the grounds for his case against Tocqueville.

His case was that of an ardent Pan-Anglian and his book the most important document of the Pan-Anglian age. In faulting Tocqueville for not having adequately understood the Englishness of American life, Bryce wished to help restore America to the English-speaking community of peoples.[41] He wished no less to lend his support to the growing group of Pan-Anglians who, during those years of deepening international crisis, were calling for a rapprochement between Great Britain and the United States.[42] *The American Commonwealth* underscored the basis for rapprochement: the shared ethnicity of the two nations as well as their common language, law, literature, and history. In our own day, said Bryce, "for the purposes of thought and arts, the United States is part of England, and England is part of the United States" (3:552). That each nation had its own type of politics should not obscure the fact that both were democracies. One could now see, in the half-century since Tocqueville, that democracy was a variable growth. And therefore, Bryce insisted repeatedly, it would be wrong to cite democracy as the mainspring of American institutions. What mattered far more, to his way of thinking, was America's English legacy. In that legacy he found his own explanation of what Tocqueville had hailed as America's great achievement: ensuring liberty in a regime of democracy. For Bryce the achievement was far from being uniquely American. Bringing with them the English common law, Magna Carta, the Bill of Rights, and wide borrowings from the English constitution, the English of America implanted liberty in the very texture of their political institutions.

That *The American Commonwealth* celebrated the shared legacy of the United States and Great Britain explains, in significant measure, the great acclaim that greeted its appearance. It was prominently reviewed in both countries.[43] Bryce's American friends sent him their warm congratulations, hailing both the book and the approval of the critics. Seth Low, who had been mayor of the city of Brooklyn, was delighted by "the splendid reception given to your book on both sides of the water." Henry Villard, a prominent journalist and financier, said he was merely joining "the international chorus of the admirers of your new work" in declaring it "the ablest book ever written in this country. . . . Everybody on this side and especially all those whose opinion is of value have reached this conclusion." Woodrow Wilson wrote to express his "sincere admiration for the great work which every intelligent man among us on this side of the sea would now feel it a distinct discredit not to have read." Albert Bushnell Hart, a foremost member of America's new generation of historians and political scientists, praised Bryce for "the effect of your own profound studies in stirring up Americans to think about and write about their own government." Bryce's correspondents sounded three closely related themes about the *Commonwealth*: that it spoke to and for the groups who were shaping public opinion in America; that it was spurring them to reconsider their own politics and constitution; and that, in effect, it signified a changing view of the relation between the kindred societies.[44]

After a century of diplomatic and ideological conflict, a new amity was arising between America and Britain. Bryce both expressed and hailed the growing friendship. It is "one of the most remarkable events of our time," he said, "that a cordial feeling should now exist between the two chief branches of the English race." *The American Commonwealth* was virtually a public act in the British-American relationship. The reviews of Bryce's work that appeared widely in the most important journals of both countries not only served as a transatlantic symposium on the relationship but also helped to renew and extend it. A most impressive success, *The American Commonwealth* acted as the best evangel of Bryce's Pan-Anglian doctrine. He was called on to revise it several times. It appeared in cheap editions and in a one-volume abridgment was used extensively in American universities and high schools. During the three decades from 1888 to 1918, when Bryce was virtually the embodiment of the British-American relationship, *The American Commonwealth* sold some 212,000 copies, a high figure for those days, and no small record for a treatise on institutions that approached its subject with a hard, factual sobriety and that asked of its readers no less than it gave them. Half-a-century after its publication, Harold J. Laski called *The American Commonwealth* "a real event in the history of the relations between Great Britain and the United States."[45]

That it was a "real event" testified to Bryce's role and contribution. He rationalized the new relationship between America and Britain. He gave the British ruling classes a basis for a new orientation toward the transatlantic republic. And he gave America's governors, particularly her genteel reformers and progressives, the text for a new civism, one especially encouraging and useful when social strife and immigrant hordes seemed to be violating the integrity of their Roman republic. Powerful men in both countries could, with Bryce as their text, proceed to build a connection of binational powers, assured by the intelligence that theirs was not a new work but merely one of renovation. It is hard to imagine a man more strategically placed than Bryce to undertake the Anglo-American ambassadorship he served for well over four decades. To list his friends and connections would be to name the scores, indeed the hundreds, of men who served at the center of American and British public life: in all levels of government, in all tiers of jurisprudence, in the colleges and universities, in the many fields of literature and journalism.

Here could be found the measure of his difference from the author of *Democracy in America*. Each man conducted an embassy for an idea. Bryce sounded the virtues of Pan-Anglian institutions in the democratic age; Tocqueville, the threat of democracy to liberty. To Bryce, the examples of America and England seemed to throw into question Tocqueville's fears about the course of democracy no less than the accuracy of his portrait of America. The challenge that Bryce had directed against Tocqueville's premises had a certain validity. But what Bryce could not have foreseen, writing as he was for his own decade and purpose, was that it was precisely those premises that would make the *Democracy* a vital document for later times. Tocqueville's intent was surely edificatory and his focus was less on America than on democracy. But if he was seeking a solution for the problems of the democratic revolution in France, his intelligences could be applied to those problems wherever and whenever they arose. His *Democracy* took on new life in the twentieth century, when the spread of democratic despotism fulfilled the worst of his fears about preserving liberty. What further enhanced the vogue of his work was that, by speculating in the large about democracy, he far transcended the confines of his time and place; he had offered not so much conclusive answers as challenging questions.

Because of the difference in the substance and purport of their masterpieces, the services each man gave his cause differed widely. Far more than Tocqueville, Bryce was at the center of the politics of his society; and he was far better situated than Tocqueville to practice what he was preaching. He incarnated the Pan-Anglian idea, working for it on a lifelong mission. More than consummate expression, he gave it a powerful direction in England and America. The very identity of the book and its author's service, however, set a term to the durability of *The American Commonwealth*. That it so closely fit the needs of the Pan-Anglian age defined its limits: it did not survive either its age or its author. The reason lay in something more than its fading purpose. Bryce had written a Baedeker to late-nineteenth-century America, and as America changed, the Baedeker itself became history. But to say that the Pan-Anglian age has long since passed would be to miss the point that its idea has been translated and sustained. In terms of the Darwinian doctrine to which Bryce subscribed, his *Commonwealth*, while registering the differences between America and England as two varieties of a polity, emphasized that in their evolutionary descent they were withal members of the same species. Arguing their shared legacy, he argued their need for surviving by mutuality. The gospel of Bryce's age became the actuality of a later one. Two world wars transformed the partnership of equals that Bryce had evangelized into a grand American alliance in which Britain prominently belonged. It would not have surprised him that Dilke's vision of a Greater Britain had been realized as a Greater America. This gave an enduring vitality to the message, if not quite the details, of his *American Commonwealth*.

Notes

ABRAHAM S. EISENSTADT, Introduction

1. André Jardin, *Alexis de Tocqueville 1805–1859* (Paris, 1984), 505–506.

2. George Wilson Pierson, *Tocqueville and Beaumont in America* (New York, 1938), 7–9.

3. Olivier Zunz, "Tocqueville and the Writing of American History in the Twentieth Century: A Comment," *The Tocqueville Review* 7 (1985/ 86):131–132.

4. François Furet, "The Intellectual Origins of Tocqueville's Thought," *The Tocqueville Review* 7 (1985/86):124.

5. Ibid., 119.

6. Jean-Claude Lamberti, *Tocqueville et les deux démocraties* (Paris, 1983), 13.

7. Ibid., 309, 311–313. Continuously concerned with this problem, Tocqueville kept revising his ideas about the forms and dangers of democratic despotism; see James T. Schleifer, *The Making of Tocqueville's Democracy in America* (Chapel Hill, N.C., 1980), 142–156, 173–187.

8. Lamberti, *Tocqueville,* 310.

9. The most useful book on this rich, highly important subject is Frank E. Manuel, *The Prophets of Paris* (Cambridge, Mass., 1962).

10. Lamberti, *Tocqueville,* 20.

11. Furet, "Intellectual Origins," 119.

12. Theodore Caplow, "The Current Relevance of *Democracy in America*," *The Tocqueville Review* 7 (1985/86):138–139.

13. Lamberti, *Tocqueville,* 11–12, 307.

14. Ibid., 302.

15. Ibid., 15–17; Furet, "Intellectual Origins," 120–121.

16. Lamberti, *Tocqueville,* 15.

17. From his close friend Louis de Kergolay, who was traveling in Germany in late 1836 and early 1837, Tocqueville received a letter that anticipated several of the features of Hitler's "democratic despotism" with remarkable accuracy: cited in Schleifer, *Making,* 175.

18. Jardin, *Alexis de Tocqueville,* 257–258. Jardin cites (pages 260–261) a highly important letter that Tocqueville wrote to a

reviewer of his 1840 *Democracy,* spelling out his great fear of the possibility of "universal slavery" under the regime of the coming democracy. See also: Schleifer, *Making,* 185–187.

19. Lamberti, *Tocqueville,* 15.

20. *Democracy in America,* ed. J. P. Mayer and Max Lerner, trans. George Lawrence (New York, 1966), 643–680, esp. chaps. 6–8.

21. See Lamberti, *Tocqueville,* 308.

22. Schleifer, *Making,* 259.

23. While the principal concern of the *Review* is with comparative sociology, particularly that of France and America, it has expanded its purview to include the fostering and publishing of studies of Tocqueville.

24. Lamberti, *Tocqueville,* 9–10.

25. The Tocqueville revival, it should again be noted, is not a uniquely American or French phenomenon. During the past few decades, the *Democracy* has appeared in complete or abridged editions in several countries, including Italy, the Federal Republic of Germany, Mexico, Brazil, and Israel.

GITA MAY, "Tocqueville and the Enlightenment Legacy"

1. *The Old Regime and the French Revolution,* trans. Stuart Gilbert (New York, 1955), xv.

2. *Selected Letters on Politics and Society,* trans. James Toupin and Roger Boesche (Berkeley, 1985).

3. Cf. *The Old Regime and the French Revolution,* x: "I see the spirit which sponsored the conception, birth, and fruition of the Revolution gaining ground, and little by little all its salient features taking form under my eyes. For it was not merely foreshadowed in the years preceding it; it was an immanent reality, a presence on the threshold. These records disclose not only the reasons of the events accompanying its outbreak, but also, and perhaps even more clearly, those of its aftereffects on the destinies of France."

4. *Democracy in America,* trans. Henry Reeve, 2 vols. (New York, 1974), 2:396. Henceforth all quotations from this work will refer to this edition and will be identified by volume and page in the body of the text.

BERNARD E. BROWN, "Tocqueville and Publius"

I am grateful to Seymour Drescher, Abraham S. Eisenstadt, James T. Schleifer, and Arthur Schlesinger, Jr., for their helpful comments on the first version of this paper.

1. Alexis de Tocqueville, *De la Démocratie en Amérique*, 2 vols. (Paris, 1951), 1:169. I translate "un beau livre" as "a great book," in the same sense in which "les beaux esprits se rencontrent" is best rendered as "great minds think alike."

2. In William W. Story, ed., *Life and Letters of Jospeh Story*, 2 vols. (Boston, 1851), 2:330.

3. George W. Pierson, *Tocqueville and Beaumont in America* (New York, 1938), 730–735.

4. Citations from James T. Schleifer, *The Making of Tocqueville's Democracy in America* (Chapel Hill, N.C., 1980), 98, 101. In general, see ibid., 87–101, 145–148. See also the material from "cahier E" reprinted in *Voyages en Sicile et aux Etats-Unis*, vol. 5 of Tocqueville's *Oeuvres complètes* (Paris, 1957), 266–270.

5. See, for example, Robert A. Dahl, *A Preface to Democratic Theory* (Chicago, 1956), especially chap. 1; and James MacGregor Burns, *The Deadlock of Democracy* (Englewood Cliffs, N.J., 1963). Their orientation owes much to Charles Beard, *An Economic Interpretation of the Constitution of the United States* (New York, 1913).

6. *De la Démocratie en Amérique*, 1:224.

7. Ibid., 1:235. On the *loi Defferre*, see Mark Kesselman, "The Tranquil Revolution at Clochemerle: Socialist Decentralization in France," in Philip Cerny and Martin Schain, eds., *Socialism, the State, and Public Policy in France* (New York, 1985), 166–185. Concerning the origins of the *loi Defferre*, Kesselman observes: "the rationale for decentralization can be traced back to Tocqueville, who unfavorably compared the French situation, where the bureaucracy absorbed much of society's vital substance, with the decentralized American system." Ibid., 180.

8. Cited by Schleifer, *Making*, 140.

9. The founders of the American republic paid little attention to Rousseau. One of the few observers to note the similarities is Cecilia Kenyon. See her essay, "Alexander Hamilton: Rousseau of the Right," *Political Science Quarterly* 73 (June 1958):161–179.

10. *The Federalist,* Number 51, cited in *De la Démocratie en Amérique,* 1:397–398.

11. Jefferson's theory is set forth in his *Notes on Virginia,* central passages of which are reproduced by Madison in *The Federalist,* Number 48.

12. *De la Démocratie en Amérique,* 1:398.

13. Alexis de Tocqueville, *Democracy in America,* ed. Phillips Bradley, 2 vols. (New York, 1945), 1:259.

14. *De la Démocratie en Amérique,* 1:384. My italics.

15. Ibid., 1:385.

16. Ibid., 1:387–388.

17. Ibid., 1:598.

18. Ibid., 1:396.

19. Ibid., 1:178.

20. Ibid., 1:179.

21. Ibid., 1:180, 181, 184, 185.

22. Ibid., 1:590, 594, 596–597.

23. See also the account by George W. Pierson, *Tocqueville and Beaumont in America,* 607.

24. Tocqueville's citations from Hamilton's papers 73 and 12 are in *De la Démocratie en Amérique,* 1:320, 348.

25. Ibid., 1:473. My italics.

26. In Tocqueville, *Ecrits et discours politiques* (Paris, 1985), 42. This is tome 3, vol. 3 of the *Oeuvres complètes.*

27. Tocqueville, *Souvenirs,* ed. Luc Monnier (Paris, 1942), 189.

28. *De la Démocratie en Amérique,* 1:389.

29. Ibid., 1:288–289.

30. Ibid., 1:465.

31. Ibid., 1:450–451, 456–457. See also Doris S. Goldstein, *Trial of Faith: Religion and Politics in Tocqueville's Thought* (New York, 1975), especially chap. 2.

32. André Jardin, *Alexis de Tocqueville, 1805–1859* (Paris, 1984), 100–101.

33. *De la Démocratie en Amérique,* 1:392.

34. See Francis Lieber, *Stranger in America,* 2 vols. (London, 1835), 2:77–78. Lieber's impressions were cited in John Stuart Mill, "State of Society in America," *London Review,* 2 (January 1836):

365–389, reprinted in J. S. Mill, *Essays on Politics and Society* (Toronto, 1977), 91–115.

35. *De la Démocratie en Amérique*, 1:465.

36. Ibid., 1:389.

37. Ibid., 1:390–391.

38. From Mill's review of "De Tocqueville's Democracy in America, II" in *The Edinburgh Review* 72 (October 1840):20. Reprinted in Mill, *Essays on Politics and Society*, 175–176.

39. *De la Démocratie en Amérique*, 1:285.

40. See James Fenimore Cooper, *The American Democrat* (reprint New York, 1931); also John P. McWilliams, Jr., *Political Justice in a Republic: James Fenimore Cooper* (Berkeley, 1972); and Robert E. Spiller, *Fenimore Cooper: Critic of His Times* (New York, 1931). On Francis Lieber, see his *On Civil Liberty and Self-Government*, 3d ed. (Philadelphia, 1877), especially 398–409. The first edition was published in 1853.

41. *De la Démocratie en Amérique*, 2:21, 22. My italics.

42. Ibid., 1:424 (on immigration); ibid., 2:430–437 (on "the despotism to be feared by democratic nations"). Tocqueville's remarks on later immigration are cited by Seymour Drescher, *Dilemmas of Democracy: Tocqueville and Modernization* (Pittsburgh, 1968), 277.

43. *De la Démocratie en Amérique*, 1:219. This clearly was the model Tocqueville had in mind for constituent assemblies in France. Note how Tocqueville's description of the constitutional convention follows that of John Jay in Number 2:

This convention, composed of men who possessed the confidence of the people, and many of whom had become distinguished by their patriotism, virtue, and wisdom, in times which tried the minds and hearts of men, undertook the arduous task. In the mild season of peace, with minds unoccupied by other subjects, they passed many months in cool, uninterrupted, and daily consultation; and finally, without having been awed by power, or influenced by any passion except love for their country, they presented and recommended to the people the plan produced by their joint and very unanimous councils.

44. *De la Démocratie en Amérique,* 1:167.

45. Tocqueville, *Souvenirs,* 162.

46. Ibid., 166, 169.

47. Ibid., 74–75.

48. See Tocqueville's letter to Mill, 3–5 December 1835, in *Correspondance anglaise, Oeuvres complètes,* 6:302–304.

49. *De la Démocratie en Amérique,* 1:7.

SEYMOUR DRESCHER, "Comparison and Synthesis in *Democracy in America*"

I wish to thank Abraham S. Eisenstadt and William Stanton for their critical readings and stylistic suggestions on an earlier draft of this essay.

1. *De la Démocratie en Amérique,* 4 vols. (Paris, 1835–1840).

2. See *Democracy in America,* ed. J. P. Mayer and Max Lerner; trans. George Lawrence (New York, 1966), 383, author's preface to vol. 2.

3. See most recently, John Patrick Diggins, *The Lost Soul of American Politics: Virtue, Self-Interest, and the Foundations of American Liberalism* (New York, 1984), chap. 8; Robert N. Bellah, Richard Madsen, William M. Sullivan, Anne Swidler, and Steven M. Tipton, *Habits of the Heart: Individualism and Commitment in American Life* (Berkeley, 1985), preface and passim; and Max Lerner, "Introduction: Tocqueville and America," in *Democracy in America* (Mayer and Lerner ed.), xliv, xlv.

4. See James T. Schleifer, *The Making of Tocqueville's Democracy in America* (Chapel Hill, 1980), part I and chap. 20, esp. 279–286. See also G. W. Pierson, "Le 'second voyage' de Tocqueville en Amérique" in *Alexis de Tocqueville: Livre du centenaire, 1859–1959* (Paris, 1960), 71–85.

5. "Tocqueville's Two *Démocraties,*" *Journal of the History of Ideas* 25 (April–June 1964):201–216. See also Cushing Strout, "Tocqueville's Duality: Describing America and Thinking of Europe," *American Quarterly* 21 (Spring 1969):87–99.

6. Jean-Claude Lamberti, *Tocqueville et les deux démocraties* (Paris, 1983), 173–184; André Jardin, *Alexis de Tocqueville, 1805–*

1859, (Paris, 1984), chap. 15; *Alexis de Tocqueville: De la Démocratie en Amérique; Souvenirs; L'Ancient Régime et la Revolution,* intro. J. C. Lamberti and Françoise Mélonio (Paris, 1986). See especially Mélonio's "Introduction à la seconde *Démocratie*," 397–425.

7. Jardin, *Tocqueville,* 240; Mélonio, "Introduction a la seconde *Démocratie*," 398. Qualitative analysis reinforces quantitative measurements. See Drescher, "Tocqueville's Two *Démocraties*" and Mélonio, "Introduction," 404: "Thus experience led Tocqueville to modify his conceptions of democracy between 1837 and 1840 or rather to differently conceive the relation between equality of conditions and political democracy, between equality and liberty. This evolution is as perceptible in his correspondence as in his manuscripts and then in the definitive draft."

8. Yale manuscripts for *Democracy in America,* drafts for the preface, C. V. k. Paq. 7, cahier I, 50; also cited in Drescher, "Tocqueville's Two *Démocraties*," 202, and Schleifer, *Making,* 29 and note, correcting Drescher's dating.

9. Yale manuscripts, C. V. k. Paq. 7, 53, cited in Schleifer, *Making,* 29 and note. See also Tocqueville to John Stuart Mill, 18 December 1840, in Alexis de Tocqueville, *Oeuvres* (Paris, 1951–), vol. 6 *Correspondance anglaise* (1954), 1:330.

10. Schleifer, *Making,* 280.

11. *Democracy* (1835) (Mayer ed.), 12–14.

12. *Democracy* (1835) (Mayer ed.), 12, 20.

13. Schleifer, *Making,* 279.

14. See especially *Democracy* (1835) (Mayer ed.) 63–70, 75, 78–81, 84–88, 241–242.

15. *Democracy* (1835) (Mayer ed.), chap. 5.

16. *Democracy* (1835) (Mayer ed.), 365.

17. *Democracy* (1835) (Mayer ed.), 87; Schleifer, *Making,* 140 and note. Schleifer cites this sentence as being on pages 95–97 of Tocqueville's *Democracy* (Mayer ed.). My edition has the quotation on page 87.

18. *Democracy* (Mayer ed.), 87–88.

19. Tocqueville, "Etat social et politique de la France avant et dupuis 1789," in *Oeuvres,* vol. 2, *L'Ancien Régime et la Revolution,* 1:57; first published as "Political and Social Condition of France, First Article" in *The London and Westminster Review,* 3 (April 1836):

137–169. See also *Oeuvres*, 2, 1:54–55. S. Drescher, *Dilemmas of Democracy: Tocqueville and Modernization* (Pittsburgh, 1968), 35 and note discusses the shifting weight given to centralization between 1835 and 1840.

20. *Democracy* (1835) (Mayer ed.), 286–290.

21. *Democracy* (1840) (Mayer ed.), 663; compare with *Democracy* (1835) (Mayer ed.), 5.

22. *Democracy* (1840) (Mayer ed.), 655.

23. See Koenraad W. Swart, "Individualism in the Mid-Nineteenth Century (1826–1860)," *Journal of the History of Ideas* 23 (January–March 1962):77–90; and above all, Jean-Claude Lamberti, *La Notion d' individualisme chez Tocqueville* (Paris, 1970). On the dating of the shift see Schleifer, *Making*, 252 and note.

24. *Democracy* (1840) (Mayer ed.), 477–478.

25. Schleifer, *Making*, 238–240.

26. *Democracy* (1835) (Mayer ed.), 224, 280.

27. *Democracy* (1835) (Mayer ed.), 223.

28. *Democracy* (1835) (Mayer ed.), 279.

29. *Democracy* (1835) (Mayer ed.), 280, 343, 345, 368–370.

30. Schleifer, *Making*, 281.

31. Ibid., 239–240.

32. Tocqueville, "Etat Social," 60–62.

33. Drescher, *Tocqueville and England* (Cambridge, Mass., 1964), chap. 5.

34. In addition to Tocqueville's notes on England, see Beaumont's notes of his voyages to England and in Ireland 1835 and 1837, Yale Manuscripts C.X.3. "en quoi les Whigs sont Démocrates;" C.X.5, 18 May 1837, on centralization in Ireland. On centralization in relation to England's New Poor Law, see C.X.5, Beaumont's conversation with Nassau Senior, Paris, 27 October 1836; for Tocqueville's notes on English and French trends toward centralization, see C.V.k. Paq. 7, 41, 42; C.V.d., 41; C.V.g. Paq. 9, cahier 2, 52–53; ibid., 123.

35. Yale MSS. C.V.d. Paq. 5, 30, conversation with Adolphe Thiers, 27 May 1837.

36. Tocqueville to Mill, 10 February 1836, *Oeuvres*, 6, 1:307. On the whole process of Tocqueville's transition, see S. Drescher, *Dilemmas*, 35–44.

37. "Tocqueville's Two *Démocraties*," 206 and note.

38. *Democracy* (1840) (Mayer ed.), 605–606, 652.

39. *Democracy* (1840) (Mayer ed.), 645.

40. *Democracy* (Mayer ed.), 475, 652. In the latter passage both the idea of individual rights and the taste for local liberties are described as drawn from the aristocracy of England.

41. Diggins, *Lost Soul,* 238–239. In Tocqueville's own assessment, Americans could lose their participatory republicanism only in the wake of the most profound and total social revolution, not insensibly. He found "no reason to foresee such a revolution," nor could he detect any symptom of it. See *Democracy* (Mayer ed.), 364. Another conflation of French and American individualism occurs in Leo Marx's "A Visit to Mr. America," *New York Review of Books,* 12 March 1987, 36–38. Marx formulates a "Tocquevillian" "claim that the political culture of the Unites States" was more conducive to individualism "than that of any other Western nation." (36) Tocqueville, in fact, explicitly claims the opposite—that the political culture of the United States was less conducive to individualism. See *Democracy* (Mayer ed.) 2, part 2, especially chapters 3, 4, 8, 14.

42. Bellah, *Habits,* chap. 1.

43. Stanley Hoffman, "Fragments Floating in the Here and Now: Is There a Europe, Was There a Past, and Will There Be a Future? Or the Lament of a Transplanted European," in *Culture and Society in Contemporary Europe: A Casebook,* ed. Stanley Hoffman and Paschalis Kitromilides (London, 1981), 230.

ARTHUR SCHLESINGER, JR., "Individualism and Apathy in Tocqueville's *Democracy*"

1. Tocqueville to Louis de Kergolay, January 1835, Alexis de Tocqueville, *Selected Letters on Politics and Society,* ed. Roger Boesche (Berkeley, 1985), 94.

2. A. O. Hirschman, *The Passions and the Interests* (Princeton, 1977), 60–61.

3. *Democracy in America,* ed. Phillips Bradley, 2 vols. (New York, 1945), 1, chap. 14.

4. Tocqueville to Ernest de Chabrol, 9 June 1831, *Selected Letters,* 38.

5. Ibid.

6. James T. Schleifer, *The Making of Tocqueville's Democracy in America* (Chapel Hill, 1980), 242–243.

7. *Journey to America,* ed. J. P. Mayer (New Haven, 1959), 210–211.

8. *Democracy in America,* 1, chap. 5. Unless otherwise indicated, all further references are to the *Democracy.*

9. *Democracy* (Bradley ed.) 1, chap. 14.

10. Ibid., 1: chap. 15.

11. Ibid., 1: chap. 3.

12. Ibid., 2: second book, chap. 2.

13. Ibid., 2: second book, chap. 14.

14. Ibid., 2: second book, chap. 10.

15. Ibid., 2: third book, chap. 19.

16. *The Old Regime and the French Revolution,* trans. Stuart Gilbert (Garden City, N.Y., 1955), 13.

17. *Democracy* (Bradley ed.) 2: appendix BB.

18. Ibid., 2: second book, chaps. 2, 4.

19. Ibid., 2: second book, chap. 14.

20. Ibid., 2: Appendix BB.

21. Ibid., 2: fourth book, chap. 6.

22. Ibid., 2: third book, chap. 21.

23. Ibid., 2: first book, chap. 10.

24. "The Perpetuation of our Political Institutions," in *Abraham Lincoln: Selected Speeches, Messages, and Letters,* ed. T. Harry Williams (New York, 1957), 6.

25. Seymour Drescher, "Tocqueville's Two Democracies," *Journal of the History of Ideas* 25 (April-June 1964):201–216.

26. Tocqueville to Pierre-Paul Royer-Collard, 20 August 1837, *Selected Letters,* 118.

27. Tocqueville to Louis de Kergolay, 18 October 1847, *Selected Letters,* 193.

28. From *Journeys to England and Ireland* in *Alexis de Tocqueville on Democracy, Revolution, and Society,* ed. John Stone and Stephen Mennell (Chicago, 1980), 305–306.

29. *Democracy* (Bradley ed.), 2: second book, chap. 20.

30. Ibid., 1: chap. 3.

31. Ibid., 2: second book, chap. 4.

32. Ibid., 2: second book, chap. 4.

33. Ibid., 2: second book, chap. 4.

34. Ibid., 2: second book, chap. 7.

35. Ibid., 2: second book, chap. 4.

36. Tocqueville to Mill [June 1835], *Selected Letters*, 101.

37. *Democracy* (Bradley ed.), 2: second book, chap. 17.

38. Ibid., 1: chap. 14.

39. Ibid., 2: second book, chap. 14.

40. "The Conservative," in *The Portable Emerson*, ed. Mark van Doren (New York, 1946), 89–91.

41. *History of the United States*, 9 vols. (New York, 1889–1891), 6:123.

42. A. O. Hirschman, *Shifting Involvements: Private Interest and Public Action* (Princeton, 1982).

43. *Democracy* (Bradley ed.) 2, second book, chap. 13.

44. *Old Regime*, 209.

MELVIN RICHTER, "TOCQUEVILLE, NAPOLEON, AND BONAPARTISM"

1. Entry for 19 August 1850 in *Correspondence & Conversations of Alexis de Tocqueville with Nassau William Senior*, ed. M.C.M. Simpson, 2 vols. (London, 1872), 1:113.

2. Entry for 15 August 1833 in *Oeuvres complètes*, ed. J. P. Mayer, 18 vols. (Paris, 1949–), 5:2, 11–12. This edition is still in progress. Henceforth it will be cited as *Oeuvres* (Mayer ed.) to distinguish it from the older *Oeuvres complètes*, ed. Gustave de Beaumont, 9 vols. (Paris, 1861–1863), henceforth cited as *Oeuvres* (Beaumont ed.). All translations, unless otherwise noted, are by Melvin Richter.

3. Tocqueville to Corcelle, 17 June 1853, *Oeuvres* (Mayer ed.), 15:2, 76.

4. *Oeuvres* (Mayer ed.), 2:2, 29. For the convenience of readers, I shall cite texts whenever translated by John Lukacs, *Tocqueville, "The European Revolution," and Correspondence with Gobineau* (New York, 1959), 154. Hereafter cited as Lukacs, *Tocqueville*.

5. Dieter Groh, "*Cäsarismus*," in *Geschichtliche Grundbergriffe*, ed. Otto Brunner, Werner Conze, and Reinhart Koselleck, 7 vols. (Stuttgart, 1972–), 1:726–771.

6. I follow the method for dealing with concepts and their history developed in my "Conceptual History [*Begriffsgeschichte*] and Political Theory," *Political Theory* 14 (November 1986):604–637, and "*Begriffsgeschichte* and the History of Ideas," *Journal of the History of Ideas* 48 (April-June 1987):247–263.

7. For a discussion of Bonapartism as a political movement, see Theodore Zeldin, *Politics and Anger* (Oxford, 1979), 140–205. An older view closer to Tocqueville's are the lectures of H.A.L. Fisher, *Bonapartism* (Oxford, 1914). The best historiographical study of Napoleon is Pieter Geyl, *Napoleon: For and Against* (London, 1949). This work, however, does not consider Tocqueville's treatment of Napoleon and Bonapartism.

8. It was not until around 1880 that the concept of "imperialism" took on its present meanings. Groh, "Cäesarismus," 727.

9. In a fragmentary note, he directed himself "to narrate and judge at the same time." *Oeuvres* (Mayer ed.), 2:2, 302; Lukacs, *Tocqueville*, 145.

10. I have argued this point in my "Toward a Concept of Political Illegitimacy," *Political Theory* 10 (1982):185–214.

11. *Oeuvres* (Mayer ed.), 1:330, 413, 430.

12. *Oeuvres* (Mayer ed.), 1:1, 330; *Oeuvres* (Beaumont ed.), 1:342.

13. Jean-Claude Lamberti, *Tocqueville et les deux démocraties* (Paris, 1983). This is now being translated for publication by the Harvard University Press.

14. Seymour Drescher, "Tocqueville's Two *Démocraties*," *Journal of the History of Ideas* 25 (1964):201–216.

15. These statements occur in the preface to the 1840 volumes: *Oeuvres* (Mayer ed.), 1:1,7; the preface to the 12th edition: *Oeuvres* (Mayer ed.), 1:1, xliii–xliv; the preface to *L'Ancien Régime et la Révolution, Oeuvres* (Mayer ed.), 2:1, 75; Stuart Gilbert, trans., *The Old Regime and the Revolution* (New York, 1955), xiv–xv. This translation is seriously misleading. I refer to it for the benefit of those who have access to nothing better.

16. James Schleifer, *The Making of Tocqueville's Democracy in America* (Chapel Hill, 1980), 285.

17. François Furet, "*Naissance d'un paradigme: Tocqueville et le voyage en Amérique (1825–1831),*" *Annales* 39 (1984):225–239.

18. Melvin Richter, "Comparative Political Analysis in Montesquieu and Tocqueville," *Comparative Politics* 1 (1969):129–160.

19. Tocqueville to Reeve, 15 November 1839, *Oeuvres* (Mayer ed.), 6:1, 47.

20. Drescher, "Tocqueville's Two *Démocraties*, 204–205, 214.

21. Lamberti, *Tocqueville et les deux démocraties*, 290, 311.

22. Ibid., 311.

23. Ibid., 311.

24. Ibid., 174, 173–181, 281.

25. *Oeuvres* (Mayer ed.), 1:1, 447.

26. Letter to Paul Clamorgan, Paris, 17 April 1842. In *Alexis de Tocqueville als Abgeordneter*, ed. Joachim Kuhn (Hamburg: Hauswedell, 1972), 75. Translation adapted from *Alexis de Tocqueville. Selected Letters on Politics and Society*, trans. R. Boesche and J. Toupin (Berkeley and Los Angeles, 1985), 158. Clamorgan, Tocqueville's electoral agent, seems to have been an admirer of Napoleon.

27. *Oeuvres* (Mayer ed.), 1:2, 89–92. This subject is discussed in James Schleifer's valuable essay in this volume.

28. *Oeuvres* (Mayer ed.), 1:2, 305.

29. *Oeuvres* (Mayer ed.), 2:2, 267–298; Lukacs, *Tocqueville*, 117–142.

30. *Oeuvres* (Beaumont ed.), 9:14.

31. *Oeuvres* (Mayer ed.), 1:1, 413.

32. *Oeuvres* (Beaumont ed.), 9:16, 17–18, 19.

33. Ibid., 19.

34. *Oeuvres* (Mayer ed.), 2:1, 72; *Old Regime* (Gilbert trans.), xi.

35. *Oeuvres* (Beaumont ed.), 19–20.

36. Ibid., 21.

37. Ibid., 17.

38. *Oeuvres* (Mayer ed.), 1:2, 290–291.

39. *Oeuvres* (Mayer ed.), 2:1, 108–114.

40. *Oeuvres* (Beaumont ed.), 9:16–17.

41. *Oeuvres* (Mayer ed.), 1:2, 339; I here use the translation of *Democracy in America*, trans. Phillips Bradley, 2 vols. (New York, 1966),

2:334. Hereafter cited as *Democracy* (Bradley ed.). Compare this passage to *Oeuvres* (Beaumont ed.), 9:20.

42. *Oeuvres* (Mayer ed.), 1:2, 339; *Democracy* (Bradley ed.), 2:334.

43. *Oeuvres* (Beaumont ed.), 9:21.

44. *Oeuvres* (Mayer ed.), 1:1, 6; *Democracy* (Bradley ed.), 1:8–9. I am here using the Bradley translation in my citation.

45. *Oeuvres* (Beaumont ed.), 9:18–19.

46. "La pensée politique de Tocqueville sous la monarchie de juillet," in *Oeuvres* (Mayer ed.), 2:2, 16.

47. Tocqueville reported to the Academy of Moral and Political Sciences on Macarel's *Cours de droit administratif. Oeuvres* (Beaumont ed.), 9:60–75.

48. Ibid., 65.

49. Ibid., 63.

50. Ibid., 63–64.

51. Ibid., 71–72.

52. Ibid., 74.

53. Ibid.

54. *Oeuvres* (Mayer ed.), 1:2, 354. Tocqueville's report on Cherbuliez was written in 1847 and delivered on 15 January 1848.

55. Ibid., 2:359–361.

56. Ibid., 1:xliii–xliv.

57. "*l'Etat social et politique de la France avant et depuis 1789,*" *Oeuvres* (Mayer ed.), 2:1, 31–76. For an extended comparison of Tocqueville's essay and book, see François Furet, "*Tocqueville est-il un historien de la Révolution française?*" *Annales* 25 (1970): 435–451.

58. Tocqueville to Kergorlay, 15 December 1850, *Oeuvres* (Mayer ed.), 13:2, 229–234.

59. Tocqueville to Madame Phillimore, 20 June 1852, *Oeuvres* (Beaumont ed.), 7:282–283.

60. Letter from Tocqueville to Montalembert, 10 July 1856, in ibid., 7:388–390.

61. Letter to Corcelle, 17 September 1853, ibid., 6:257.

JAMES T. SCHLEIFER, "Tocqueville as Historian"

1. For the general examination, see Marvin Zetterbaum, "Tocqueville: Neutrality and the Use of History," *American Political Science Review* 58 (September 1964):611–621; Zetterbaum's argument is also included in his *Tocqueville and the Problem of Democracy* (Stanford, 1967).

For the more specific studies, see: Albert Salomon, "Tocqueville, Moralist and Sociologist," *Social Research* 2 (November 1935): 405–428; idem, "Tocqueville's Philosophy of Freedom," *The Review of Politics* 1 (October 1939): 400–431; Edward Gargan, "The Formation of Tocqueville's Historical Thought," *The Review of Politics* 24 (January 1962):48–61; idem, "Tocqueville and the Problem of Historical Prognosis," *American Historical Review* 68 (January 1963): 332–345; Melvin Richter, "Tocqueville's Contribution to the Theory of Revolution," *Revolution,* ed. Carl Friedrich (New York, 1966), 75–121; idem, "The Uses of Theory: Tocqueville's Adaptation of Montesquieu," in *Essays in Theory and History* (Cambridge, Mass., 1970), 74–102; idem, "Toward a Concept of Political Illegitimacy," *Political Theory* 10 (May 1982):185–214; Roger Boesche, "The Strange Liberalism of Alexis de Tocqueville," *History of Political Thought* 2 (November 1981):495–524; idem, "Why Could Tocqueville Predict So Well?" *Political Theory* 11 (February 1983):79–103; François Furet, "Tocqueville and the Problem of the French Revolution," in *Interpreting the French Revolution,* trans. Elborg Forster (Cambridge, 1981); idem, "La Révolution sans la Terreur? Le débat es historiens du XIXe siècle," *Le Débat* 13 (June 1981): 40–54; idem, "Naissance un paradigme: Tocqueville et le voyage en Amérique, 1825–1831," *Annales* 39 (March-April 1984):225–239; also see Sasha Reinhard Weitman, "The Sociological Thesis of Tocqueville's *The Old Regime and the Revolution*," *Social Research* 33 (Autumn 1966): 389–403.

2. Consult especially the pertinent portions of Pierre Birnbaum, *Sociologie de Tocqueville* (Paris, 1970), particularly chaps. 2, 5, 6; Seymour Drescher, *Tocqueville and England* (Cambridge, Mass.,

1964), particularly chap. 10 and idem, *Dilemmas of Democracy: Tocqueville and Modernization* (Pittsburgh, 1968); Pierre Manent, *Tocqueville et la nature de la démocratie* (Paris, 1982), particularly chap. 7; and Jean-Claude Lamberti, *Tocqueville et les deux Démocraties* (Paris, 1983), particularly 56–57, 213–216, and 301–313, hereafter cited as Lamberti, *Tocqueville et les deux Démocraties*.

3. Alexis de Tocqueville, *Democracy in America*, ed. Phillips Bradley, 2 vols., Vintage ed. (New York, 1945), 2:90–93; hereafter cited as *Democracy* (Bradley ed.).

Although this brief chapter encapsulates much of Tocqueville's theory, several other portions of the *Democracy* also offer significant elements; see especially *Democracy* (Bradley ed.): the 1835 "Introduction," 1:3–17, and the 1840 "Preface"; "Origin of the Anglo-Americans, and Importance of This Origin in Relation to Their Future Condition" and "Social Condition of the Anglo-Americans," 1:27–56; "Principal Causes Which Tend to Maintain the Democratic Republic in the United States," 1:298–342; "Why Great Revolutions Will Become More Rare," 2:265–278; and the famous concluding paragraph, 2:352.

4. Yale Tocqueville Manuscripts Collection, Drafts, C V g, "Rubish," original autograph drafts of the 1840 *Democracy*, Box 3, for the chapter on historians in democratic times; (hereafter cited as Yale, Drafts, C V g, "Rubish"). The first earlier title is in the margin of the first page of the chapter; the second is on the chapter jacket-sheet. All translations from the working papers of the *Democracy*—drafts, "Rubish," and Original Working Manuscript—are mine.

5. Also consult Tocqueville's well-known, concise statement about general and particular causes and historical causation in *The Recollections of Alexis de Tocqueville*, trans. Alexander Teixeira de Mattos, edited and introduced by J. P. Mayer, Meridien ed. (New York, 1959), 63–64. See, as well, Tocqueville's "Preface" to the 1840 text, *Democracy* (Bradley ed.), 2:v–vi, where he again stresses the plurality of causes.

6. *Democracy* (Bradley ed.), 2:91.

7. Although Tocqueville implies in his chapter that historians of aristocratic times are morally superior to those of democratic periods,

he does complain that the former have failed to give sufficient attention to general causes.

8. *Democracy* (Bradley ed.), 2:92.

9. Ibid., 2:93.

10. See James T. Schleifer, *The Making of Tocqueville's "Democracy in America"* (Chapel Hill, 1980), especially chaps. 3 and 4; (hereafter cited as Schleifer, *Making*).

11. See the key subchapters, *Democracy* (Bradley ed.), 1:330–342.

12. Yale, Drafts C V g, "Rubish," Box 3, for the chapter on historians in democratic times; Tocqueville's own emphasis.

13. Ibid.; Tocqueville's own emphasis.

14. Ibid.; comment in margin.

15. See especially Yale, Drafts, C V g, "Rubish," Box 3, the entire chapter on historians in democratic times.

16. Yale Tocqueville Manuscripts Collection, Original Working Manuscript of the *Democracy*, C VI a, Box 1, for the chapter "Social Condition of the Anglo-Americans" (hereafter cited as Yale, Original Working Ms., C VI a).

17. Yale, Original Working Ms, C VI a, Box 2, for the subchapter "Situation of the Black Population in the United States. . . ."

18. Ibid.; comment in margin.

19. Yale Tocqueville Manuscripts Collection, Drafts of the *Democracy*, C V k, cahier 1, 46–47, from drafts for the 1840 "Preface"; (hereafter cited as Yale, Drafts).

20. Yale, Drafts, C V k, cahier 2, 37–41. This essay is addressed specifically to issues of governmental principles and institutions; the following sentences precede the essay: "Utility of varying the means of government. Ideas which are too general in matters of government, like those which are too specific, are a sign of the weakness of the human mind. Belong to intelligence only half-matured. Danger of letting any single social principle determine, absolutely and without challenge, the direction of society."

21. See especially Roger Boesche, "Why Could Tocqueville Predict So Well?" *Political Theory* 11 (February 1983):79–103; (hereafter cited as Boesche, "Why Could Tocqueville Predict So Well?").

22. Marvin Zetterbaum in his work has stressed the idea that

Tocqueville's appeals to religion and to God are essentially utilitarian and that Tocqueville saw religion primarily as a "salutary myth," useful for balance in a democratic society; he deemphasizes any personal religious conviction that Tocqueville may have had. See Zetterbaum, *Tocqueville and the Problem of Democracy* (Stanford, 1967).

23. For articles dissenting from the overly utilitarian interpretation of Zetterbaum, see Catherine Zuckert, "Not by Preaching: Tocqueville on the Role of Religion in the American Democracy," *Review of Politics* 43 (April 1981):259–280; James T. Schleifer, "Tocqueville and Religion: Some New Perspectives," *The Tocqueville Review* 4 (Fall-Winter 1982):303–321; and Françoise Mélonio, "La Religion selon Tocqueville: Ordre moral ou esprit de liberté?" *Etudes* (January 1984):73–88.

24. Yale, Original Working Ms., C VI a, Box 3, for the chapter on historians during democratic times; cf. *Democracy* (Bradley ed.), 2:91. Why did Tocqueville delete this additional criticism? Perhaps because it was a distraction from his argument. It introduced still another, separate idea: not just that historians in democratic times too readily went looking for general causes, but also that they often fixed upon specious ones.

25. *Democracy* (Bradley ed.), 2:92.

26. Yale, Original Working Ms., C VI a, Box 3, for the chapter on historians during democratic times.

27. Yale, Drafts, C V g, "Rubish," Box 3, for the chapter on historians during democratic times.

28. Melvin Richter, "The Uses of Theory: Tocqueville's Adaptation of Montesquieu," in *Essays in Theory and History* (Cambridge, Mass., 1970).

29. Boesche, "Why Could Tocqueville Predict So Well?" 82.

30. Also consult Tocqueville's chapter, "Why Great Revolutions Will Become More Rare," from the 1840 text, which implies an entire theory of historical causation, of how and why profound changes do or do not occur; *Democracy* (Bradley ed.), 2:265–278. And see especially Lamberti, *Tocqueville et les deux Démocraties*, chap. 8.

31. *Democracy* (Bradley ed.), 2:215–221, "How Equality of Condition Contributes to Maintain Good Morals in America." For the earlier version, see Yale, Original Working MS., C VI a, Box 4, for that chapter.

32. Yale, Original Working Ms. C VI a, Box 4, for the chapter "How Equality of Condition Contributes to Maintain Good Morals in America." Compare the published text, *Democracy* (Bradley ed.), 2:215, where Tocqueville does not mention conscience.

33. Yale, Drafts, C V g, "Rubish," Box 4, for the chapter entitled "How Democracy Renders the Habitual Intercourse of the Americans Simple and Easy," *Democracy* (Bradley ed.), 2:178–180.

34. Yale, Drafts, C V k, cahier 1, 37.

35. Yale, Drafts, C V g, "Rubish," Box 3, for the chapter entitled "How Religion in the United States Avails Itself of Democratic Tendencies." See *Democracy* (Bradley ed.), 2:21–29.

36. See Schleifer, *Making,* especially chaps. 3, 4, and 5. Also consult Tocqueville's brief discussion, in the 1840 text, of metempsychosis, a doctrine that he professes to prefer to materialistic theories; *Democracy* (Bradley ed.), 2:154–156.

37. Yale, Drafts, C V k, cahier 1, 37.

38. Mignet's *History of the French Revolution* was first published in 1824. On Mignet, see François Furet, "La Révolution sans la Terreur? Le débat des historiens du XIXe siècle," *Le Débat* 13 (June 1981):40–54; and Stanley Mellon, *The Political Uses of History: A Study of Historians in the French Restoration* (Stanford, 1958). Also consult André Jardin's biography, the first comprehensive one we have, *Alexis de Tocqueville, 1805–1859* (Paris, 1984), for further information about the connections between the two men; (hereafter cited as Jardin, *Tocqueville*).

39. Yale, Original Working Ms., C VI a, Box 3, from the chapter on historians during democratic times.

40. Yale, Drafts, C V a, cahier unique, 58.

41. Yale, Drafts, C V g, "Rubish," Box 4, for the concluding chapter, "General Survey of the Subject"; *Democracy* (Bradley ed.), 2:349–352.

42. Ibid., for the penultimate chapter, "Continuation of the Preceding Chapters"; *Democracy* (Bradley ed.), 2:340–348.

43. Yale, Drafts, C V h, cahier 4, 33.

44. Yale, Drafts, C V g, "Rubish," Box 3, for the chapter on historians during democratic times.

45. Yale, Drafts, C V a, cahier unique, 58.

46. *Democracy* (Bradley ed.), 2:352.

47. Yale, Drafts, C V k, cahier 1, 42; for the 1840 preface.

48. Yale, Original Working Ms., C VI a, Box 3, from the chapter on historians during democratic times.

49. Most of these methodological traits are also evident in the *Ancien régime*. But in that later work, Tocqueville also presented a further principle: "I am dealing here with classes as a whole, to my mind, the historian's proper study." Consult *The Old Regime and the French Revolution*, trans. Stuart Gilbert (Garden City, New York, 1958), 122.

50. This general trait may be qualified a bit however. See Roger Boesche, "Tocqueville and *Le Commerce*: A Newspaper Expressing His Unusual Liberalism," *Journal of the History of Ideas* 44 (April-June 1983):277–292; and consult some of Tocqueville's contributions to *Le Commerce*, especially his article of 7 January 1845.

51. Yale, Drafts, C V h, cahier 3, 99.

52. Yale, Original Working Ms., C VI a, Box 1, for the 1835 "Introduction."

53. *Democracy* (Bradley ed.), 1:227–233.

54. Yale, Drafts, C V h, cahier 3, 74–77.

55. On his redefinition of republican virtue, see especially Doris Goldstein, "Alexis de Tocqueville's Concept of Citizenship," *American Philosophical Society Proceedings* 108 (February 1964):39–53; on religion and despotism, see *Democracy* (Bradley ed.), 1:97.

56. Tocqueville's attention to ideas in history also led him to an examination of what later came to be called the sociology of knowledge: recognition of the connection between the positions, functions, and roles of groups (or classes) in society and the ideas held by those groups and the study of how ideas circulate from one group to others in society. As noted above, in the *Ancien régime* Tocqueville particularly stressed the role of classes and "class-consciousness."

57. In addition to the articles by Richter, Furet, and Boesche cited in the opening note, see the pertinent portions of Raymond Aron, *Les Etapes de la pensée sociologique* (Paris, 1967), especially 25–76; Jean-Jacques Chevallier, *Les Grandes oeuvres politiques: De Machiavel à nos jours* (Paris, 1962), especially 101 and 129–138; and Jardin, *Tocqueville*, especially 326. Also consult Montesquieu, *Consid-*

érations sur les causes de la grandeur et de la décadence des Romains and *De l'Esprit des lois*.

58. Aron, *Etapes*, 43–49 and 56–60.

59. His attitude was shaped in part by his dislike of Machiavelli "who is, after all," Tocqueville wrote in a draft fragment, "only a superficial man, skilled at discovering secondary causes, but from whom great general causes escape." Yale, Drafts, C V g, "Rubish," Box 4, from the chapter "Some Considerations on War in Democratic Communities"; *Democracy* (Bradley ed.), 2:297–302.

60. *Democracy* (Bradley ed.), 2:265–278, "Why Great Revolutions Will Become More Rare."

61. Yale, Original Working Ms., C VI a, Box 4, from the chapter on great revolutions.

62. Yale, Drafts, C V g, "Rubish," Box 4, from the chapter on great revolutions.

63. *Democracy* (Bradley ed.), 1:327.

64. Perhaps one of the best examples of Tocqueville's shift away from classical examples concerns his changing images of the despotism that democratic peoples had most to fear. In 1835, he described one form of democratic despotism as similar to the worst tyranny of the Roman emperors, *Democracy* (Bradley ed.), 1:340–341. But by 1840 he emphasized the newness of conditions and repudiated his own earlier classical analogy, ibid., 2:334. Cf. Schleifer, *Making,* chaps. 11–13.

65. See particularly the special issue of the *Journal of Modern History* 44 (December 1972), 448–541, which is devoted to a discussion of the Annales school and contains: Fernand Braudel, "Personal Testimony," 448–467; H. R. Trevor-Roper, "Fernand Braudel, the *Annales,* and the Mediterranean," 468–479; J. H. Hexter, "Fernand Braudel and the *Monde Braudellien,*" 480–541. Also consult Marc Bloch, *The Historian's Craft,* trans. Peter Putnam, intro. Joseph Strayer, Vintage ed. (New York, 1953) (hereafter cited as Bloch, *Historian's Craft*); François Furet, *In the Workshop of History,* trans. Jonathan Mandelbaum (Chicago, 1984), especially the "Introduction" and Part I, E. Le Roy Ladurie, *The Territory of the Historian,* trans. Ben and Sian Reynolds (Chicago, 1979), especially chaps. 1, 2, and 3;

and Georg Iggers, *New Directions in European Historiography* (Middletown, Conn., 1975), chap. 2, 43–79.

66. On the parallel between *moeurs* and *mentalité*, see, for example, Lamberti, *Tocqueville et les deux Démocraties*, 312; and Boesche, "Why Could Tocqueville Predict So Well?"

67. H. R. Trevor-Roper, "Fernand Braudel, the *Annales*, and the Mediterranean," *Journal of Modern History* 44 (December 1972):469.

68. In addition to Braudel's works, see the articles by Braudel and Hexter from the *Journal of Modern History,* cited in note 65.

69. J. H. Hexter, "Fernand Braudel and the *Monde Braudellien,"* *Journal of Modern History* 44 (December 1972):500.

70. Consult Yale, Original Working Ms., C VI a, Box 3, for the chapter on historians during democratic times; and Yale, Drafts, C V g, "Rubish," Box 3, for the same chapter.

71. Bloch, *Historian's Craft*, 26.

72. However, various observers have noted that the quantitative imperative is perhaps not as powerful now as it has been during earlier stages of the school's development; see for example Robert Darnton, "Intellectual and Cultural History," in *The Past Before Us: Contemporary Historical Writing in the United States,* ed. Michael Kammen (Ithaca, 1980), 345.

73. One of the best indications of those resonances is the increasing interest in Tocqueville of François Furet, a leading figure of the *Annales* school and recently elected president of the Commission nationale pour la publication des oeuvres complètes d'Alexis de Tocqueville. The result has been a succession of perceptive and stimulating essays by Furet on various aspects of Tocqueville and his work; see the articles cited above as well as Furet, *Workshop,* chap. 10, "The Conceptual System of *Democracy in America."*

ROBERT NISBET, "TOCQUEVILLE'S IDEAL TYPES"

1. Alexis de Tocqueville, *Democracy in America,* ed. Phillips Bradley, 2 vols. (New York, 1945), 2:17, 69.

2. Ibid., 1:14.

3. Ibid., 2:11.

4. *Tocqueville and Beaumont in America* (New York, 1938), 756.

5. Ibid., 761–762.

6. Ibid., 759.

7. I have dealt with the significance for political thought of Robert de Lamennais in "The Politics of Social Pluralism: Some Reflections on Lamennais" in *The Journal of Politics* 10 (November 1948):764–786.

8. Paul Janet, "Alexis de Tocqueville et la science politique aux XIXe siècle," *Revue des Deux Mondes* 34 (1861):116.

9. *The Making of Tocqueville's Democracy in America* (Chapel Hill, 1980), 259.

DANIEL T. RODGERS, "Of Prophets and Prophecy"

1. James Bryce, "The Predictions of Hamilton and Tocqueville," *Johns Hopkins University Studies in Historical and Political Science* 5 (1887): 329–381.

2. Alexis de Tocqueville, *Democracy in America,* ed. Phillips Bradley (New York, 1945), 2:486, 447; Tocqueville, *Democracy in America,* ed. Richard D. Heffner (New York, 1956), 9, 16; Robert Nisbet, *The Sociological Tradition* (New York, 1966); Tocqueville, *Democracy in America,* ed. Thomas Bender (New York, 1981), xl.

3. *Democracy* (Bradley ed.), 2:452.

4. David Riesman et al., *The Lonely Crowd: A Study of the Changing American Character* (New Haven, 1950).

5. *Democracy* (Bender ed.), xl, xlvi; Richard Sennett, "What Tocqueville Feared" in *On the Making of Americans: Essays in Honor of David Riesman,* ed. Herbert J. Gans (Philadelphia, 1979); Robert Nisbet, "Many Tocquevilles," *American Scholar* 46 (1976):64–71.

6. Cf. François Furet, "The Conceptual System of 'Democracy in America'" in his *In the Workshop of History* (Chicago, 1984), 193–196.

7. Alexis de Tocqueville, *Journey to America,* trans. George Lawrence, ed. J. P. Mayer (New Haven, 1960), 156.

8. Ibid., 80, 95, 159–160.

9. Alexis de Tocqueville, *Democracy in America,* trans. George Lawrence, ed. J. P. Mayer (Garden City, 1969), 254–255.

10. Herbert B. Adams, "Jared Sparks and Alexis de Tocqueville," *Johns Hopkins University Studies in Historical and Political Science* 16 (1898): 605; Anon., "European Views of American Democracy:

M. de Tocqueville," *United States Magazine and Democratic Review* 1 (1837):102–107.

11. Alexis de Tocqueville, *Democracy in America, with an Original Preface and Notes by John C. Spencer* (New York, 1838), 1:451–454; Anon., "Democracy in America," *American Quarterly Review* 19 (1836):151–154.

12. Daniel C. Gilman, "Alexis de Tocqueville and His Book on America—Sixty Years After," *Century* 56 (1898):712.

13. Mary P. Ryan, *Cradle of the Middle Class: The Family in Oneida County, New York, 1790–1865* (Cambridge, England, 1981).

14. *Democracy* (Mayer ed.), 645.

15. Seymour Drescher, "Tocqueville's Two Democracies," *Journal of the History of Ideas* 25 (1964):201–216.

16. James T. Schleifer, *The Making of Tocqueville's "Democracy in America"* (Chapel Hill, 1980), 122.

17. *Democracy* (Mayer ed.), 9.

18. Ibid., 638.

19. Nisbet, *Sociological Tradition*, 121–122; Hannah Arendt, *On Revolution* (New York, 1963), 23.

20. *Democracy* (Mayer ed.), 673.

21. George W. Pierson, *Tocqueville in America* (Garden City, 1959), 457–465.

22. John S. Mill, "De Tocqueville on Democracy in America [II]" in *The Collected Works of John Stuart Mill* (Toronto, 1963–   ), 18:196.

SEAN WILENTZ, "On Tocqueville and Jacksonian America"

1. Important critical appraisals of the Tocqueville revival and its aftermath include those by Max Beloff, "Tocqueville and the Americans" (1951), reprinted in idem., *The Great Powers: Essays in Twentieth Century Politics* (London, 1959); and Lynn L. Marshall and Seymour Drescher, "American Historians and Tocqueville's *Democracy*," *Journal of American History* 55, 3 (December 1968):512–532. A full evaluation of more recent scholars' uses and abuses of Tocqueville remains to be written.

2. John Higham, *Writing American History: Essays on Modern Scholarship* (Bloomington, Ind., 1970), 159.

3. Robert Bellah et al., *Habits of the Heart: Individualism and Commitment in American Life* (Berkeley, 1985); Peter Steinfels, "Up from Individualism," *The New York Times Book Review*, 14 April 1985, 1.

4. Richard Sennett, *The Fall of Public Man* (New York, 1977); Alexis de Tocqueville, *Democracy in America*, ed., Thomas Bender (New York, 1981); John Patrick Diggins, *The Lost Soul of American Politics: Virtue, Self-Interest, and the Foundations of Liberalism* (New York, 1984).

5. Robert V. Remini, *Andrew Jackson and the Course of American Democracy, 1833–1845* (New York, 1984), 616.

6. Richard Reeves began the current round of Tocquevillian punditry with his *American Journey: Travelling with Tocqueville in Search of Democracy in America* (New York, 1982). More recently, James Reston has written that Tocqueville's observations "are still as fresh as this morning's newspaper" ("Democracy in America," *The New York Times*, 2 July 1986). A few weeks later, Arthur M. Schlesinger, Jr., remarked that "[t]he reader of Alexis de Tocqueville is constantly astonished to recognize the lineaments of modern America in his great work" ("The Challenge of Change," *The New York Times Magazine*, 27 July 1986, 20).

7. See, for example, James T. Schleifer's frequent comments about *Democracy*'s shortcomings in his *The Making of Tocqueville's "Democracy in America"* (Chapel Hill, 1980). Schleifer's balanced evaluation is at once intensely admiring and painstakingly critical of Tocqueville's achievement. For an earlier critical appreciation of *Democracy*, see Jack Lively, *The Social and Political Thought of Alexis de Tocqueville* (New York, 1962).

8. Christopher Lasch, *The Culture of Narcissism: America in an Age of Diminished Expectations* (New York, 1978), 29–30.

9. Alexis de Tocqueville, *Democracy in America*, ed. J. P. Mayer (New York, 1969), 209. Unless otherwise noted, all subsequent citations of *Democracy* will be to this edition. The most sustained challenge to Tocqueville on these matters is Edward Pessen, *Riches, Class, and Power Before the Civil War* (Lexington, Mass., 1973).

10. In addition to Pessen's work, see Jeffrey G. Williamson and Peter H. Lindert, *American Inequality: A Macroeconomic History* (New York, 1980), esp. 36–46. Williamson and Lindert, drawing on several

local studies, estimate that the concentration of wealth in America grew especially uneven from the 1820s to the 1840s.

11. *Democracy* (Mayer ed.), 294.

12. Paul E. Johnson, *A Shopkeeper's Millennium: Society and Revivals in Rochester, New York, 1815–1837* (New York, 1978), 136–137.

13. Johnson, *Shopkeeper's Millennium*; Mary P. Ryan, *Cradle of the Middle Class: The Family in Oneida County, New York, 1790– 1865* (Cambridge, 1981); Carroll Smith Rosenberg, *Disorderly Conduct: Visions of Gender in Victorian America* (New York, 1985).

14. Donald Matthews, *Religion in the Old South* (Chicago, 1978); Eugene D. Genovese, *Roll, Jordan, Roll: The World the Slaves Made* (New York, 1974); Lawrence W. Levine, *Black Culture and Black Consciousness: Afro-American Folk Thought from Slavery to Freedom* (New York, 1977); Albert Raboteau, *Slave Religion* (New York, 1980).

15. *Democracy* (Mayer ed.), 317. On slave families, see especially Herbert G. Gutman, *The Black Family in Slavery and Freedom, 1750– 1920* (New York, 1976).

16. *Democracy* (Mayer ed.), 600–603.

17. See Nancy F. Cott, *The Bonds of Womanhood: "Woman's Sphere" in New England, 1780–1830* (New Haven, 1977).

18. Catharine Beecher, *A Treatise on Domestic Economy* (Boston, 1842), 26–34.

19. On these conflicts, see especially Christine Stansell, *City of Women: The Female Laboring Poor in New York, 1789–1860* (New York, 1986).

20. *Democracy* (Mayer ed.), 398.

21. Ibid.

22. See, for example, John Ashworth's sweeping analysis of conflicting party and factional ideologies in his *"Agrarians" and "Aristocrats": Party Political Ideology in the United States, 1837–1846* (London, 1985).

23. Robert V. Remini approvingly repeats this remark as the opinion of "one wag" in *Jackson*, 613.

24. On the Progressive historians' neglect of Tocqueville, see Marshall and Drescher, "American Historians," 513–515.

25. Several works have contributed to this reading of *Democracy*,

including George W. Pierson, *Tocqueville and Beaumont in America* (New York, 1938); Louis Hartz, *The Liberal Tradition in America: An Interpretation of American Political Thought Since the Revolution* (New York, 1955); Schleifer, *Making*; Diggins, *Lost Soul*. Works of relevance to specific points are cited below.

26. By now, an enormous literature has explored the vicissitudes of republicanism in early America. For an introduction, see Robert Shalhope, "Republicanism in Early America," *William and Mary Quarterly* 38 (1982):334–356.

27. Schleifer, *Making*, 235.

28. Tocqueville quoted in J. P. Mayer, *Alexis de Tocqueville: A Biographical Study in Political Science* (New York, 1960), 13.

29. See above all Linda K. Kerber, *Federalists in Dissent: Imagery and Ideology in Jeffersonian America* (Ithaca, 1970); and Daniel Walker Howe, *The Political Culture of the American Whigs* (Chicago, 1979).

30. *Democracy* (Mayer ed.), 179.

31. On Choate, see Jean V. Matthews, *Rufus Choate: The Law and Civic Virtue* (Philadelphia, 1980).

32. *Democracy* (Mayer ed.), 525–528.

33. On earlier developments, see David Hackett Fischer, *The Revolution of American Conservatism: The Federalist Party in the Era of Jeffersonian Democracy* (New York, 1965).

34. Daniel Webster, "The Basis of the Senate," in *The Writings and Speeches of Daniel Webster* ed. Fletcher Webster, 18 vols. (Boston, 1903), 5:15.

35. Rufus King to Christopher Gore, 3 February 1822, quoted in Shaw Livermore, Jr., *The Twilight of Federalism: The Disintegration of the Federalist Party, 1815–1830* (Princeton, 1962), 124.

36. *Democracy* (Mayer ed.), 238.

37. Ibid., 251.

38. Webster quoted in Diggins, *Lost Soul*, 108.

39. Calvin Colton, *The Junius Papers: Number VII* (New York, 1844).

40. For further quotations, see Sean Wilentz, *Chants Democratic: New York City & the Rise of the American Working Class, 1788–1850* (New York, 1984).

41. For an overview, see Howe, *American Whigs*.

42. See Ashworth, *"Agrarians."*

43. In this instance, I have quoted the more felicitous translation in Alexis de Tocqueville, *Democracy in America,* ed., Phillips Bradley (New York, 1954), 1:412.

44. *Democracy* (Mayer ed.), 363.

45. The classic works on these topics are Fletcher M. Green, *Constitutional Development in the South Atlantic States, 1776-1860: A Study in the Evolution of Democracy* (Chapel Hill, 1930), and idem., "Democracy in the Old South," *Journal of Southern History* 12 (1946):3-23. These should be supplemented by some recent studies of the southern yeomanry and the second party system in the South: Steven Hahn, *The Roots of Southern Populism: Yeoman Farmers and the Transformation of the Georgia Upcountry, 1850-1890* (New York, 1983); J. Mills Thornton III, *Politics and Power in a Slave Society: Alabama, 1800-1860* (Baton Rouge, 1978); Harry Watson, *Jacksonian Politics and Community Conflict: The Emergence of the Second Party System in Cumberland County, North Carolina* (Baton Rouge, 1981). See also Watson's intelligent synthesis, "Conflict and Collaboration: Yeomen, Slaveholders, and Politics in the Antebellum South," *Social History* 10 (1983):273-298. On the origins of these paradoxes, see Edmund S. Morgan, *American Slavery, American Freedom: The Ordeal of Colonial Virginia* (New York, 1975).

46. See Eugene D. Genovese, *From Rebellion to Revolution: Afro-American Slave Revolts in the Making of the Modern World* (Baton Rouge, 1979); Ira Berlin et al., eds., *Freedom: A Documentary History of Emancipation, 1861-1867,* series 1, vol. 1, *The Destruction of Slavery* (Cambridge, 1985).

47. On Tocqueville's appreciation of these matters, see Schleifer, *Making,* 168.

48. *Democracy* (Mayer ed.), 278, n. 1.

49. Thomas Hamilton, *Men and Manners in America,* 2 vols. (London, 1833), 1:59ff.

50. John Stuart Mill, "M. de Tocqueville on Democracy in America," *Edinburgh Review* 72 (1840):1.

51. Tocqueville quoted in Jean-Claude Lamberti, *Tocqueville et les Deux Démocraties* (Paris, 1983), 26.

52. *Democracy* (Mayer ed.), 555-558.

53. See, among other recent works, Alan Dawley, *Class and Community: The Industrial Revolution in Lynn* (Cambridge, Mass., 1976); Bruce Laurie, *Working People of Philadelphia, 1800–1850* (Philadelphia, 1980); Wilentz, *Chants Democratic*.

54. On the south, see Hahn, *Roots*; Watson, "Conflict and Collaboration"; as well as the various works Watson cites. On the north, see the classic works by Paul W. Gates, *The Farmer's Age: Agriculture, 1815–1860* (New York, 1951), and idem., *History of Public Land Law Development* (Washington, D.C., 1968), as well as John Mack Faragher, *Sugar Creek: Life on the Illinois Prairie* (New Haven, 1986). Allan Kulikoff's forthcoming study of the rise and fall of the American yeomanry promises to throw a great deal of additional light on this subject, particularly on the connections between economic change, family life, and gender relations in the countryside.

55. James Bryce, *The American Commonwealth*, 2 vols. (London and New York, 1888–1889).

ABRAHAM S. EISENSTADT, "Bryce's America and Tocqueville's"

I have been helped by the comments of Glenn C. Altschuler and James T. Schleifer, and particularly by those of John W. Brennan. I am also grateful to the National Endowment for the Humanities for having supported the research on which this essay is based.

1. Edmund Ions, *James Bryce and American Democracy 1870–1922* (London, 1968), 118. For studies at the Johns Hopkins University in the 1880s, see *Historical Scholarship in the United States, 1876–1901: As Revealed in the Correspondence of Herbert B. Adams,* ed. W. Stull Holt (Baltimore, 1938), 7–18, and essays by J. M. Vincent and Richard T. Ely in *Herbert B. Adams* (Baltimore, 1902), 2–23, 27–49.

2. H.A.L. Fisher, *James Bryce,* 2 vols. (New York, 1927), 1:222–123, 135–138, chaps. 4, 8, 9, 11; Ions, *Bryce,* 100–101, chaps. 4–8.

3. Ions, *Bryce,* 126. A detailed presentation of Bryce's 1883 seminar lecture on Tocqueville's *Democracy* may be found in notebook N–28 of the Albert Shaw Papers at the New York Public Library. Shaw, who was editor of the *Review of Reviews* from 1894 until

1937, was a student at the Johns Hopkins University in the early 1880s.

4. James Bryce, *The Predictions of Hamilton and De Tocqueville,* Johns Hopkins University Studies in Historical and Political Science, fifth series, vol. 9 (Baltimore, 1887), 5, 51; James Bryce, *Studies in History and Jurisprudence,* 2 vols. (New York, 1901), 1:301. The sixth essay of the latter work, entitled "The United States Constitution as Seen in the Past: The Predictions of Hamilton and Tocqueville," is a slightly revised version of Bryce's 1887 *Predictions.*

5. Bryce, *The Predictions,* 23–24.

6. Max Lerner, "Introduction: Tocqueville and America," in Alexis de Tocqueville, *Democracy in America,* ed. J. P. Mayer and Max Lerner, trans. George Lawrence (New York, 1966), xxvii–xxviii. (Lerner's "Introduction" was published separately as *Tocqueville and American Civilization,* New York, 1969). One significant example of Bryce's problems in acculturation is the difficulty he had as a Scottish Presbyterian in standing for and receiving a scholarship at Trinity College, at Oxford, for refusing to sign the Thirty-nine Articles: see Fisher, *James Bryce,* 1:36–43 and Ions, *Bryce,* 45, 50.

7. Lerner, "Introduction: Tocqueville and America," xxviii–xxix.

8. Fisher, *James Bryce,* 1:136–137; Ions, *Bryce,* 45–46, 72–73, 78, 122.

9. Bryce to Mrs. Sarah Whitman, 6 October 1884, Bryce Papers, Bodleian Library, Oxford University.

10. On the role of America as a model for British reform, there are several important general works, including Frank Thistlethwaite, *The Anglo-American Connection in the Early Nineteenth Century* (Philadelphia, 1959); David Paul Crook, *American Democracy in English Politics 1815–1850* (Oxford, 1965); Max Berger, *The British Traveller in America, 1836–1860* (New York, 1943); Richard L. Rapson, *Britons View America* (Seattle, 1971); Henry T. Tuckerman, *America and Her Commentators* (New York, 1864; reprinted New York, 1961); John Graham Brooks, *As Others See Us* (New York, 1908); and Allan Nevins, ed., *America Through British Eyes* (New York, 1948).

11. Bryce to Higginson, 13 December 1885; Bryce to Theodore Stanton, 24 September 1889. Bryce Papers.

12. Ions, *Bryce,* 126–129.

13. Particularly relevant to the ongoing controversy over English democracy are the *Essays on Reform* (London, 1867), to which Bryce contributed an important piece ("The Historical Aspect of Democracy") sustaining the argument for enlarging the franchise; the essays are reprinted in W. L. Guttsman, ed., *A Plea for Democracy* (Bristol, 1967). In the vast literature on the ferment of mid- and late-Victorian political reform, some of the signal works are G. Kitson Clark, *The Making of Victorian England* (Cambridge, 1962), chap. 8; Asa Briggs, *The Age of Improvement* (London, 1959), chaps. 5, 10; Robert Blake, *Disraeli* (London, 1966); Maurice Cowling, *Disraeli, Gladstone, and Revolution* (Cambridge, 1967); Geoffrey Best, *Shaftesbury* (London, 1964); Peter Stansky, ed., *The Victorian Revolution* (New York, 1973), esp. the articles by MacDonagh, Parris, Tholfsen, Cornford, and Roach; and two older, still useful classics, John Morley, *The Life of William Ewart Gladstone*, 3 vols. (London, 1903) and Elie Halevy, *Victorian Years 1841–1895* (London, 1951).

14. Bryce, *The Predictions*, 23.

15. Ibid., 23, 25, 24, 28.

16. James Bryce, *The American Commonwealth*, 3 vols. (London, 1888), I, 5, 6. All references to volumes and page numbers in parentheses in the text refer to this work.

17. Bryce to Theodore Stanton, 13 October 1887; Jesse Macy to Bryce, 15 October 1888, Bryce Papers; 1:5. What Bryce meant by the word "commonwealth" may be found in an essay he wrote in 1867, arguing for extending the franchise. He distinguished sharply between "government by class" and "a Commonwealth [which] knows nothing of classes." The latter is "a society of individual men, the good of each of whose members is the good of all. To this idea England strove, in the days of Cromwell and Milton, to give a visible form. And in this idea is to be found the simplest and the most potent safeguard against an unjust exercise of power by rich and poor, for it is the idea of a true Commonwealth—it is at once the condition and the pledge of national unity." See James Bryce, "The Historical Aspect of Democracy," 178–180.

18. Bryce, *American Commonwealth*, 3:133, 120–128, 141.

19. Jack Lively, *The Social and Political Thought of Alexis de Tocqueville* (Oxford, 1965), 97; see Benjamin E. Lippincott, *Victorian Critics of Democracy* (Minneapolis, 1937).

20. Fisher, *James Bryce*, 1:50.
21. Bryce, *American Commonwealth*, 3: chap. 97.
22. Bryce, *The Predictions*, 25–26.
23. Ibid. It is not directly germane to our concern with Bryce's charge against Tocqueville to ascertain how far in actual fact the latter was familiar with the Englishness of the Americans. What Tocqueville knew is very closely explored by Seymour Drescher in his altogether excellent monograph on *Tocqueville and England* (Cambridge, Mass., 1964). As Drescher discloses, the French master's visits to England in 1833 and 1835, from which he hoped to cull evidence to support his theories, had the effect of making him modify his views on democracy, aristocracy, and the democratic revolution. What is clear from Drescher is that by the time of his 1840 *Democracy,* Tocqueville knew considerably more than before about the extent of English attitudes and values among the Americans and surely about the similarity between "American ways" and those of the English middle class. How then shall we explain Bryce's charge? First: it is safe to surmise that Bryce did not have available to him the Tocqueville materials that, writing eight decades later, Drescher did. Second: in his charge against the author of the *Democracy*, Bryce entered, as we have noted, a careful modification about the degree of Tocqueville's familiarity with the English. Third: the relevance of English mores to American figures more centrally in the 1835 *Democracy* than in its 1840 sequel; and Tocqueville did not have that closer knowledge of the English when he wrote the first part of the *Democracy* that he was to gain by the time he wrote the second.
24. Bryce, *American Commonwealth*, 3:63; 1:408, 34. What Bryce says in this paragraph and the next is correctly seen by H. A. Tulloch as part of an altering English perception of American history and institutions, particularly of race, the Revolution, and the Constitution. See Tulloch, "Changing British Attitudes towards the United States in the 1880s," *The Historical Journal* 20 (December 1977):825–840.
25. Bryce, *American Commonwealth*, 3:62; 1:22–23, 473, 29, 35, 474.
26. Ibid., 3:62; Bryce, "The Historical Aspect of Democracy," 167–180. Very important in arguing for the reform bill of 1867 were the younger members of England's intelligentsia and professoriat,

particularly those centered at Oxford and Cambridge, about whom Christopher Harvie has written a most valuable monograph: *The Lights of Liberalism—University Liberals and the Challenge of Democracy 1860–86* (London, 1976). Chaps. 1, 2, and 6 are especially relevant.

27. Bryce, *American Commonwealth*, 3:62–63; Bagehot, "Introduction to the second edition," *The English Constitution and Other Political Essays* (reprint New York, 1924), 6–8; 3:30–31, 3–12, 13.

28. Gilder to Bryce, 4 January 1906; Putnam to Bryce, 29 June 1898; Roosevelt to Bryce, 2 June 1911. Bryce Papers. On the sources and aspects of the Pan-Anglian movement, see Charles Wentworth Dilke, *Greater Britain: A Record of Travel in English-Speaking Countries during 1866 and 1867*, 2 vols. (London, 1868); Andrew Carnegie, *Triumphant Democracy* (New York, 1886), esp. chaps. 1, 2, 20; Robert Kelley, *The Transatlantic Persuasion: The Liberal-Democratic Mind in the Age of Gladstone* (New York, 1968), xiii–xxiii, 403–418; A. S. Eisenstadt, *Charles McLean Andrews: A Study in American Historical Writing* (New York, 1956), 205– 219; Richard Heathcote Heindel, *The American Impact on Great Britain, 1898–1914: A Study of the United States in World History* (Philadelphia, 1940), 128, 130–131; Barbara Miller Solomon, *Ancestors and Immigrants* (Cambridge, Mass., 1956), 59–81; Cushing Strout, *The American Image of the Old World* (New York, 1963), 132–156; G. D. Lillibridge, *Beacon of Freedom: The Impact of American Democracy upon Great Britain 1830– 1870* (London, 1955).

29. Bryce to Theodore Stanton, 13 October 1887, Bryce Papers.

30. Bryce, *The Predictions*, 24, 27–28.

31. Ibid., 27–28.

32. Cited in John Stone and Stephen Mennell, eds., *Alexis de Tocqueville on Democracy, Revolution, and Society* (Chicago, 1980), 25.

33. Fisher, *James Bryce*, 1:237.

34. Bryce, *American Commonwealth*, 1:373, 384–385, 386, 388–389, 390; 2: chap. 58.

35. Ibid., 1:225–229, 240–242, chap. 17.

36. Ibid., chaps. 19, 25, 26, 95. On Bryce's views about government by the "best men," see David C. Hammack, "Elite Perceptions of

Power in the Cities of the United States, 1880–1900: The Evidence of James Bryce, Moisei Ostrogorskii, and their American Informants," *Journal of Urban History* 4 (August 1978):369–171.

37. Fisher, *James Bryce*, 1:238; in the preface to *The American Commonwealth*, Bryce cites the names of twenty-five Americans to whom he was particularly indebted. For the Mugwump mentality, see Richard Hofstadter, *The Age of Reform* (New York, 1955), chap. 4; Ari Hoogenboom, *Outlawing the Spoils: A History of the Civil Service Reform Movement, 1865–1883* (Urbana, 1961), 179–197; Geoffrey Blodgett, *The Gentle Reformers: Massachusetts Democrats in the Cleveland Era* (Cambridge, Mass., 1966); John G. Sproat, *"The Best Men" Liberal Reformers in the Gilded Age* (New York, 1968), 4–10, 46–69; John Tomisch, *A Genteel Endeavor: American Culture and Politics in the Gilded Age* (Stanford, 1971), esp. 73–93; and Walter T. K. Nugent, *From Centennial to World War: American Society 1876–1917* (Indianapolis, 1977), 37–65. Hammack enters a caveat about regarding Bryce simply as "a captive of the Mugwumps" in "Elite Perceptions of Power," 366.

38. Bryce, *The Predictions*, 23.

39. Bryce, *American Commonwealth*, 1: chaps. 13, 10, 5, 7; 2: chaps. 36, 44, 48.

40. Ibid., 3: chap. 97; 3:356, 331, 363.

41. The idea of a community of English-speaking peoples was variously voiced during the late nineteenth and early twentieth centuries in the writings of Charles Dilke and Andrew Carnegie, which we have already noted as well as in Josiah Strong, *The United States and the Future of the Anglo-Saxon Race* (London, 1889); James Fullarton Muirhead, *The Land of Contrasts* (London, 1900); William T. Stead, *The Americanization of the World* (New York, 1902); and H. G. Wells, *The Future in America* (New York, 1906).

42. The need for rapprochement and, indeed, possible alliance between Britain and America was urged, again in different ways, by the above writers, as well as by Edward A. Freeman, John Fiske, Joseph Chamberlain, Alfred T. Mahan, and James Bryce. Some important early twentieth-century statements of the argument for rapprochement or alliance are to be found in John R. Dos Passos, *The Anglo-Saxon Century* (New York, 1903); William Archibald Dunning, *The British*

Empire and the United States (New York, 1914); Sinclair Kennedy, *The Pan-Angles* (New York, 1914); and George Louis Beer, *The English-Speaking Peoples* (New York, 1917). The best single treatment of Anglo-American diplomacy during these years is Bradford Perkins, *The Great Rapprochement: England and the United States 1895–1914* (New York, 1968).

43. Francis W. Coker, "How Bryce Gathered His Materials and What Contemporary Reviewers Thought of the Work," in *Bryce's 'American Commonwealth' Fiftieth Anniversary*, ed. Robert C. Brooks (New York, 1939), 159–160.

44. Low to Bryce, 6 July 1889; Villard to Bryce, 3 July 1889; Hart to Bryce, 29 September 1903. Bryce Papers.

45. Bryce, *American Commonwealth*, 3:257; the figures are from *Bryce's 'American Commonwealth' Fiftieth Anniversary*, 239; Laski, *The American Democracy* (New York, 1948), 16.

Index